Acclaim for *George C. Marshall and the Early Cold War*

"This is a timely and important book. Marshall was present and effective at the creation of all of the Cold War national security policies and institutions that established U.S. international leadership. This entire policy and institutional architecture is now in doubt. If it is to be reformed or replaced, it will need a person of Gen. Marshall's caliber to lead such an effort. This book is an important revival and analysis of Marshall's historic role."
—**Gordon Adams**, author of *Buying National Security: How America Plans and Pays for Its Global Role and Safety at Home*

"*George C. Marshall and the Early Cold War* is an engaging collection of scholarly essays that ably demonstrates the impact of George C. Marshall on the emerging Cold War. Together they shed new light on the pervasive influence that this remarkable American had on the tumultuous times that followed the end of hostilities in Europe and the Pacific. This is an excellent book that is strongly recommended for any reader interested in the growth of the United States as a world power in the aftermath of World War II and the seminal role that George C. Marshall played in those momentous events."
—**James H. Willbanks**, author of *A Raid Too Far: Operation Lam Son 719 and Vietnamization in Laos*

". . . an excellent collection of essays that explores the various dimensions of Marshall's career during the early Cold War. *George C. Marshall and the Early Cold War* is a must-read for anyone interested in a range of controversial issues that continue to plague America, from the politics of grand strategy and military mobilization to the difficulty of mediating international conflict and the complexity of managing alliances."
—**Steven Casey**, author of *Selling the Korean War: Propaganda, Politics, and Public Opinion in the United States, 1950–1953*

"Balanced and objective, *George C. Marshall and the Early Cold War* could not be more relevant. Marshall's leadership and world view are prescient to today's complex security environment."
—**William Thomas Allison**, author of *American Military History: A Survey from Colonial Times to the Present*

D1593232

"Although George C. Marshall remains an enigmatic figure, this outstanding book presents his personal relationships, his significant contributions, and gives the reader ample evidence of his remarkable importance to the early Cold War era. Marshall is brought to the forefront of the Cold War in this new and momentous contribution to our understanding of this singularly important individual."
—**Brian Laslie**, author of *Architect of Air Power: General Laurence S. Kuter and the Birth of the US Air Force*

"This book is a must-read for anyone interested in how the United States developed and implemented the policies that eventually allowed us to prevail in the Cold War."
—**Lawrence Korb**, author of *Reshaping America's Military: Four Alternatives*

"Contributing to the substantial work on George C. Marshall, the authors in their highly readable *George C. Marshall and the Early Cold War* provide revealing perspectives on Marshall's largely underreported influence on important components of U.S. history following World War II."
—**Major General Jeffrey E. Phillips**, United States Army (Retired)

"This wide-ranging book demonstrates that General George C. Marshall, 'organizer of victory' in World War II, was also the indispensable man for American national security in the early years of the Cold War. With scholarly rigor and cogent analysis, the authors show how Marshall shaped U.S. diplomacy, defense policy, and the structure of government in this crucial but less-studied period."
—**Charles A. Stevenson**, author of *Warriors and Politicians: U.S. Civil-Military Relations under Stress*

"In this comprehensive, often searching appraisal of Marshall's successful and failed efforts at reforming institutionalized power in postwar America, several crucial points stand out. There were, in fact, multiple Marshall Plans for advancing national security. While his European Recovery Program was a great achievement, all of us still pay the price for his failure, on three separate occasions, to convince Congress to adopt Universal Military Training. William A. Taylor reminds us that the past is forever bleeding into the present."
—**Barry F. Machado**, author of *In Search of a Usable Past: The Marshall Plan and Postwar Reconstruction Today*

"This volume's conclusions highlight Marshall's indispensable role in establishing the national security strategy and structure for the Cold War. *George C. Marshall and the Early Cold War* is an admirable ensemble of well-researched and well-written essays on an almost-forgotten era of the Cold War."

—**Jonathan House**, author of *Military History of the Cold War, 1944–1962*

GEORGE C. MARSHALL AND THE EARLY COLD WAR

GEORGE C. MARSHALL AND THE EARLY COLD WAR

Policy, Politics, and Society

Edited by
WILLIAM A. TAYLOR

Foreword by MARK A. STOLER

UNIVERSITY OF OKLAHOMA PRESS : NORMAN

*This book is published with the generous assistance of
The McCasland Foundation, Duncan, Oklahoma.*

Elements from Chapter 5 were previously published in Frank A. Settle Jr.'s book *General
George C. Marshall and the Atomic Bomb* (Santa Barbara, Calif.: Praeger, 2016) and appear
here in a condensed and substantially revised form.

Library of Congress Cataloging-in-Publication Data

Names: Taylor, William A., 1975– editor. | Stoler, Mark A., author of foreword.
Title: George C. Marshall and the early Cold War : policy, politics, and society /
    edited by William A. Taylor ; foreword by Mark A. Stoler.
Description: Norman : University of Oklahoma Press, [2020] | Includes index
    and bibliographic references. | Summary: "This edited volume highlights and
    contextualizes George C. Marshall's roles in American diplomatic and military
    affairs in the post–World War II and early Cold War era."—Provided by publisher.
Identifiers: LCCN 2019053422 | ISBN 978-0-8061-6543-1 (paperback)
Subjects: LCSH: United States—Foreign relations—20th century. | Marshall, George C.
    (George Catlett), 1880–1959—Influence. | Cold War. | World politics—1945–1955. |
    United States—Military policy—History—20th century.
Classification: LCC E744 .G465 2020 | DDC 327.73009/04—dc23
LC record available at https://lccn.loc.gov/2019053422

To Mom and Dad Lesniewski,
Linda and Dennis

"General Marshall's leadership takes its authority directly from his great strength of character. I have never known a man who seemed so surely to breathe the democratic American spirit. He is a soldier, and yet he has a profound distaste for anything that savors of militarism. . . . During a long lifetime I have had considerable experience with men in Government. General Marshall has given me a new gauge of what such service should be. The destiny of America at the most critical time of its national existence has been in the hands of a great and good citizen. Let no man forget it."

—Henry L. Stimson, secretary of war, 1945

CONTENTS

FOREWORD

"I have seen a great many soldiers in my day," seventy-seven-year-old Secretary of War Henry L. Stimson told Army Chief of Staff Gen. George C. Marshall on May 8, 1945, the day Nazi Germany officially surrendered, "and you, sir, are the finest soldier I have ever known." That was a sentiment shared by most members of Congress, the public, and Presidents Franklin D. Roosevelt and Harry S Truman. "He would tell the truth even if it hurt his cause," Speaker of the House Sam Rayburn remembered. "Congress always respected him" for that "and would give him things they would give no one else." Administration officials agreed. "Let General Marshall, and only General Marshall, do all the testifying in connection with the Bill you are about to send up for additional appropriations for the Army," Secretary of the Treasury Henry Morgenthau advised Roosevelt in May 1940. "I feel I could not sleep at night with you out of the country," President Roosevelt admitted to Marshall in late 1943. "Wherever this man goes he inspires reverence," Roosevelt's press secretary noted in his diary; "may God spare him."[1]

Time magazine aptly summarized that reverence and the reasons for it in naming Marshall its "Man of the Year" in early 1944. Marshall, it claimed, had been primarily responsible for the actualizing of America's potential strength, which had turned the tide of the war. Beyond that, not since George Washington had Americans so trusted a soldier, and "never in U.S. history has a man enjoyed such respect on Capitol Hill." According to one member of Congress, only Marshall "could at any time get a unanimous vote of confidence." Devoid of any political ambition, he was "*civis Americanus*," a "trustee for the nation," and "the closest thing to the indispensable man."[2]

On November 26, 1945, Marshall officially retired from the army. "In a war unparalleled in magnitude and horror," President Truman read in awarding him his only military decoration of the war, a second oak leaf cluster to his 1919 Distinguished Service Medal, "millions of Americans gave their country outstanding service. General of the Army George C. Marshall gave it victory."[3]

Along with that victory went extraordinary power on the world scene. "The United States stands at this time at the pinnacle of world power," Winston Churchill would assert in early 1946. But "with primacy in power," he warned, "is also joined an awe-inspiring accountability for the future."[4] From 1939 to 1945, Marshall had played a central role in the creation of this American power. Now, unexpectedly, he would for the next six years play an equally central if different role in the appropriate use of that power—first as special presidential envoy to China, then as secretary of state, and finally as secretary of defense.

While this unexpected and successful shift from military to diplomatic and political affairs surprised many, it did not surprise those who had worked with Marshall during World War II. As Gen. Walter Bedell Smith later and accurately stated, "His whole service had been a preparatory course for high-level negotiations."[5] In World War I Marshall had negotiated with French officers on an almost daily basis. As aide to postwar army chief of staff Gen. John J. Pershing, he would deal with statesmen as well as soldiers and political issues at the highest levels. He would also deal with a host of thorny politico-military issues during his 1924–27 service in China. And during World War II he would negotiate not only with the members of Congress, but also with the British military chiefs on the Anglo-American Combined Chiefs of Staff, with his Soviet and other Allied counterparts, with British prime minister Winston Churchill, and with Soviet leader Joseph Stalin.

As William A. Taylor accurately notes in his introduction, scholarship on Marshall's pivotal role in the post–World War II years has received less attention than his World War II years. This volume seeks to remedy that shortcoming in the literature by focusing on numerous issues and events from 1945 to 1951 in which Marshall played a key role: the fight for universal military training; the effort to mediate the Chinese Civil War; the rise of American military airpower; the postwar U.S. military structure as enunciated in the National Security Act of 1947; the development of the atomic bomb and postwar nuclear policy; the European Recovery Program that bears his name; the formation of NATO and its military command; the Korean War; and racial integration in the U.S. Army. Admittedly, not all Marshall's efforts ended in success. But many if not most of them did. And the failures, most notably in regard to universal military training and the Chinese Civil War, are in many ways as instructive as the successes.

Aside from his pre–Cold War experiences previously mentioned, what factors led Marshall to play such a central role in these postwar issues and events? For the most part they were the same characteristics that had marked his entire career. As the late Larry I. Bland, my distinguished predecessor as editor of the *Papers of George Catlett Marshall*, once emphasized to me in this regard, Marshall in a sense spent the first four decades of his career preparing for the years 1939–51.

First, it is important to recognize Marshall's extraordinary talents as a *manager* as well as a soldier. In this respect, Marshall was the epitome of the twentieth-century staff officer, and his exceptional management talents were as valuable in the postwar world as they had been before 1945. Such management skills had become necessary in twentieth-century military organizations, as they had in large business organizations, because of the increasing size and complexity of such entities. Eliot Cohen and John Gooch have noted in this regard that "the modern commander is much more akin to the managing director of a large conglomerate enterprise than ever he is to the warrior chief of old. He has become the head of a complex military organization, whose many branches he must oversee and on whose cooperation, assistance, and support he depends for success." Marshall himself pointedly and publicly noted in this regard in June 1940 that "the flag-waving days of warfare are gone. The successful army of today is composed of specialists, thoroughly trained in every detail of military science, and above all, organized into a perfect team."[6]

Early in his career those managerial talents led to army assignments far beyond his lowly rank and, with those assignments, close association with many of the most important and high-ranking officers in the pre–World War II army. Two of them with whom he worked during World War I deserve special mention as important mentors: Fox Conner, who would also mentor Dwight Eisenhower in the 1920s, and John J. Pershing, who would also become a virtual surrogate father for Marshall.

Marshall also possessed extraordinary personal presence. "The moment General Marshall entered a room," Dean Acheson wrote, "everyone in it felt his presence. It was a striking and communicated force. His figure conveyed intensity, which his voice, low, staccato, and incisive, reinforced. It spread a sense of authority, and of calm."[7]

Marshall was also utterly honest and willing to talk back to his superiors, no matter what their rank and position. That would include Pershing, first as commander of the American Expeditionary Forces in World War I and then as army chief of staff, and Presidents Franklin Roosevelt and Harry Truman. Equally if not more important, these individuals did not relieve him when he challenged or disagreed with them. And as former Secretary of Defense Robert Gates noted more than a decade ago, Roosevelt's trust in Marshall was based not only on such candor "but also because once a decision was made, FDR could count on Marshall to do his utmost to carry out a policy—even if he disagreed with it—and make it work."[8] So could Pershing and Truman.

Vitally important to Marshall's importance and successes were both his lifelong commitment to selfless public service and his refusal to run for political office—or participate in any way in partisan politics. Indeed, he refused even to vote on the grounds that he was a servant to the Republic and took orders from the president, his commander-in-chief, no matter what that individual's political party. He also had to work with the House and Senate, no matter which party held a majority in each chamber. As he quipped when asked about his own "political faith," "My father was a democrat, my mother a republican, and I am an Episcopalian."[9]

This did not mean, however, that Marshall lacked ambition—just that his ambitions were limited to his military career and were largely if not totally fulfilled when he became army chief of staff. Nor did it mean that he was politically naive and failed to understand American politics. To the contrary, his nonpartisanship coexisted with an extraordinary understanding of the American political process and its importance to his work. Without that understanding he never could have won the respect of Congress and obtained its willingness to grant his requests both during and after World War II. Indeed, his rejection of partisan politics and with it any idea of running for political office was a key part of the image he presented that enabled him to obtain what he desired from Congress. Any "public suggestion" in 1941 that he run for president, "even by mere rumor or gossip," he noted, "would be fatal to my interests." And in January 1947, when he emphatically asserted to the press just before becoming secretary of state that under no circumstances would he be a candidate for political office, he thereby, as James Reston of the *New York Times* realized, reassured the politically vulnerable President Truman (who had not been elected to the presidency at that time) as well as the Republican-controlled Congress, with which he had to work, that under no circumstances could he be considered a political rival.[10]

Others had recognized the depth of Marshall's political understanding while he was still chief of staff. One subordinate noted that he possessed "an uncanny eye for the political angle of every problem." Another labeled him in this regard "the most accomplished actor in the Army. . . . Everybody thinks MacArthur is, but he's not. The difference between them is that you always *know* MacArthur is acting!"[11]

Equally important was Marshall's related understanding of, as well as respect for, civilian democratic values in general, and particularly in American society—even when those values differed from his own as a soldier or when they negatively affected him personally. "God bless American democracy," he wrote in mid-1948. "I approve of it highly but suffer from it extremely."[12] Where Marshall had obtained this respect is unclear—perhaps as early as his cadet days at the Virginia Military Institute and/or his numerous early assignments with the National Guard; perhaps after World War I when he worked with Pershing, who had become army chief of staff; perhaps when in the 1930s he worked with the New Deal's Civilian Conservation Corps; and perhaps from all these experiences. Whatever the sources, he was a fierce defender of those values. Indeed, they help to explain his unsuccessful struggle to obtain congressional approval for universal military training—which he viewed as the only appropriate military policy for American democracy.

In international affairs Marshall was a true multilateralist who at least since World War I had understood the need for allies. And within this context he was also a strong proponent of a "Europe First" grand strategy that translated both during and after World War II into massive U.S. economic and military aid to European allies, from Lend-Lease through the European Recovery Program and NATO. That strategy was linked to Marshall's understanding of the limits of power and the need to match ends to means—the essence of sound strategic thinking.

As expressed during and after World War II, the emphasis on Europe was based on geography, power, threat assessment, and values. Europe was far closer to the United States than Asia. It also contained enormous industrial power and, with that, great potential military power. Consequently, any hegemonic European power—be it Nazi Germany during World War II or the Communist Soviet Union after the war—posed the greatest potential threat to American security. Many of the nations within Western Europe also shared with the United States democratically elected governments and democratic values.

None of this was true in Asia. Only Japan could be considered an Asian economic power, and much of that power had been destroyed during the war. China was at the time far from being the economic power it is today—or an economic power of any sort. Nor was it a democracy. And Marshall had had firsthand experiences with the limits of American power regarding that troubled country—as early as his 1924–27 assignment with the Fifteenth Infantry Regiment in Tientsin and then during World War II as well as during his ensuing 1945–46 China mission.

Undergirding all Marshall's beliefs and actions was an understanding of history and a related, extraordinary ability to see beyond the immediate consequences to the long-term consequences of actions. For Marshall, history was so much more than the meaningless rote memorization of facts—a method of teaching history common during his lifetime that he condemned on numerous occasions. Rather, history was a process with important lessons for the present. "In order to take full part in the life which is before you," he advised students at Princeton University on February 22, 1947, "I think you must in effect relive the past." And he did not mean just the recent past—or "that one should be interested in the past only as a guide to the future." Rather, as he pointed out, "one usually emerges from an intimate understanding of the past with its lessons and its wisdom, with convictions which put fire in the soul. I doubt seriously whether a man can think with full wisdom and with deep convictions regarding certain of the basic international issues today who has not at least reviewed in his mind the period of the Peloponnesian War and the fall of Athens."[13]

Marshall's ability to see beyond immediate to long-term consequences of actions was illustrated by his refusal in 1940 to support greater funding for the army than he had requested, even though "numerous congressmen, mostly senators," favored such a move. With many others opposed even to the requested amount, Marshall concluded that it was "very necessary for me to build up their confidence in me for future demands."[14] Even more telling of this ability was the charge he gave in early 1943 to Maj. Gen. John Hilldring, whom he had placed in command of the newly created Civil Affairs Division within the Army General Staff. "I'm turning over to you today a sacred trust," Hilldring remembered Marshall telling him, "and I want you to bear that in mind every day and every hour you preside over the military government and civil affairs venture." The American people "do not distrust us and do not fear us. Our countrymen, our fellow citizens, are not afraid of us. They don't harbor any ideas that we intend to alter the government of the country or the nature of this government in any way. This is a sacred trust that I turn over to you today." The "enormous corps of military governors" that Hilldring was training and would "dispatch all over the world" could "damage this high regard in which the professional soldiers in the Army are held by our people, and it could happen, it could happen, Hilldring, if you don't understand what you are about, and . . . that this reputation we have is of enormous importance. . . . This is my principal charge to you, this is the thing I never want you to forget in the dust of battle and when the pressures will be on you."[15]

That Marshall would emphasize this at all in the midst of a world war is impressive and noteworthy in and of itself. That he would do so at this relatively early time in the war—before the battle for French North Africa had even ended, let alone before the ensuing invasions of Sicily, Italy, and France—verges on the extraordinary. For good reason, Richard Neustadt and Ernest May cited this episode as a classic example of what they labeled "thinking in time streams" and how history can and should be used, rather than misused, by policy makers.[16]

The chapters in this volume are filled with other examples of Marshall's ability to think in this way and see "the big picture." They are also filled with examples of Marshall's other exceptional abilities and characteristics that enabled him to play such a central role in key U.S. postwar policies after his military career had ended.

NOTES

1. Henry L. Stimson and McGeorge Bundy, *On Active Service in Peace and War* (New York: Harper & Brothers, 1947), 664; Forrest C. Pogue, *George C. Marshall*, vol. 3: *Organizer of Victory, 1943–1945* (New York: Viking, 1973), 131; Larry I. Bland, Sharon R. Ritenour, and Clarence E. Wonderlin Jr., eds., *The Papers of George Catlett Marshall*, vol. 2: *"We Cannot Delay," July 1, 1939–December 6, 1941* (Baltimore: Johns Hopkins University Press, 1986), 214; Larry I. Bland and Mark A. Stoler, eds., *The Papers of George Catlett Marshall*, vol. 6: *"The Whole World Hangs in the Balance," January 8, 1947–September 30, 1948* (Baltimore: Johns Hopkins University Press,

2014), 54; William D. Hassett, *Off the Record with F.D.R., 1942–1945* (New Brunswick, N.J.: Rutgers University Press, 1958), 249.

2. *Time* 43 (January 3, 1944): 15–18.

3. Forrest C. Pogue, *George C. Marshall*, vol. 4: *Statesman* (New York: Viking, 1987), 1.

4. Winston Churchill, "The Sinews of Peace," March 5, 1946, https://winstonchurchill .org/resources/speeches/1946–1963-elder-statesman/the-sinews-of-peace/.

5. Walter Bedell Smith, *My Three Years in Moscow* (Philadelphia: Lippincott, 1950), 216.

6. Eliot Cohen and John Gooch, "Military Misfortunes: The Anatomy of Failure in War," quoted in Lt. Col. Donald Dreschler and Col. Charles D. Allen (U.S. Army, ret.), "Why Senior Military Leaders Fail," *Armed Forces Journal* (July/August 2009): 34; Bland, Ritenour, and Wonderlin, *Papers of George Marshall*, 2:249.

7. Dean Acheson, *Present at the Creation: My Years in the State Department* (New York: W. W. Norton, 1969), 140–41.

8. Robert Gates, "Reflections on Leadership," in *Parameters* (Summer 2008): 11.

9. Bland, Ritenour, and Wonderlin, *Papers of George Marshall*, 2:616.

10. Ibid., 2:388; Bland and Stoler, *Papers of George Marshall*, 6:8.

11. Paul M. Robinett Diary, January 30, 1941, George C. Marshall Library, Lexington, Va.; William Frye, *Marshall: Citizen Soldier* (Indianapolis: Bobbs-Merrill, 1947), 258.

12. Bland and Stoler, *Papers of George Marshall*, 6:484.

13. Ibid., 6:49.

14. Ibid., 6:687–88.

15. Pogue, *George C. Marshall*, 3:458–59.

16. Richard E. Neustadt and Ernest R. May, *Thinking in Time: The Uses of History for Decision Makers* (New York: Free Press, 1986), 247–56.

ACKNOWLEDGMENTS

This work has been a collaborative project from start to finish. Throughout the process, I have been fortunate to work with and receive support from a wonderful group of mentors, colleagues, friends, and family. Mark A. Stoler, the eminent scholar of George C. Marshall, graciously agreed to write the foreword for this volume. I am honored and humbled to work together with him and benefit from his many cogent insights. Jeremy P. Maxwell first suggested this work and affably agreed to contribute his chapter early, along with mine, for peer review at the proposal stage. Jeremy's work ethic and commitment to the historical profession have proven prodigious; he remains a colleague and close friend. All the contributors to this volume have been a complete joy to work with. They embody the breadth of the historical profession, representing military, diplomatic, and institutional historians and spanning universities large and small, as well as professional military education. I am proud to call them all colleagues and friends.

The George C. Marshall Foundation and Virginia Military Institute (VMI) have proven remarkably supportive of this project as well as of my work in general. Early in my academic career, the foundation provided me with a George C. Marshall/Baruch Fellowship, which afforded extensive research at the George C. Marshall Library on the campus of VMI in Lexington, Virginia, and reinforced my interest in and rigorous study of Marshall. Throughout this current project and my two previous books that have dealt with George C. Marshall, *Every Citizen a Soldier* (College Station: Texas A&M University Press, 2014) and *Military Service and American Democracy* (Lawrence: University Press of Kansas, 2016), Paul B. Barron, former director of library and archives, along with Jeffrey Kozak, current director of library and archives, and Cara C. Sonnier, digital communications librarian, provided guidance and assistance. Jeffrey Kozak recently left the Marshall Foundation to become the archivist at the VMI Library, and Paul Barron temporarily has returned to serve as acting archivist at the foundation until a new permanent archivist can be found. In addition to aiding me during my multiple research trips to the library and archives, they also provided high-quality photographs of Marshall and his associates at pivotal moments in his career that appear throughout this volume. An earlier version of my Chapter 1, "The Obligation to Serve: Marshall and Universal Military Training," won second prize out of approximately sixty entries in the John A. Adams '71 Center for Military History and Strategic Analysis at Virginia Military Institute Cold War Essay Contest in 2018. Bradley L. Coleman, director of the center, administered the research award, provided the honorary plaque, and proved a pivotal supporter, valued colleague, and dear friend.

The entire team at University of Oklahoma Press has been wonderful to work with. Adam Kane, editor-in-chief, believed in this project from the start and provided useful direction and sustaining encouragement throughout the process. I am most grateful for his friendship. Stephanie E. Evans, editor for this volume, helped shepherd the project from manuscript to book. Dale Bennie, sales and marketing manager; Katie Baker, publicity manager; and Amy L. Hernandez, marketing assistant, ensured that the resulting volume received widespread attention.

The students, staff, faculty, and administrators at Angelo State University have supported my work since my arrival here, encouraging me to pursue new directions in my research and to integrate those results into my teaching. Brian J. May, president, has led the university through significant growth with exceptional vision. The entire senior leadership team, including Donald R. Topliff, provost and vice president for academic affairs; Micheal W. Salisbury, dean of the College of Graduate Studies and Research; and John E. Klingemann, dean of the College of Arts and Humanities, have fostered my research and have helped me to pursue it. Colleagues in my department, especially Bruce E. Bechtol Jr., Anthony N. Celso, and Kenneth J. Heineman, have proven gracious mentors and valued associates. Many Angelo State University staff members also played important roles: Thomas G. Nurre Jr. broadly marketed my work and accomplishments; Purnell J. Curtis provided excellent technology support, especially regarding illustrations; and Vianey Sanchez ensured that administrative matters were completed in a timely and efficient manner.

Brian D. Laslie and another anonymous reviewer offered lucid insights and positive feedback at the beginning of this project; I am most grateful for their many recommendations, helpful suggestions, and energizing inspiration to start off on a clear path with a sound vision. Upon completion of the manuscript, Laslie and Jonathan M. House thoroughly reviewed it as part of the formal peer review process, providing valuable direction and cogent ideas for refinement; I am most appreciative of their wise guidance. In addition to the formal peer review process, many other colleagues graciously spent their time and effort to review the manuscript, including Gordon Adams, William T. Allison, Steven Casey, Bradley L. Coleman, Sheldon A. Goldberg, Justin Hart, Lawrence J. Korb, Maj. Gen. Dennis Laich, Barry F. Machado, Maj. Gen. Jeffrey E. Phillips, Charles A. Stevenson, Lawrence B. Wilkerson, and James H. Willbanks. I am most honored and humbled to receive their very positive endorsements.

As with all my work, my family has provided the most sustenance. My wife, Renee M. Taylor, and our two kids, Madison G. Taylor and Benjamin A. Taylor, always have heartened me to follow my projects wherever they lead. I am most grateful for their unconditional love. My parents, Richard A. Taylor and L. Diane Taylor, emboldened me to follow my dreams, which in my case led me first into military service and then into academia. They have consistently provided excellent role models for me to emulate. My other parents, the Lesniewskis, to whom I have dedicated this book, have welcomed me into their family as one of their own. I am fortunate to call them Mom and Dad and wish them all the best as they pursue their own dreams and embark on new journeys.

Even with the backing of such an amazing group of mentors, colleagues, family, and friends, any errors that remain are mine alone.

ACRONYMS AND ABBREVIATIONS

ACTS	Air Corps Tactical School
AEC	Atomic Energy Commission
AWPD	Army War Plans Division
AWPD-1	Air War Plan Document-1
CBO	Combined Bomber Offensive
CCP	Chinese Communist Party
CCS	Combined Chiefs of Staff
CEEC	Committee of European Economic Cooperation
CFM	Conference of Foreign Ministers
CIA	Central Intelligence Agency
CJCS	Chairman, Joint Chiefs of Staff
CIG	Central Intelligence Group
DCI	Director of Central Intelligence
DDEL	Dwight D. Eisenhower Library

DOD	Department of Defense
ECA	Economic Cooperation Administration
EDC	European Defense Community
ERA	European Recovery Act
ERP	European Recovery Program
ETO	European Theater of Operations
GCML	George C. Marshall Library
GMD	Guomindang (Chinese Nationalist Party)
HSTL	Harry S. Truman Library
IADA	International Atomic Development Authority
JCAE	Joint Committee on Atomic Energy
JCPOA	Joint Comprehensive Plan of Action
JCS	Joint Chiefs of Staff
JSSC	Joint Strategic Survey Committee
KPA	Korean People's Army
MFNAP	Marshall Foundation National Archives Project
NARA	National Archives and Records Administration
NATO	North Atlantic Treaty Organization
NME	National Military Establishment
NSC	National Security Council
NSRB	National Security Resources Board
OCS	Officer Candidate School
OEEC	Organization of European Economic Cooperation
OSS	Office of Strategic Services
PACUT	President's Advisory Commission on Universal Training
PCC	Political Consultative Conference
PCI	Italian Communist Party
PPS	Policy Planning Staff
ROK	Republic of Korea
SHAPE	Supreme Headquarters Allied Powers Europe
UMT	Universal Military Training
UMTS	Universal Military Training and Service
UN	United Nations
UNAEC	United Nations Atomic Energy Commission
UNC	United Nations Command
UNRRA	United Nations Recovery and Rehabilitation Administration

USAAC	U.S. Army Air Corps
USAAF	U.S. Army Air Forces
USAID	U.S. Agency for International Development
USSBS	U.S. Strategic Bombing Survey
USSR	Union of Soviet Socialist Republics

INTRODUCTION

Entering a New Storm

This book tells the compelling story of George C. Marshall's influence after World War II, generally ranging from 1945 to his death in 1959. It argues that Marshall's many significant policymaking positions throughout this period, including U.S. Army chief of staff, special presidential envoy to China, secretary of state, and secretary of defense, among others, placed him at the center of a tumultuous yet formative period of American history.[1] Few U.S. policy makers have ever held such important and diverse stations; fewer still have ever done so at such a critical juncture of U.S. history. As a result, Marshall achieved unique personal accolades. He remains the lone American to have served as army chief of staff, secretary of state, and secretary of defense and is the only career soldier to have received the Nobel Peace Prize. More important, these positions allowed Marshall entrée to the halls of U.S. policy and power, where he directly shaped the early Cold War through his own decisions and indirectly affected the early Cold War through his extended network of colleagues, many of whom also served as senior policy makers. While voluminous scholarship on Marshall analyzes his leadership during World War II, scholars have placed less emphasis on his enduring bearing on the critical years that followed, which would eventually become known as the early Cold War. This volume seeks to reveal the myriad ways that Marshall influenced events in the aftermath of World War II and became one of the most dominant and consequential leaders of the early Cold War. Two characteristics stand out about this turbulent time: it was a storm in both its chaos and its consequences, and Marshall was at the center of it all.

George Catlett Marshall was born on December 31, 1880, in Uniontown, Pennsylvania.[2] The youngest of three siblings, Marshall took an early interest in martial affairs and reported in September 1897 while still a teenager to Virginia Military Institute (VMI) in Lexington, Virginia. He excelled in military training, although not academics, eventually serving as first captain, the highest rank that a cadet could attain at this school. In 1901, he graduated from VMI and received on February 2, 1902, a commission as a second lieutenant in the U.S. Army. Thereafter, Marshall embarked upon one of the most lengthy and highly storied military careers in U.S. history, eventually becoming one of only five soldiers ever to attain the five-star rank of general of the army.[3] In the process, Marshall deployed with the Thirtieth Infantry Regiment during the Philippine insurrection; attended stateside at the Army Service Schools in Fort Leavenworth, Kansas, first as a student and then as an instructor; became a trusted adviser to Gen. John J. Pershing, commander of the American Expeditionary Forces (AEF) in France during World War I and afterward upon their return to the United States; operated with the Fifteenth Infantry Regiment in Tientsin, China; led numerous military officers as assistant commandant of the Infantry School at Fort Benning, Georgia; and eventually became U.S. Army Chief of Staff on September 1, 1939. He functioned in this critical post for the entirety of World War II, planning, implementing, and leading the United States toward victory in a total and global war.[4]

As America emerged from World War II, a series of momentous policy debates quickly surfaced, including over universal military training, China's fierce civil war, creation of an independent air force, unification of the armed services and design of the National Security Act of 1947, control of atomic weapons, implementation of the momentous European Recovery Program, formulation of the North Atlantic Treaty, strategy for the Korean War, and racial integration of the U.S. military. A better understanding of earlier attempts by policy makers, regularly centered around Marshall, to provide national

U.S. Army Chief of Staff George C. Marshall. Circa 1945. U.S. Army Signal Corps. Courtesy George C. Marshall Library, Lexington, Va.

security contextualizes the implications of such highly relevant current issues as military service, foreign policy, technological innovation, joint operations, weapons of mass destruction and proliferation, diplomacy and postconflict resolution, alliances, mobilization, and citizenship, as well as their sway on America historically and today.

This volume explores such vital themes in three ways. First, each chapter provides robust context on a specific policy. Each chapter presents extensive background, illuminating how the topic climaxed after World War II and why it was critical at that time. Each chapter considers contemporary arguments for and against the matter and explores why individuals and groups held their views. Since World War II, most Americans have understood that their country has fundamental national security needs. These same Americans also have understood that individual liberty is an essential component of America's national character. Individuals and groups, however, have disagreed regarding the proper balance of these two seminal concepts, especially when it comes to military policy. The same dynamic holds true today.

Second, this work reinforces the central role that Marshall played relative to each specific issue. Each chapter traces his influence on other individuals and groups and how his relationships channeled his views outward to reach a broader audience. As one of the most well known and widely respected leaders of his day, Marshall shaped events through his words and deeds, but also through his extensive contacts, including with many colleagues who also held senior policymaking positions during the early Cold War. Each chapter demonstrates Marshall's prominent stance regarding the topic and articulates how he guided it. As a result, the book examines policy with regard to rhetoric and reality as well as individuals and society. Americans have voiced differing views concerning the place of the military in American society. This book surveys Marshall's positions, assesses why he held them, and analyzes how he forged the crucial policies that took shape in times of peace and war.

Third, this collection studies the impact of Marshall's legacy on America during the early Cold War. Each chapter evaluates how Marshall guided the theme specifically and American society generally. This involvement included both successes and failures. On most occasions, Marshall's authority proved pivotal to overall success. In some cases, however, even Marshall's prodigious stature failed to secure his preferred goal. Universal military training and his mission to China were but two examples. In those instances, however, Marshall's clout was indispensable in molding the debate, even in a losing cause. These disputes still changed America significantly, as evidenced by the fact that the inability to achieve UMT resulted in the institution of the draft from 1948 to 1973 and the disappointment of his mission to China altered the dynamics of the Cold War through the emergence of Communist China on the international stage and through domestic recriminations against those who were unsuccessful in preventing that outcome, including Marshall. Even in failure, therefore, Marshall's shadow loomed large. In the vast majority of concerns, however, Marshall's desired outcome came to fruition. Each chapter considers the broader significance of the particular problem for American society during the early Cold War. Accordingly, this book investigates the relationship between policy, politics, and society. It uses the significant, powerful, and vital persona of George C. Marshall and his personal relationships with key policy makers to demonstrate his effect on America after World War II. In this way, the book highlights crucial questions involving military policy for American democracy and sparks public debate about their implications for today and the future.

George C. Marshall remains a pivotal figure in twentieth-century American history. One of the most widely respected leaders of his day, Marshall served as army chief of staff from 1939 to 1945, special presidential envoy to China from 1945 to 1947, secretary of state from 1947 to 1949, and secretary of defense from 1950 to 1951. *Time* magazine named Marshall "Man of the Year" in 1943 and 1947, and in 1953 he was awarded the Nobel Peace Prize for the Marshall Plan. As a result, he served at the center of critical events during a turbulent and seminal crucible in American history. Literature on Marshall includes four major categories: biographies, World War II, the Marshall Plan, and leadership. Little work has been done, however, to explore his intimate involvement after World War II across the spectrum of major challenges that transformed America during the early Cold War and that had far-ranging implications for decades, reverberating down to the present day. Marshall's public service in a plethora of senior policymaking positions and vast authority on a broad range of significant subjects illustrates his central station at the intersection of American policy, politics, and society.

This book consists of nine topical chapters that follow a general chronological order, focusing primarily on the decade 1945 to 1955. Each chapter outlines a specific matter that was significant to American policy, politics, and society during the early Cold War over which Marshall held some sway. Each chapter provides an overview of the issue, recounts the ensuing debates around it, and examines how the resulting policy manifested itself in American society during times of peace and war. The undergirding theme of each chapter is how Marshall influenced the subject directly and through his relationships with other senior policy makers and thereby created a lasting legacy regarding that specific matter and early Cold War America in general.

In this introduction, "Entering a New Storm," William A. Taylor sets the context for the volume and provides the undergirding methodology and overall themes of this work. In chapter 1, "The Obligation to Serve," Taylor explores Marshall's pivotal, and ultimately unsuccessful, role in the campaign for universal military training (UMT) after World War II, including his indispensable bonds with John M. Palmer and James W. Wadsworth Jr. In chapter 2, "To Mediate Civil War," Katherine K. Reist recounts Marshall's special mission to China and its implications for America and the early Cold War more generally as he mediated between Nationalist leader Chiang Kai-shek (Jiang Jieshi) and Communist leader Mao Zedong. In chapter 3, "The Advocate of Airpower," John M. Curatola reconnoiters Marshall's role in the emergence of the air force as an independent military service, charting his mentorship of such aviation leaders as Henry H. "Hap" Arnold and Larry Kuter. In chapter 4, "Military Posture for Peace," Sean N. Kalic surveys the National Security Act of 1947 and Marshall's sway over it, including the inspiration of Marshall's ideas on Dwight D. Eisenhower and Ferdinand Eberstadt as they framed this pivotal milestone that produced much of the national security apparatus for the period of the Cold War—and indeed today. In chapter 5, "To Harness Atomic Power," Frank A. Settle Jr. studies Marshall's centrality to atomic weapons during the early Cold War through his long-standing grooming of Robert A. Lovett and his close friendship with Bernard Baruch. In chapter 6, "The Patient Is Sinking," Michael Holm reveals the diplomatic and economic aspects of the plan that bears Marshall's name and the effect of his collaboration with Dean Acheson and Paul Hoffman on its ultimate success. In chapter 7, "An Alliance by Default," Ingo Trauschweizer demonstrates Marshall's imprint on the formation of the North Atlantic Treaty in 1949 and the subsequent reverberations of this crucial event for the early Cold War, encompassing Marshall's interactions with George F. Kennan and Charles Bohlen. In chapter 8, "Return to the Pentagon," Jared Dockery illustrates Marshall's importance to the Korean War as President Truman recalled him to serve as secretary of defense and to prosecute the war during its most precarious stage, including his guidance of J. Lawton Collins and his role in the controversial dismissal of Gen. Douglas MacArthur, supreme commander, Allied Powers; commander-in-chief, United Nations Command; commander-in-chief, Far East; and commanding general, U.S. Army, Far East. In chapter 9, "The Freedom to Serve," Jeremy P. Maxwell illuminates Marshall's impression on American military service during the Korean War and shows how his relationships with senior commanders, especially Matthew B. Ridgway, paved the way for racial integration throughout the U.S. military and countered the views of other senior military leaders, including Edward M. Almond, who were staunchly against racial integration. In the conclusion, "Good and Faithful Servant," William A. Taylor closes this work with some reflections about Marshall's life, legacy, and relevance for today.

Taken together, these chapters reveal several significant themes. First, this work uncovers multifaceted ways in which U.S. leaders planned for national security during the early Cold War, including not only such military calculations as mobilization but such economic ones as costs and such political ones as priorities. The debates regarding UMT revealed tensions regarding how the United States prepared for conflict during times of peace and war. Questions such as who should serve and how proved essential. Ultimately, these debates represented far more than merely mobilization or even military service; they touched on broader questions about the correct size of the U.S. military, how much Americans were willing to pay in taxes to sustain their armed forces, and the delicate balance between national security and civil liberties in American democracy. Second, this volume exposes the difficulties in discerning how to mediate foreign conflicts—or whether even to attempt to do so in the first place—through the American experience with the Chinese Civil War. Such struggles, especially when outsiders attempted to fit them nicely within broader labels, often revealed local and opportunistic forces at work. China's competing leaders usually courted U.S. support for tangible benefits—whether they consistently or even actually intended to follow through is less certain. As a result, diplomacy was critical as was the foresight to separate regional dynamics from global dichotomies and to assess culture within a society and understand how it related to national interests and possible courses of action. Third, this collection assesses how to incorporate technological advances into future military plans, not only in technical matters but also in discerning both the promises and the limitations of such technology. Ultimately, U.S. leaders needed to ascertain the myriad other changes necessary to maximize technological revolutions, including personnel, training, organizations, and strategy. Fourth, this anthology considers the best organization to solve national security threats and to ensure a coherent, coordinated, and effective application of U.S. instruments of power to grand strategy in order to achieve policy goals in both peace and war. Such reform not only coordinated individual military services into a joint effort, but also ensured that other aspects of grand strategy—including diplomacy, information, and economics—played vital roles as well. Fifth, this book portrays the magnitude of weapons of mass destruction, proliferation, and arms control upon the advent of the atomic age. Preventing their use and propagation were not only existential military problems; they also involved pursuing diplomacy and building consensus at the highest levels of international affairs. Only by contemplating the peaceful potential of nuclear power and respecting the underlying security dilemma nuclear weapons had been developed to address could U.S. policy makers ensure that prudent, pragmatic, and effectual controls were put in place to limit their escalation or use. Sixth, this volume establishes the potency of U.S. leadership in the postwar world, including not only the clear articulation of formidable ideals that resonated with allies but also sustained efforts to aid allies in ways that demonstrated the tangible value of these principles. Doing so reinforced the importance of nonmilitary means, including diplomacy, information, and economic aid to extend, maintain, and bolster America's standing on the world stage. The result not only benefited U.S. allies in dire need of assistance but also strengthened the United States in return. Seventh, this collection emphasizes the enduring value of alliances, not just militarily but also politically, economically, and even psychologically, as during the early Cold War. Alliances reinforced relationships and encouraged pursuit of common goals, while promoting shared values and endorsing broad principles. In more quantifiable terms, alliances allowed cost sharing regarding international security and buttressed global deterrence. Ultimately, the North Atlantic Treaty reassured allies, deterred adversaries, and augmented national and international security, while ensuring economic prosperity and social stability in the contest of systems that developed during the early Cold War. Eighth, this anthology exposes the dangers of unpreparedness when dealing with brazen and aggressive adversaries through consideration of the Korean War. Once that war had broken out, the possibilities of stopping enemy offensives, rallying allies, and mobilizing a nation became tenuous at best. In the process, this volume uncovers the delicate balance between civil and military leaders engaged in prosecuting war and the absolute necessity of civilian control in order to avoid a military strategy that discounted geopolitical factors and risked escalation—both conventional and nuclear. Ninth, this book reveals the challenges of guaranteeing that a military is representative of the society that it protects and the beliefs that it espouses. In the face of systemic, severe, and long-standing racism within the U.S. military, civilian and military leaders during the early Cold War years sought ways to rectify these shortcomings and ensure that military service discarded practices such as racial segregation that were anathema to American ideals.

By providing a comprehensive historical account of George C. Marshall's central role in shaping America during the early Cold War, this book fills a significant void in the scholarship of American military history specifically and American history generally. It utilizes the specific historical context of Marshall's position at the apex of policymaking and his extensive associations with senior leaders to explore broader questions about American power and the place of the military within American society. Previous historians have produced accounts of Marshall either in other time periods or with a narrow topical focus. They have explored the interwar period, World War II, the Marshall Plan, or Marshall's leadership.[5] They have seldom, however, examined the broader story of Marshall's unique role within American society at the dawn of the Cold War. They also have neglected to connect the historical narrative to current issues facing the nation; attending to such connections makes this collection relevant, timely, and in fact crucial to questions of national security, diplomacy, economics, politics, and social issues. The contributions in this volume demonstrate two important dynamics: Marshall continues to have an enduring relevance to policy, politics, and society, and little work has been done on his influence on postwar America. While Marshall deserves extensive attention for the categories discussed above, his impact on America during the early Cold War was vast, encompassing the most significant issues of that formative chapter in American history. These vital topics are what *George C. Marshall and the Early Cold War* is all about.

NOTES

1. Marshall served as army chief of staff from 1939 to 1945, as special presidential envoy to China from 1945 to 1947, as secretary of state from 1947 to 1949, as president of the American Red Cross from 1949 to 1950, as chair of the American Battle Monuments Commission from 1949 to 1959, as secretary of defense from 1950 to 1951, and won the Nobel Peace Prize in 1953.

2. There are many vital biographies that chronicle Marshall's life. The most detailed among them is Forrest C. Pogue, *George C. Marshall*, 4 vols. (New York: Viking, 1963–87). Other fine examples include Debi Unger and Irwin Unger with Stanley Hirshson, *George Marshall: A Biography* (New York: HarperCollins, 2014); Ed Cray, *General of the Army: George C. Marshall, Soldier and Statesman* (New York: Cooper Square, 1990); and Mark A. Stoler, *George C. Marshall: Soldier-Statesman of the American Century* (Boston: Twayne, 1989).

3. On five-star rank, see Christopher R. Gabel, "George Catlett Marshall," in *Generals of the Army: Marshall, MacArthur, Eisenhower, Arnold, Bradley*, ed. James H. Willbanks (Lexington: University Press of Kentucky, 2013), 19–61.

4. On Marshall's contributions as army chief of staff, see Forrest C. Pogue, *George C. Marshall*, vol. 2, *Ordeal and Hope, 1939–1942* (New York: Viking, 1966), and vol. 3, *Organizer of Victory, 1943–1945* (New York: Viking, 1973); Mark A. Stoler, "George C. Marshall and the 'Europe-First' Strategy, 1939–1951: A Study in Diplomatic as well as Military History," *Journal of Military History* 79, no. 2 (April 2015): 293–316; Mark A. Stoler, *Allies and Adversaries: The Joint Chiefs of Staff, the Grand Alliance, and U.S. Strategy in World War II* (Chapel Hill: University of North Carolina Press, 2000).

5. There are many significant works that examine Marshall's military influence on World War II as army chief of staff and senior planner of the American war effort. Examples include Winston Groom, *The Generals: Patton, MacArthur, Marshall and the Winning of World War II* (Washington, D.C.: National Geographic, 2015); Stephen R. Taaffe, *Marshall and His Generals: U.S. Army Commanders in World War II* (Lawrence: University Press of Kansas, 2011); and Andrew Roberts, *Masters and Commanders: How Four Titans Won the War in the West, 1941–1945* (New York: HarperCollins, 2009). Key books that examine Marshall's diplomatic influence as secretary of state and primary architect of the European Recovery Program, also known as the Marshall Plan, include Benn Steil, *The Marshall Plan: Dawn of the Cold War* (New York: Simon & Schuster, 2018); Michael Holm, *The Marshall Plan: A New Deal for Europe* (London: Routledge, 2017); Nicolaus Mills, *Winning the Peace: The Marshall Plan and America's Coming of Age as a Superpower* (Hoboken, N.J.: John Wiley & Sons, 2008); Greg Behrman, *The Most Noble Adventure: The Marshall Plan and the Time When America Helped Save Europe* (New York: Free, 2007); and Michael J. Hogan, *The Marshall Plan: America, Britain, and the Reconstruction of Western Europe, 1947–1952* (Cambridge: Cambridge University Press, 1987). In addition, important accounts that examine Marshall's leadership as both a general and civilian include Charles F. Brower, ed., *George C. Marshall: Servant of the American Nation* (New York: Palgrave Macmillan, 2011); H. Paul Jeffers with Alan Axelrod, *Marshall: Lessons in Leadership* (New York: St. Martin's Press, 2010); Gerald M. Pops, *Ethical Leadership in Turbulent Times: Modeling the Public Career of George C. Marshall* (Lanham, Md.: Lexington Books, 2009); and Jack Uldrich, *Soldier, Statesman, Peacemaker: Leadership Lessons from George C. Marshall* (New York: AMACOM, 2005).

THE OBLIGATION TO SERVE

Marshall and Universal Military Training

It was April 1951, and a vicious war raged across the Korean Peninsula. The United States needed many more soldiers to sustain the war effort there, and controversy erupted across America regarding either enacting universal military training (UMT) or renewing the Selective Service System, reopening the contentious debate that had seethed after World War II.[1] George C. Marshall, secretary of defense, advocated UMT, as he always had, characterizing it as "The Obligation to Serve." Marshall explained that such a system was "in the best democratic tradition" and reassured critics that its benefits would far outweigh its costs. "It is within our capacity to support through the years," Marshall promised. He cataloged UMT's many advantages, including speeding mobilization, providing a General Reserve, and stabilizing the ebb and flow of national security that came with transitions from war to peace. Marshall argued that UMT would ensure "a posture of strength to discourage aggression, a reserve of power to marshal in an emergency."[2]

Marshall lamented the failure of the earlier campaigns for UMT, one after World War I and another after World War II, and connected them directly to the mobilization problems that he now faced for the Korean War as secretary of defense. He chided, "Our failure to provide for Universal Military Training in 1920 and the tragic repetition of that error in 1945 and 1946 are largely responsible for the call we must make on our young men today." Moreover, Marshall argued that UMT would have prevented many of the difficulties of the Korean War. He maintained, "I am convinced that it would not now be necessary to interrupt the normal course of their lives if we had taken the conservative, wise action—an effort that was defeated largely by emotional rather than logical reactions."[3] As events unfolded, Marshall would be disappointed once again, when in response to the crisis on the Korean Peninsula Congress passed on June 7, 1951, the Universal Military Training and Service Bill. President Harry S. Truman signed it into law twelve days later, achieving UMT in name only and unintentionally cementing the use of selective service in America for much of the Cold War.[4] These final gasps of the campaign for UMT, which echoed the much stronger movement for it immediately after World War II that culminated in its critical demise in 1948, illustrated two important facts of American history. First, the campaign for UMT had long-standing, widespread, and vigorous support. Second, George C. Marshall was at the center of it all.

Although it lasted many years and assumed multiple forms, at its core the campaign for UMT sought to have every eighteen-year-old male in America undergo one year of mandatory military training, at the conclusion of which they would choose from multiple options, including serving in active forces, mustering into reserve units, or returning to their civilian lives. Led by Marshall, a plethora of senior military officers, especially within the army, first planned the program in great detail, then recruited allies across American military, government, and society, and finally campaigned for the program, always vigorously and at times overzealously.[5] UMT had many supporters at the highest levels of American government and society, including President Harry S. Truman; Henry L. Stimson, secretary of war; John J. McCloy, undersecretary of war; Walter L. Weible, director of military training; and John MacAuley Palmer, special assistant to the army chief of staff, among others. None was as vocal or as influential as George C. Marshall, first as army chief of staff, then as secretary of state, and finally as secretary of defense. The debates over UMT also reverberated throughout American society, becoming the national high school debate topic during the academic year 1945–46 and remaining a major question in American society for nearly a decade after World War II.[6] Discussing the postwar role of the army and illustrating the vital importance that he placed on the citizen-soldier concept and by extension UMT, Marshall captured the essence of the program by arguing for "the citizen-soldier upon whom, in my view, the future peace of the world largely depends."[7] In its starkest form, supporters characterized the campaign by the phrase: "The young people of today are the soldiers of tomorrow."[8]

Marshall had been an advocate of UMT for most of his adult life. As a result, the context for the campaign after World War II dated back to before World War I in a drive known as the Plattsburg Movement because organizers located one of the main training camps at Plattsburg, New York.[9] Marshall participated in the program and quickly became an ardent booster. It was also at this time that he struck up a friendship with John McAuley Palmer that would last the remainder of his life and became most consequential for UMT.[10] Their relationship spanned more than four decades; Palmer recounted that it began at the Fort Leavenworth Service Schools around 1909 when he was president of the local branch of the Infantry Association and Marshall was its secretary and "a likely young lieutenant, still in his twenties."[11] Palmer reminisced, "This little group of Infantry officers started something new in our service history when it rejected the old slogan, 'Infantry Increase' and came out for 'A well-balanced Army.'" Palmer linked their efforts to the National Defense Act of 1920, which in its original form had sought the enactment of UMT. He explained that he and Marshall, aided by other members of the branch such as Zeke Williams, Bill Bjornstad, and Charley Lincoln, "did some spade work on military policy which, ten years later, became the indispensable basis for all of the really constructive features in the National Defense Act of 1920."[12] In addition to becoming lifelong friends, Marshall and Palmer also became two of the most significant proponents of UMT in America.[13] Their work on UMT after World War I in the form of the National Defense Act was a formative moment in their lives, one that would resonate for them for decades as a lost opportunity: it continued to inform their approach to the same task after World War II. Palmer discussed the problem confronting the army after the war. "To anyone who can see the whole thing in perspective, the organization problem after World War II is, *in essence*, the same as the organization problem after World War I," Palmer confided to Marshall.[14]

Marshall, convinced of the merits of UMT and now connected to the intellectual prophet behind the idea, needed political allies with access in Washington

George C. Marshall (*right*) and John M. Palmer in General Marshall's office.
U.S. Army Signal Corps. Courtesy George C. Marshall Library, Lexington, Va.

if he were to enact it. James W. Wadsworth Jr. became such a supporter. He represented the Thirty-Ninth District of New York and was one of the most knowledgeable figures on national security in the U.S. Congress. "As usual, I am after information about the Army. My thirst for information in that field is insatiable!" he exclaimed to Marshall prior to World War II.[15] Wadsworth's family had been wealthy and influential for generations, and he claimed a family connection to UMT that dated back to George Washington in the form of his relative Jeremiah Wadsworth.[16] As a result, for much of his adult life Wadsworth pursued and supported UMT with a personal zeal, hoping to secure the legacy that his forebear had been unable to generations before. Of significance, Marshall venerated Wadsworth. "As you know, I have long been a very honest, and frank admirer of yours; I believe I have told you that I thought you understood more about the Army than most of the officers in the Army," Marshall extolled.[17] As a result, the National Defense Act of 1920 brought together Marshall, Palmer, and Wadsworth as key boosters in support of UMT. The event would also become the prism through which they would view their subsequent efforts after World War II. For example, Palmer asked Marshall to review his writings on the National Defense Act of 1920 and confirm them; Wadsworth had already done so. Marshall declared that he would be "delighted to read them."[18] Such coordination would characterize their efforts in the early Cold War.

Marshall, along with Palmer and Wadsworth, would consistently cling to the National Defense Act of 1920, and their failure to secure UMT through it, as a key lesson in their campaign after World War II. At the height of the latter campaign, Marshall, along with Secretary of War Henry L. Stimson, Secretary of the Navy Frank Knox, and Chief of Naval Operations Ernest J. King, held an "off-the-record" meeting to promote UMT with representatives of major national women's organizations. On April 26, 1945, at 11:30 A.M. in Room 3E-869 of the Pentagon, Marshall reflected on the National Defense Act of 1920 and articulated to the group his interpretation of its relevance. Marshall reiterated, "I came back after it was over in 1919 and happened to be with General Pershing in the adoption of a very reasonable Defense Act of 1920, and then I was with him during its complete emasculation. I saw there was nothing left but the wording of the law. Then, out with troops, I saw the results of that." Marshall bemoaned the National Defense Act of 1920 as an opportunity lost; it would reinforce his passion for UMT for the remainder of his life. Marshall regretted America's unpreparedness and argued that UMT was the solution. Marshall doubted that enough Americans would volunteer, but more importantly, he feared the parsimony of the U.S. Congress. Events would prove both his trepidations to be legitimate. Marshall prescribed a remedy. If enacted, UMT would build the mobilization potential of the nation through the creation of a large pool of trained personnel known as a General Reserve. It would occur "on a time basis," in that it would take several years to fill the pool, but once complete, it would be capable of "converting a potential into an actual" because the General Reserve could be mobilized in the case of war. Foremost in Marshall's calculus was Congress's ability, but more important its willingness, to fund a large army. Marshall pointed out the vast debt that the country had amassed as a result of World War II and the civilian standard of living that would have to compete with extensive defense appropriations. Marshall explained, "I can put it this way on a purely business proposition—if you do not have compulsory training, you are not going to have an adequate army of any kind. It is one or the other." Marshall reiterated the case that the country could not afford a large army, only UMT, but this was a risky proposition. When pressed on the plan's shortcomings, Marshall fired back, "If you don't have a solution, don't destroy any solution anybody else offers."[19]

Marshall grieved the inability of the National Defense Act of 1920 to enact UMT. He recalled, "The most instructive aspect of this matter to my mind was the fact that General Pershing with his prestige, certainly with a great experience, was powerless to intervene." Marshall feared that he would be in the same position after World War II that Pershing had found himself following World War I. Marshall dreaded that the defeat of UMT would lead to unnecessary deaths of untrained soldiers and unsustainable debt for the nation. Marshall avowed, "So as we see it, certainly as I see it, we either abandon the policy of maintaining, as I have termed it, a respectable military posture or we adopt universal military training."[20] In other words, Marshall argued that without either a large army or UMT, the United States would not have a "respectable military posture." With a plan for a large standing army, however, Congress either would not fund it—the most likely option according to Marshall—or the United States would go bankrupt if Congress did finance it, which Marshall considered unlikely. Therefore, UMT was Marshall's answer to postwar security for military, economic, political, and social reasons.

John McAuley Palmer, who would become special adviser to Marshall on UMT and later serve as consultant on military history for the Library of Congress, felt the same way about the National Defense Act of 1920. Palmer had long served in an unofficial role as the intellectual proponent behind the plan, but before the end of World War II he would assume an official role advising Marshall.[21] When discussing the problems with the National Defense Act of 1920, Palmer maintained that the intransigence was primarily due to army reluctance to move away from a large professional standing army. Palmer recalled,

> For it was largely the War Department's demand for a system based on a large standing army and its hostile attitude toward the development of our traditional "citizen forces" which made it impossible to secure a complete and final legislative solution of our military problem (including universal military training) in the National Defense Act of 1920. In fact, most of the constructive features of the Act of 1920 entered the law, not upon the recommendation of the War Department but in spite of its unsympathetic attitude.[22]

During the interwar period Marshall and Palmer continued to refine their conceptions of military service, especially UMT.[23] As a lieutenant colonel, Marshall served as aide-de-camp to John J. Pershing, general of the armies. On September 10, 1923, Marshall presented his recommendations concerning the interwar army. Throughout his speech, Marshall also explored the Citizens' Military Training Camps and their contribution to the Organized Reserves.[24] During his musings on army organization, Marshall contended that more emphasis needed to be placed on reserve forces: "The great problem at present is to arrive at a definite policy regarding the method of developing the Reserve organizations. We have been experimenting for three years and the time has come to reach a decision."[25]

Marshall and Palmer also maintained their close and warm friendship based on mutual respect.[26] Palmer spent much of the interwar period perfecting his conception of UMT. There were precedents for such a solution; Palmer based many of his ideas on the Swiss system that existed at that time, but he adapted it to suit American democracy.[27] Significantly, he also widely publicized his ideas through his extensive published works.[28] As a result of his voluminous and successful writing, Palmer's significance also rose.[29] Throughout the interwar period, Palmer established himself as an erudite intellectual in the army and the most knowledgeable expert on UMT. He provided all his work to Marshall, who in turn disseminated it widely and thereby became the most recognized military champion of UMT, greatly influencing the direction, scope, and reach of the nationwide campaign.

As the 1930s waned and the world found itself again awash in conflict, Palmer's ideas became increasingly contrasted with those of an earlier army intellectual, Emory Upton.[30] Upton was a proponent of a professional army, and his views contrasted with Palmer's. "A few days ago I took up the cudgels for you in a modest way. One of my disciples, a man of some influence, wrote me that you were apparently against what he called the 'Washington-Palmer idea' and that you were really building up an 'Uptonian' regular army," Palmer notified Marshall. Furthermore, Palmer informed Marshall that he had chided the man that

> you are clear off as to what General Marshall is doing. Marshall *is* increasing the regular army but not in the vicious way that was adopted in 1861 and 1917. He is increasing it by bringing citizen officers and soldiers into it for the period of the emergency (essentially as Washington and Knox proposed in 1790) and not by making it a scheme for the permanent promotion of *all* regular army officers without reference to their individual merits. In this way he is fitting an expanding regular army into the original Washingtonian pattern.[31]

Marshall thanked Palmer for his steadfast support. "I need it these days because I am getting knocks from every side," Marshall admitted.[32]

On November 13, 1941, Marshall recalled Palmer to active duty as a brigadier general. His orders were simple: craft the War Department's plan for UMT. Marshall relayed to Palmer,

> Orders were supposed to have issued today placing you on active duty. The understanding is, pursuant to our telephone conversation, that you have no obligations of office or office hours, that you are merely available to me for consultation in the matter of Army organization as pertaining to the citizen forces, and that you are immediately available as a consultant to the Executive Committee of the National Guard people, who have already requested your advice.[33]

With this pivotal move based on the two generals' long-standing and close friendship, Marshall launched the opening salvo in the campaign for UMT, which would become the basis for all army plans for the immediate post–World War II era. Throughout the crusade, Palmer's unique personal and intellectual role resembled that of a prophet, while Marshall's stature proved critical to disseminating rationales and garnering support.[34]

On August 25, 1944, George C. Marshall, army chief of staff, issued War Department Circular No. 347. The order made UMT official army policy for the post–World War II era and promulgated this ideal throughout the army and into American society.[35] While most observers understandably interpreted the order as solely Marshall's because he signed the policy document, it was Palmer who conceived it, advocated it, and convinced Marshall of its merits. Palmer jested with Marshall, "While we were in New Hampshire, my daughter Mary read me an article from the *New York Times* giving your views on national military policy as expressed in a recent War Department Circular. 'Why Daddy,' she said, 'General Marshall's views are very similar to yours, aren't they?'"[36]

As army chief of staff, Marshall's ability to promulgate UMT as policy throughout the army proved most significant for UMT. Palmer conceded, "The circular appears at a psychological moment in our campaign for sound post-war organization. It should put an end to a divergency of views which has thwarted the establishment of a sound military system since the war of 1812." For his part, Marshall sought to give Palmer credit for the circular, only to have his friend dutifully refuse for the betterment of the campaign. "I was greatly touched," Palmer relayed, "when [William F.] Tompkins told me that you asked him to have credit given me for my part in its preparation. I told him that this is not the time for such credit. The country has hailed the pronouncement as the 'Marshall Plan.' With your great prestige back of it, I hope to live to see the accomplishment of what I have worked for all my life. That is all I ask."[37]

During the spring and summer of 1945, Congress weighed in on UMT specifically and the American postwar defense establishment generally. Congress held highly anticipated and widely followed hearings on the spectrum of issues facing America after World War II; the intent was to formulate postwar plans. The Select Committee on Postwar Military Policy of the House of Representatives, known informally as the Woodrum Committee after its chair, Clifton A. Woodrum (D-Va.), heard from numerous advocates for and against UMT, and more than a hundred witnesses appeared before the committee.[38] The august group examined one central question: "Should the United States adopt as a matter of broad policy a system of universal military training in the postwar period?"[39]

Marshall and Palmer prepared together for the Woodrum Committee. Palmer helped Marshall sharpen his advocacy of UMT. Palmer argued that America's experience in World War I and World War II proved that UMT was essential for postwar America. "Any military organization short of this will obviously be an inadequate half-measure," he averred. Palmer grounded his argument for UMT in the views of George Washington. "Our present plan for a military system based upon universal military training is nothing more or less than a modern adaptation of the plan of 1790," he argued. Palmer compared possible scenarios with and without UMT, claiming that UMT would enhance mobilization, arguing that a sense of complacency would quickly pervade postwar America, and concluding with a rousing endorsement of UMT: "In my opinion, whatever the details of our future plans may be, they should rest upon a definite decision by the Congress in favor of universal military training."[40]

After weeks of organizing, preparing, and posturing, the Woodrum Committee held its hearings. No witness was more anticipated or more respected than George C. Marshall.[41] On June 16, 1945, Marshall delivered his much anticipated testimony before a standing-room-only crowd. It was 4:00 P.M. on a Saturday afternoon, yet the expectant audience remained to hear the main attraction: Marshall's recommendations for U.S. national security after World War II.[42] Marshall left no doubt as to his endorsement; he strenuously promoted UMT. Marshall contended, "A large standing Army is not an acceptable solution for three reasons: Its cost would be prohibitive; the necessary men to fill its ranks could not be hired in time of peace; and it would be repugnant to the American people. Therefore some other solution must be found." The order of Marshall's protest against a "large standing Army" was most telling. Congressional appropriations were at the heart of Marshall's dismissal of such a path forward. "Whatever military system we plan we must have a thorough understanding of the practicality of obtaining the annual appropriations necessary," he cautioned. After cataloging various options, Marshall insisted that UMT was the only viable one and recommended making it the foundation of U.S. national security after the war. Marshall insisted, "I know of no other system other than universal military training that will meet the requirements I have just outlined." Marshall explained why UMT was necessary: it would strengthen the peace process, it would address the key historical lessons of both World War I and World War II, it "would be a supremely democratic procedure," and it would require training only and not military service. Most important, "It would be far more economical than any other method for maintaining military power."[43]

Marshall reinforced his support for UMT in his final biennial report as army chief of staff, much of which was devoted to consideration of national security for postwar America. In it, Marshall established himself as the most visible, vocal, and respected advocate of the plan in the country, and supporters lauded his position. Palmer analyzed in prodigious detail Marshall's report. He continued to contrast Marshall with George Washington, arguing that Marshall had accomplished what Washington had failed to. "You have translated Washington's philosophy into the language and thought of the atomic age," Palmer effused and contended that Marshall's biennial report would propel UMT toward its successful enactment.[44]

Marshall also clearly highlighted his view of deterrence: weakness invited war, while preparedness prevented it. "We must, if we are to realize the hopes we may now dare have for lasting peace, enforce our will for peace with strength. We must make it clear to the potential gangsters of the world that if they dare break our peace they will do so at their great peril," Marshall presaged. Rather, he claimed that a clear military policy, based on the twin pillars of scientific research and a citizen army, would ensure national security. Marshall emphasized the latter: "The importance of scientific research is the most obvious to the civilian, but the importance of a peacetime citizen army based on universal military training is of greater importance, in my opinion."[45]

With the atomic bombing of Hiroshima on August 6, 1945, and that of Naga-saki three days later, the agonizing years of destruction of World War II soon came to a conclusion. The attention of Americans quickly shifted to postwar policy. Some observers argued that the advent of the atomic age made UMT anachronistic: large armies were a thing of the past. In the face of such pro-nouncements, Marshall continued his staunch support. "Development of the atomic bomb has increased, rather than decreased, the importance of the soldier who fights on the ground, in the opinion of Gen. George C. Marshall," reported the *New York Times*. Marshall cautioned doubters, "People overlook the fact, when they are talking about mechanized or technological warfare, that more men are required than in the past." Marshall reminded them of the augmented number of support personnel, or "tail-to-tooth" ratio, that had emerged during World War II and would likely increase in any future conflict.[46]

At the end of World War II, Marshall's prestige was unsurpassed. Americans lauded him as the senior planner of the American war effort. Even comic books hailed him as one of the greatest American heroes of all time.[47] To some observ-ers, however, Marshall's job was not yet done; they urged him to implement UMT. "Congressional doubts and anxieties about universal military training can best be resolved by an assurance that General Marshall himself will conduct the program. The assurance would give to the whole country a firm confidence that the program would be conducted upon a sound, constructive and demo-cratic basis," opined the *Washington Post*. Some observers feared that the largest army America had ever mobilized was shrinking precipitously at the same time that America's place in the world had climaxed and international affairs were not only uncertain, but increasingly tense. "America's military might was built with great speed. But today it is being torn down with even greater speed. The fact is a cause of grave concern to President Truman, to General Marshall and to thinking citizens in every facet of our national life," concluded the *Post*.[48]

Marshall courted and received political support for UMT. President Harry S. Truman proved a consistent supporter of UMT, formally requesting its enact-ment eight times during his presidency.[49] Truman recounted, "I believe now there is a good chance to obtain a reasonable training law. I am going to put forth every effort possible to get that done."[50] To demonstrate his commitment, Truman formed the President's Advisory Commission on Universal Training (PACUT), known colloquially as the Compton Commission after Karl T. Comp-ton, its chair and the president of the Massachusetts Institute of Technology.[51]

The Compton Commission considered four major problems: the necessity of UMT for national security, its particular form for national security, its desirability for social purposes, and alternative measures to improve American society.[52] The respected body held many meetings, including thirteen official ones from December 20, 1946, to April 19, 1947.[53] To aid its consideration of UMT in postwar America, the group also investigated military service in more than fifty other countries.[54]

Marshall and Palmer both provided extensive feedback to the Compton Commission; no one's input, however, was more influential than Marshall's.[55] As secretary of state, Marshall's commitment to UMT had only increased. "Secretary Marshall replied very emphatically that as Secretary of State he feels the need of universal military training even more urgently than he felt it as Chief of Staff." In addition to the extensive military experience that he brought to bear, Secretary of State Marshall advocated UMT for diplomatic reasons, especially deterrence. The consummate diplomat, Marshall provided his views to the commission in a clear, but informal, manner; he privately delivered them to the group while avoiding a public appearance. "Secretary Marshall's only reason for wishing not to appear before us at this time is the feeling that such an appearance would prejudice the case because he is a military man and his views as such are well known," Compton relayed.[56]

For his input, Palmer reinforced the comparison between UMT in postwar America and the Swiss system.[57] He urged commission members to use Switzerland as their model. Palmer claimed, "If the Commission should visit Switzerland, it would find there an up-to-date working model which has been in continuous operation and development for the century and a half since Washington submitted an American adaptation of it to the First Congress." While he admitted that he had never traveled to Switzerland, Palmer reminded them, "I have studied the Swiss military system for many years under the instruction and guidance of the only man in the world who was intimately acquainted with both the Swiss army and the American army." That man was the late Swiss military officer Col. Henri LeComte. Palmer's relationship with LeComte was personal and long-standing. Palmer recalled, "I first knew LeComte when he was a plebe at West Point and I, as a brand new cadet corporal, was one of his yearling drill-masters. After that until my graduation three years later, we became close friends."[58] Throughout his testimony, Palmer detailed the key documents outlining UMT, including his two *Saturday Evening Post* articles, Circular No. 347, and his book *America in Arms*.[59]

After extensive hearings, the Compton Commission on May 29, 1947, produced its final report, *A Program for National Security*. In it, commission members unanimously recommended that America adopt UMT. Of course, not
all observers supported the commission's recommendation.[60] A group led by
Robert M. Hutchins, chancellor of the University of Chicago, produced a scath-
ing rejoinder, known colloquially as the Hutchins report after its chair, which
criticized the Compton Commission specifically and UMT generally. Joining
Hutchins were other notables, including Democrat Sen. Edwin C. Johnson of
Colorado; Josephus Daniels, secretary of the navy during World War I; and
James G. Patton, president of the National Farmers Union. They did not limit
their critique solely to the Compton Commission but also assailed the general
concept of UMT. "We shall describe numerous fallacies and shortcomings in
this Report, including the wastefulness and futility even from a strictly military
point of view of the universal military training which the Commission strongly
recommends," Hutchins and his colleagues insisted.[61]

International tensions escalated quickly and dangerously during 1948, resulting in three war scares with the Soviet Union. In response, President Truman
called for three things: the European Recovery Program, UMT, and a temporary
resumption of selective service until UMT was operational. Amidst the chaos,
Congress again held extensive hearings to consider UMT during the spring of
1948, which produced well over one thousand pages of testimony and written
statements from every imaginable supporter and opponent. Besides Marshall,
the committee heard from James V. Forrestal, secretary of defense; Kenneth
C. Royall, secretary of the army; W. Stuart Symington, secretary of the air force;
John L. Sullivan, secretary of the navy; Karl T. Compton, chair of the President's
Advisory Commission on Universal Training; Owen J. Roberts, associate justice
of the Supreme Court; Albert Einstein, then with the Institute for Advanced
Study; Eleanor Roosevelt, former first lady; Omar Bradley, chief of staff of the
army; J. Lawton Collins, vice chief of staff of the army; Louis E. Denfeld, chief of
naval operations; Henry A. Wallace, former vice president; and George F. Zook,
president of the American Council on Education; among many others. UMT
continued to spark rigorous debate across the nation. Advocates and opponents
alike sensed that 1948 was a moment of decision, and most major public figures
weighed in during this time. In addition, churches, schools, organizations,
businesses, labor unions, and pacifist groups registered their positions.[62]

At the opening of the pivotal hearings, Sen. Chan Gurney (R-S.D.), chair of
the Senate Armed Services Committee, set an ominous tone. "It is perfectly

"We Must Be Ready to Back Up What We Say." March 18, 1948. Cartoon by
Clifford K. Berryman. Courtesy Center for Legislative Archives, U.S. National
Archives and Records Administration.

clear that a definite threat to our own security exists in the world today; it
is clear that the clouds of war are starting to gather," Gurney warned. "We
all fervently hope those clouds can be dispersed. But while we are hoping
that the storm will not overtake us, common prudence dictates that we also
'batten down the hatches' of our defense system." In addition to illuminating
the dangerous currents of international security, Gurney reminded observers
that UMT had official sanction. "The President has just told us that we need
universal military training and also the temporary reenactment of selective-
service legislation," Gurney prompted the audience. "He states that there is no
conflict between the requirements of selective service for the Regular forces
and universal training for the Reserve components because selective service
is necessary as an interim measure until the foundation of universal military
training is established."[63]

On Wednesday, March 17, 1948, at 2:30 P.M. EST, Marshall delivered his long-anticipated comments. At the outset, Marshall referenced President Truman's speech to a joint session of Congress earlier that morning. "I wish to express in person to you my own concern over the accelerated trend in Europe. In the short years since the end of hostilities this trend has grown from a trickle into a torrent," Marshall spoke with dread. "One by one, the Balkan states, except Greece, lost all semblance of national independence. Then two friendly nations—first Hungary and last week Czechoslovakia—have been forced into complete submission to the Communist control." Referring to the European Recovery Program (ERP), which would eventually bear his name, Marshall contended, "This program, I believe, is a fundamental requirement for the strengthening of the Western nations of Europe." Marshall, however, argued that other steps must be taken to ensure America's postwar security. "But this economic program in the existing situation is not a complete answer," he acknowledged. After briefly discussing the ERP, Marshall pressed for UMT. "Diplomatic action, without the backing of military strength in the present world can lead only to appeasement," he explained. "I see no possible way financially to maintain a reasonable military posture except on the foundation of universal military training." Marshall's strong advocacy of UMT as secretary of state was especially significant, given that his own Policy Planning Staff at the Department of State had recommended that he soften his testimony, which Marshall refused to do. Instead, he advocated for UMT even more strongly as secretary of state than he had before as army chief of staff. Undeterred, he stuck to his convictions and summed up the rationale for UMT. Marshall argued that UMT would ease recruiting for the active forces, would strengthen the National Guard, would improve the Reserve Officers' Training Corps, and would enhance America's commitment to international security, demonstrating it for U.S. allies abroad and Americans at home. In front of the nation, Marshall issued a clarion call for two things: the European Recovery Program and universal military training. Marshall reluctantly acknowledged the necessity of selective service, but only its "temporary application." Therefore, Marshall advocated for UMT even though he begrudgingly accepted selective service as a transitory bridge toward his ultimate goal.[64]

Most of the questions generated from the hearings centered on Marshall. In answering them, he remained steadfast. "I made a number of statements in August and September of 1945 in the general tenor of the quotation that I just read," he reminded listeners. "Then I made that statement before the

Compton Commission in May of 1947. We have now reached March of 1948. I am far more convinced now than I was then of the importance of the measures recommended." Marshall's support of UMT was consistent, and his support was growing, not waning. As secretary of state, he urged three reasons for enacting UMT, which Sen. Styles Bridges (R-N.H.) repeated for the audience. First, Marshall sought to create deterrence, which he contended would have "a great psychological effect upon the world." Second, Marshall desired to improve mobilization, which he insisted would "more adequately arm America." Third, Marshall hoped to reduce costs, which he claimed would "effectively arm [America] at a reasonable price without jeopardizing the solvency of our country."[65]

The Korean War both reinvigorated consideration of UMT in the early Cold War and blunted its chances of ultimate success. With the outbreak of fighting on the Korean Peninsula, the Senate Armed Services Committee began hearings on S. 4062, "a bill intended to inaugurate a system of universal military training consistent with the recommendations of the Compton Commission."[66] Basing its bill on the previous version that it had failed to pass in 1948, the U.S. Congress thus began serious consideration of how to handle military personnel requirements of the Korean War, thereby reigniting consideration of UMT. Not much had changed legislatively since 1948: the bill that Congress prepared in 1951 was similar to the 1948 bill in two significant ways. First, they both originally sought to implement UMT. Second, they both ultimately failed to do so and instead resumed selective service.[67] This result showed a level of continual effort on the part of the army to implement UMT for military reasons and a consistent preference on the part of Congress to privilege selective service for political calculations.

Forever hopeful, Marshall had requested "the earliest practicable date recommended for implementing Universal Military Training." Instead, the Korean War relegated UMT to await peace. "If it is the intention of the Congress to implement Universal Military Training at this time, it must of necessity take second place to meeting the emergency which is already upon us," Secretary of the Army Frank Pace admitted to Marshall, who now served as secretary of defense. As before in 1948, the activation of selective service overshadowed the possible enactment of UMT. The reasons were simple: the draft provided personnel in an immediate and calibrated way, while UMT would take several years to implement and would involve all eighteen-year-old Americans, even if that number far exceeded military requirements. While Pace recommended that it would be better for President Truman to establish a start date, he anticipated that it would have to be after the Korean War. "Nonetheless should it be required to establish a definite date in the law for the implementation of Universal Military Training, I recommend that this date should be fixed at 12 months after the termination of current combat operations, or 1 January 1952."[68] Pace's estimate portended wistful optimism about a speedy conclusion to the Korean War.

As personnel requirements skyrocketed during the Korean War, policy makers scrambled to find ways to fill them. Anna M. Rosenberg, assistant secretary of defense and a longtime confidante of Marshall's, requested information on UMT from John G. Adams, assistant general counsel for the Department of Defense, "for the use of General Marshall." She wanted to highlight the differences between the Department of Defense's plan and a congressional alternative, the Vinson plan, named after its sponsor, Rep. Carl Vinson (D-Ga.). The Pentagon's plan was to establish concurrently selective service and UMT and then gradually shift from the draft to UMT. For Marshall, Palmer, and their many allies, UMT was the long-term solution, while selective service was the temporary fix.[69] As a result, UMT remained the goal for postwar national security, especially for the army.

Adams contrasted for Rosenberg this military plan with the Vinson plan. Adams revealed angst that Congress might allow selective service to override UMT and explained to Rosenberg the reasons why. "In short, if UMT cannot begin until after the draft completely ceases, the draft may continue throughout our lifetime and the size of the standing force never be reduced. I do not believe that this country can afford indefinitely the economic and social costs of Armed Forces as big as, or bigger than, those we have today," Adams worried.[70] Ultimately, Congress convinced Marshall and his allies to accept the draft, but they anticipated that it would shift quickly to UMT. Once the draft was operational, however, Congress did not feel any urgency to make the transition. H. A. Houser, a Rosenberg staffer, relayed, "Upon adoption of the conference report by both Houses and signature of the Act by the President, the principle of UMT will have become law." Houser, Adams, Rosenberg, Palmer, and Marshall all viewed the 1951 act as the embodiment of the principle of UMT; therefore, it seemed to them a victory. It turned out to be a hollow triumph, however, because the law did not allow implementation of UMT while selective service operated, something that Houser argued was still achievable. "It is apparent, therefore, that prompt action is essential *at all stages* if it is hoped to complete the necessary action on UMT within the first session of the 82nd Congress and this is considered highly desirable," he urged Rosenberg.[71]

Even staunch proponents of UMT worried, however, that the campaign was losing momentum. On August 25, 1951, Wadsworth wrote Marshall, informing him "of the concern regarding the implementation of Universal Military Training." Wadsworth feared that if both programs ran concurrently, a young man might complete UMT and then still be drafted afterward. In essence, the dual system eliminated the underlying rationale for UMT, which was designed for peacetime. UMT would prove difficult to enact with international tensions high, as they previously were at the critical moment in 1948 and were again during the Korean War. As a result, selective service consumed it, especially with deferments exempting all but the youngest eligible Americans.[72]

George C. Marshall was critical to passage of the Universal Military Training and Service Act of 1951. Rosenberg relayed to him George Beveridge's comments in the *Washington Evening Star* about Marshall's importance in securing this pivotal act. Rosenberg disclosed that Beveridge had written on January 21, 1952, "It was General Marshall's final appeal, when he sent letters to all the members of Congress, that put the UMTS Act across at the last session. Up until then a lot of Congressmen were wavering and the bill might have been licked. I think it would have except for Marshall's final appeal."[73]

The 1951 law established a National Security Training Corps, comprised in theory of all American males between the ages of eighteen and nineteen, who were liable for six months of military training. Such training would only occur, however, when the president ceased operation of the draft. The law also established a National Security Training Commission composed of five high-profile members to oversee the program, including James W. Wadsworth Jr., chair and U.S. representative (R-N.Y.); William L. Clayton, former undersecretary of state for economic affairs; Karl T. Compton, president of MIT and previous chair of the President's Advisory Commission on Universal Training; Thomas C. Kinkaid, admiral and commander of the Seventh Fleet during World War II; and Raymond S. McLain, commander of the XIX Corps during World War II. As a result of their inability to operate concurrently and the increased use of deferments for selective service, the draft prevented UMT. "Thus, for every available registrant, four were deferred or exempted. Unless the liberal deferment provisions of the current legislation and regulations are tightened or unless inductions drop considerably, the time cannot be too far away when men 18½ to 19 years of age will become for all practical purposes the only current source of military manpower," Lewis B. Hershey warned. "When that situation obtains, Selective Service will be operating essentially on a universal military service basis with training a concomitant."[74] Basing his assessment on deferments as of June 30, 1952, Hershey argued that because selective service allowed so many deferments, it left only the very young to be drafted. With that dynamic at work, UMT remained unfeasible.

Promoters lauded the UMTS Act as a historic victory, although their optimism proved to be misplaced. In essence, they welcomed the law as establishing the principle of UMT, assuming that the mechanics to implement it logically would follow. Instead, they simply had enshrined the name of UMT on legislation that enacted selective service, which ironically would prevent any sense of urgency or further progress on UMT. "The passage of the Universal Military Training and Service law represents a step of historic significance," claimed Marshall. In a substantial understatement, Marshall admitted, "The law does not contain all the provisions the Defense Department would have desired, but I am confident that Congress will enact the necessary supporting legislation to carry into actual effect the historic principles unified in the bill. The objective of a universally shared obligation for the defense of our country on a basis that we can support is now within our grasp, for the first time since George Washington began the pursuit of this goal a century and a half ago."[75]

Observers less invested in UMT were more sanguine in their appraisals. "Whatever became of UMT?" asked Quentin R. Mott, reporter for the *Star*. "The answer is, it is still in the offing, but its approach is very slow, and not entirely sure. For the draft act signed by President Truman on June 19—which laid the groundwork for this unprecedented plan for universal training of our youth—also imposes a few hurdles for the project." Mott explained how passage of the UMTS Act ironically made its namesake an unlikely prospect at best. "But no matter how prompt the commissioners are, a combination of law and circumstances makes it highly improbable that UMT will be anything more than a paper program for some time to come," he perceived. Noting the inherent conflict between the two ideas, Mott clarified, "With a 24 months limit on service, there is going to be a big turnover a year from now. If UMT were to start taking the 18-year-olds, it would dip into the manpower pool from which Selective Service makes replacements. With such safeguards erected to prevent hasty action and all the guarantees imposed to assure full consideration, eventual adoption of UMT is still remote."[76]

The Universal Military Training and Service Act of 1951 hailed the concept of UMT without providing the enabling mechanisms for the program. The National Security Training Commission boasted, "The principle of UMT had been accepted by Congress in Public Law 51 and that there was, in consequence, no further need to entertain arguments for or against that principle. Proceeding on that premise, the Commission looked upon itself as essentially a technical body, created for the purpose of applying the accepted principle, of determining *how* a UMT program should be organized and operated." Wadsworth and his colleagues continued, "Like other untested undertakings, UMT is certain to have its growing pains, but for several reasons these should not affect its sure and steady maturation." Those reasons included the vast amount of attention, study, and debate that UMT had garnered after World War II, the comprehensive review and subsequent unanimous endorsement of UMT by the Compton Commission, and the successful validation of it embodied in the UMT Experimental Unit at Fort Knox, Kentucky.[77] With UMTS passed, supporters still believed in the training program's "sure and steady maturation" in the years ahead. They had established the principle and anticipated a future shift from selective service to UMT. "By giving approval to the principle of universal military training, through the enactment of Public Law 51, the United States has laid a foundation for enduring military strength," the group proclaimed.[78]

With time, however, it became increasingly clear that passage of the UMTS law was a Pyrrhic victory for Marshall and his many supporters. "But whatever is the best way to solve the problem, the country hasn't been sold as yet on the necessity for urgency on a 'training' program while the draft is in operation. If there's an 'emergency,' the draft is supposed to take care of it, says the observing public, and, if that isn't enough, the reserve powers in the law can be invoked to bring back into service some of the draftees who have served their time. That's an inequitable set-up but it hasn't been argued out," reported the *New York Herald Tribune*.[79] The two programs were in fundamental and perpetual conflict. Congress comfortably asked why America needed UMT if it had selective service, while Marshall and his allies always hoped to lead a shift from selective service to UMT. Congress was content to rely on selective service from 1948 to 1973, when President Richard M. Nixon and Congress replaced it with an All-Volunteer Force, which brings us back to the Korean War. As secretary of defense and the staunchest advocate of UMT in the United States, Marshall lamented an opportunity lost, much like he had after World War I. Marshall's conception of "The Obligation to Serve" had found many proponents and captured the attention of postwar America for nearly a decade, but the urgency and tensions of the early Cold War elevated selective service over UMT in an unanticipated way. Considering "The Obligation to Serve" and unaccustomed to defeat, Marshall mourned, "The history of national defense in this country has been a succession of feasts and famines that have followed each other in demoralizing sequences. For a Nation that prides itself on its hard-headed business acumen and its practical common sense, we have given the world quite an opposite impression of these qualities in our vacillations on preparedness."[80] Even in a lost cause, however, George C. Marshall remained at the center of the storm.

NOTES

1. On debates during the Korean War, see "UMT as a Must," *Washington Post*, April 18, 1951; Hanson W. Baldwin, "Manpower Bill Is Weak: Emergency Features Are Merely Adequate and Permanent Provisions Are Monstrous," *New York Times*, March 22, 1951; and "The Draft for Now," *Christian Science Monitor*, January 3, 1951. On UMT, see William A. Taylor, *Every Citizen a Soldier: The Campaign for Universal Military Training after World War II* (College Station: Texas A&M University Press, 2014). The author acknowledges the assistance of Paul B. Barron, Jeffrey S. Kozak, and Cara C. Sonnier at the George C. Marshall Library, who provided assistance on multiple research trips to the archives. The George C. Marshall Library houses all major records on Marshall's life. Most pertinent for this study were the George C. Marshall Papers and the Marshall Foundation National Archives Project (hereafter cited as MFNAP).

2. George C. Marshall, "The Obligation to Serve," *Army Information Digest* 6, no. 4 (April 1952): 8, reproduced as Xerox 3289, MFNAP, George C. Marshall Library (hereafter cited as GCML).

3. Ibid., 7.

4. On passage of the UMTS bill, see Harold B. Hinton, "Draft-U.M.T. Bill Signed by Truman: He Nominates Five to Supervise Military Training Program—Marshall Hails Law," *New York Times*, June 20, 1951; and "Draft Compromise Passed by Congress," *New York Times*, June 8, 1951.

5. Congress twice investigated the army for propagandizing for UMT. On investigations, see U.S. Congress, House, *Investigation of War Department Publicity and Propaganda in Relation to Universal Military Training: Hearings before the United States House Committee on Expenditures in the Executive Departments, Subcommittee on Publicity and Propaganda,* 80th Cong., 1st sess., June 20, July 16, 1947; 2nd sess., January 14, 1948.

6. See *Peacetime Military Training: The Nineteenth Annual Debate Handbook*, box 355, folder 095A, Record Group (RG) 165, Records of the War Department General and Special Staffs, entry 479, Security Classified Correspondence, Reports, Memoranda, and Other Papers Relating to Universal Military Training, 1944–48, National Archives and Records Administration.

7. George C. Marshall, "Biennial Report, July 1, 1943–June 30, 1945," 120, reproduced as Xerox 3208, MFNAP, GCML.

8. Walter C. Thee to Clark M. Clifford, February 2, 1947, 3, box 19, folder Universal Military Training—Message to Congress [1 of 2], Clark M. Clifford Papers, Harry S. Truman Library (hereafter cited as HSTL). There were many alternative versions of the plan, some much more radical. For example, see Walter C. Thee, Lt. Col., Quartermaster Corps, to K. L. Hastings, Col., Quartermaster Corps, Director of Personnel, Office of the Quartermaster General, January 14, 1947, 1, box 19, folder Universal Military Training—Message to Congress [1 of 2], Clark M. Clifford Papers, HSTL. In his plan, Thee advocated for military training of youths between twelve and eighteen years of age, well below the official army version that sought to train eighteen-year-olds.

9. On the Plattsburg Movement, see John Garry Clifford, *The Citizen Soldiers: The Plattsburg Training Camp Movement, 1913–1920* (Lexington: University Press of Kentucky, 1972); and William A. Taylor, "The Spirit of 1920," in *Every Citizen a Soldier*, 13–26.

10. On Palmer, see I. B. Holley Jr., *General John M. Palmer, Citizen Soldiers, and the Army of a Democracy* (Westport, Conn.: Greenwood, 1982).

11. John M. Palmer to George C. Marshall, November 13, 1944, 1, box 78, folder 23, George C. Marshall Papers (hereafter cited as Marshall Papers), GCML.

12. Ibid.

13. The third most significant was James W. Wadsworth Jr. On Wadsworth, see Martin L. Fausold, *James W. Wadsworth, Jr.: The Gentleman from New York* (Syracuse, N.Y.: Syracuse University Press, 1975).

14. John M. Palmer to George C. Marshall, November 13, 1944, 2, box 78, folder 23, Marshall Papers, GCML; emphasis in original.

15. James W. Wadsworth Jr. to George C. Marshall, December 8, 1939, 1–2, box 89, folder 30, Marshall Papers, GCML.

16. On Jeremiah Wadsworth, see Wayne Mahood, *General Wadsworth: The Life and Times of Brevet Major General James S. Wadsworth* (Cambridge, Mass.: Da Capo Press, 2003), 7–8, 9, 12, 14, 18.

17. George C. Marshall to James W. Wadsworth Jr., December 6, 1939, 1, box 89, folder 30, Marshall Papers, GCML.

18. John M. Palmer to George C. Marshall, March 15, 1940, 1, box 78, folder 17; George C. Marshall to John M. Palmer, March 19, 1940, 1, box 78, folder 17, Marshall Papers, GCML.

19. George C. Marshall, "Address by General Marshall, Women's Conference on UMT," April 26, 1945, 1–6, box 87, folder 14, George C. Marshall Papers, GCML. It is important to note that Marshall rewrote his comments after the conference. The main concepts were the same, but he smoothed the language and developed certain ideas in more detail. For instance, "If you don't have a solution, don't destroy any solution anybody else offers" became, in the released version: "If you yourself do not have a practical solution, then I beg of you to hesitate before you sweep aside the solution we propose." See the final draft included in H. M. Pasco, Lt. Col., General Staff Corps, Assistant Secretary, General Staff, "Memorandum for General Weible, by Direction of the Chief of Staff," May 12, 1945, 1, box 87, folder 15, Marshall Papers, GCML.

20. "Transcript of Committee Meeting Conference of the Secretary of War and the Secretary of the Navy and Their Staffs with Leading Educators of the Country," December 29, 1944, 15–16, 19, reproduced as Xerox 3260, MFNAP, GCML.

21. John M. Palmer, "Memorandum for the Committee on Civilian Components, Office of the Consultant in Military History, Subject: Inter-Relations between Professional and Non-Professional Personnel in the Armed Forces of a Democratic State," January 9, 1948, 1, box 78, folder 33, Marshall Papers, GCML.

22. Ibid., 2.

23. John M. Palmer to George C. Marshall, December 15, 1939, 24–28, box 78, folder 16, Marshall Papers, GCML. For example, on page 24 Marshall states, "This paragraph and the following two are more or less quotations from a paper prepared by General Palmer."

24. George C. Marshall, "The Development of the National Army, The Army War College, Washington Barracks, DC," September 10, 1923, 1–28, box 110, folder 13, Marshall Papers, GCML.

25. Ibid., 28.

26. For letters between Marshall and Palmer revealing their close friendship and mutual respect, see George C. Marshall to John M. Palmer, March 6, 1939; George C. Marshall to John M. Palmer, November 22, 1938; John M. Palmer to George C. Marshall, November 21, 1938; George C. Marshall to John M. Palmer, September 7, 1938; John M. Palmer to George C. Marshall, September 1, 1938—all located in box 78, folder 16, Marshall Papers, GCML.

27. John M. Palmer, "Memorandum for General Marshall," December 18, 1939, 1, box 78, folder 16, Marshall Papers, GCML.

28. On Palmer's interwar writings, see *America in Arms: The Experience of the United States with Military Organization* (Washington, D.C.: Infantry Journal, 1941); *Washington, Lincoln, Wilson: Three War Statesmen* (Garden City, N.Y.: Doubleday, Doran, 1930); *Statesmanship or War* (New York: Doubleday, Page, 1927); *An Army of the People: The Constitution of an Effective Force of Trained Citizens* (New York: G. P. Putnam's Sons, 1916).

29. On Palmer's influence, see "John McAuley Palmer," *Washington Post and Times Herald*, October 30, 1955; and Robert E. Runser, "Which Man's Army?" *Washington Post*, May 11, 1941.

30. On Upton, see David J. Fitzpatrick, *Emory Upton: Misunderstood Reformer* (Norman: University of Oklahoma Press, 2017); "Emory Upton and the Army of a Democracy," *Journal of Military History* 77, no. 2 (April 2013): 463–90; and "Emory Upton and the Citizen Soldier," *Journal of Military History* 65, no. 2 (April 2001): 355–89.

31. John M. Palmer to George C. Marshall, August 4, 1941, 1, box 78, folder 18, Marshall Papers, GCML; emphasis in original.

32. George C. Marshall to John M. Palmer, August 15, 1941, 1, box 78, folder 18, Marshall Papers, GCML.

33. George C. Marshall to John M. Palmer, November 13, 1941, 1, box 78, folder 18, Marshall Papers, GCML.

34. John M. Palmer to George C. Marshall, October 30, 1945, 1, box 78, folder 30, Marshall Papers, GCML.

35. On public reaction to War Department Circular No. 347, see "Marshall Plan for the Future Army," *New York Times*, September 3, 1944; and "Marshall in Favor of Small Army: Modern Democratic State No Place for Large Force, Leader Declares," *Los Angeles Times*, September 2, 1944.

36. John M. Palmer to George C. Marshall, September 14, 1944, 1, box 78, folder 21, Marshall Papers, GCML.

37. Ibid.

38. For an extensive summary of witnesses who argued for and against UMT during the Woodrum Committee hearings, see George M. Elsey, "Memorandum for Commodore Vardaman, Attachment," August 14, 1945, 1, box 89, folder National Defense—Universal Military Training (folder 1), George M. Elsey Papers (hereafter cited as Elsey Papers), HSTL.

39. U.S. Congress, House, "Universal Military Training, 79th Congress, 1st sess., House of Representatives, Report No. 857," July 5, 1945, 1, box 89, folder National Defense—Universal Military Training (folder 1), Elsey Papers, HSTL.

40. John M. Palmer, "Memorandum for the Chief of Staff, Subject: Testimony before the H. R. Select Committee on Post War Military Policy," June 12, 1945, 1–5, box 87, folder 16, Marshall Papers, GCML.

41. George C. Marshall, "Statement of General of the Army George C. Marshall, Chief of Staff, United States Army, House of Representatives, Select Committee on Postwar Military Policy," June 16, 1945, 1515, box 114, folder 41, Marshall Papers, GCML.

42. On Marshall's testimony, see "Gen. Marshall's Plea for a Peace Draft," *New York Times*, June 17, 1945; and Joseph A. Loftus, "Marshall and King Support Appeals for a Peace Draft: Forrestal and Several Chiefs of Army and Navy Also Call Compulsory Training Vital," *New York Times*, June 17, 1945.

43. George C. Marshall, "Statement by General of the Army George C. Marshall, Chief of Staff, on Universal Military Training before the Select Committee on Universal Military Training before the Select Committee on Post-War Military Policy of the House of Representatives," June 16, 1945, 2–4, box 87, folder 16, Marshall Papers, GCML.

44. John M. Palmer to George C. Marshall, September 24, 1945, 1, box 78, folder 29, Marshall Papers, GCML.

45. George C. Marshall, "The Winning of the War in Europe and the Pacific, Biennial Report of the Chief of Staff of the United States Army, 1943 to 1945, to the Secretary of War, Published for the War Department in Cooperation with the Council on Books in Wartime by Simon and Schuster," September 1, 1945, 6, box 4, folder 10, Elsey Papers, GCML.

46. "Marshall Holds Army Role Grows: Importance of Land Forces Increased by Atomic Bomb, General Testifies," *New York Times*, October 18, 1945.

47. On Marshall's appearances in comic books, see *Marshall: The Magazine of the George C. Marshall Foundation* (Spring 2017), which reveals on its cover a 1941 copy of *World Famous Heroes Magazine* on which George C. Marshall is front and center

leading a cohort of American heroes, including Paul Revere, Robert E. Peary, William A. Bishop, David Crockett, Lewis and Clark, and John Paul Jones. Also see Cara C. Sonnier, "Marshall and the Comic Books," *Marshall: The Magazine of the George C. Marshall Foundation* (Fall 2015): 24. Images of these comic books are available at https://marshallfoundation.org/blog/marshall-comic-books/ (accessed August 21, 2017).

48. "One More Job for General Marshall," *Washington Post*, October 25, 1945.

49. For a complete listing, see "Occasions of Formal Recommendation to Congress of Universal Training, by the President," August 1, 1950, 1, box 90, folder National Defense—Universal Military Training (folder 2), Elsey Papers, HSTL.

50. Harry S. Truman to Henry L. Stimson, September 6, 1950, 1, box 126, folder Military: Universal Training, Harry S. Truman Papers, President's Secretary's Files: Subject File, 1940–1953, HSTL.

51. On PACUT, see President's Advisory Commission on Universal Training, *A Program for National Security* (Washington, D.C.: Government Printing Office, 1947).

52. President's Advisory Commission on Universal Training, "Analysis of the Problems before the President's Advisory Commission on Universal Training," May 7, 1947, 1, box 12, folder Analysis of the Problems before the President's Advisory Commission on UMT [folder 1], Record Group 220, Records of Temporary Committees, Commissions, and Boards, Records of the President's Advisory Commission on Universal Training (hereafter cited as PACUT), HSTL.

53. "Cumulative Index to Hearings of the President's Advisory Commission on Universal Training," May 1, 1947, cover, box 10, folder Index to Hearings of the President's Advisory Commission on UMT—December 20, 1946–April 19, 1947, RG 220, PACUT, HSTL. For an extensive list of meetings, see 1–5. For an all-encompassing inventory of witnesses, see 6–9. The index does not include two meetings held at Princeton University in May 1947, as indicated by the handwritten note on the second copy of the index.

54. Wilbur J. Cohen, director of research, "Memorandum to Members of the Commission, Subject: Preliminary Drafts of Research Studies on Military Training in Foreign Countries," April 10, 1947, 1, box 7, folder Staff Studies—Preliminary Drafts of Research Papers on Military Training in Foreign Nations, RG 220, PACUT, HSTL. The research studies included "The Swiss System of Universal Military Training," "The Swedish System of Military Training," "Military Training and Service in Great Britain," "Compulsory Military Training in the Union of South Africa," and "Brief Summary of Military Service Requirements as of February 1947 in 53 Foreign Nations Which Have Organized Military Systems."

55. John M. Palmer, "Historical Background of Universal Training and Preparedness in the United States, Prepared for President's Advisory Commission on Universal Training," January 16, 1947, box 78, folder 32, Marshall Papers, GCML.

56. Karl T. Compton, "Memorandum, Topic: Conference with Secretary of State Marshall," January 30, 1947, 1, box 6, folder Staff Studies—Conference with Secretary of State George C. Marshall, RG 220, PACUT, HSTL.

57. John M. Palmer, "Memorandum for the President's Advisory Commission on Universal Training," box 6, folder Staff Studies—Memorandum from Brig. Gen. John

Palmer, RG 220, PACUT, HSTL. Palmer's memorandum on the Swiss system also included an appendix: John M. Palmer, "The Training of Citizen Soldiers," excerpts from Chapter 2, *Statesmanship or War* (New York: Doubleday, Page, 1927).

58. John M. Palmer, "Memorandum for the President's Advisory Commission on Universal Training," 1, 5–6, box 20, folder Bureau of the Budget—Universal Military Training, James E. Webb Papers, HSTL.

59. John M. Palmer, "Historical Background of Universal Training and Preparedness in the United States, Prepared for President's Advisory Commission on Universal Training," January 16, 1947, 8, box 78, folder 32, Marshall Papers, GCML.

60. On opposition to UMT, see William A. Taylor, "A Pig in a Poke," in *Every Citizen a Soldier*, 67–87.

61. Robert M. Hutchins, "An Analysis of the Report of the President's Advisory Commission on Universal Training," July 7, 1947, 3, 5, box 9, folder The President's Advisory Commission on Universal Military Training, Samuel I. Rosenman Papers, HSTL. For a full list of members, see 3.

62. On newspaper coverage of investigations, see Drew Pearson, "Royall Admits UMT Campaign," *Washington Post*, January 24, 1948; "Charge Army Propagandizes Training Bill to Be Probed," *Washington Post*, January 11, 1948; "Army Is Accused of Propaganda: House Group Says It Spends Money for Training Bill—Asks Action to Stop It," *New York Times*, July 24, 1947; and "Army Boosted UMT Illegally, Says Harness," *Washington Post*, June 21, 1947.

63. U.S. Senate, Committee on Armed Services, "Universal Military Training," March 17, 1948, 2, reproduced as Xerox 2985, MFNAP, GCML.

64. George C. Marshall, "Statement by the Honorable George C. Marshall, Secretary of State, before the Armed Services Committee of the Senate," March 17, 1948, 1–3, reproduced as Xerox 2985, MFNAP, GCML.

65. U.S. Congress, Senate, Committee on Armed Services, "Universal Military Training," March 17, 1948, 6, reproduced as Xerox 2985, MFNAP, GCML.

66. U.S. Congress, Senate, 82nd Cong., 1st sess., "Report No. 117, Universal Military Training and Service Act, Report of the Committee on Armed Services to Accompany S.I., Submitted by Mr. Johnson of Texas," February 21, 1951, 1–2, reproduced as Xerox 2610, MFNAP, GCML.

67. John G. Adams, assistant general counsel, "Memorandum for Honorable Marx Leva, Assistant Secretary of Defense," August 11, 1950, 1, reproduced as Xerox 2606, MFNAP, GCML.

68. Frank Pace, secretary of the army, "Memorandum for Secretary of Defense, Subject: Effective Date for Implementing Universal Military Training," August 23, 1950, 1–2, reproduced as Xerox 2606, MFNAP, GCML.

69. John G. Adams, assistant general counsel, "Memorandum for the Honorable Anna M. Rosenberg, Assistant Secretary of Defense (Manpower and Personnel)," January 11, 1952, 1, reproduced as Xerox 2610, MFNAP, GCML. On Rosenberg see John Thomas McGuire, "In the Inner Circle: Anna Rosenberg and Franklin D. Roosevelt's Presidency, 1941–1945," *Presidential Studies Quarterly* 45, no. 2 (June 2015): 396–406;

Anna Kasten Nelson, "Anna M. Rosenberg, an 'Honorary Man,'" *Journal of Military History* 68, no. 1 (January 2004): 133–161; and Anna Kasten Nelson, "Caught in the Web of McCarthyism: Anna M. Rosenberg and the Senate Armed Services Committee," *Congress and the Presidency* 30, no. 2 (Autumn 2003): 171–86.

70. John G. Adams, assistant general counsel, "Memorandum for the Honorable Anna M. Rosenberg, Assistant Secretary of Defense (Manpower and Personnel)," January 11, 1952, 2, reproduced as Xerox 2610, MFNAP, GCML.

71. H. A. Houser, "Memorandum for Assistant Secretary Rosenberg, Subject: UMTS," May 31, 1951, 1, reproduced as Xerox 2610, MFNAP, GCML; emphasis in original.

72. George C. Marshall to James W. Wadsworth Jr., August 25, 1951, 1, reproduced as Xerox 2610, MFNAP, GCML.

73. Anna M. Rosenberg to George C. Marshall, January 22, 1952, 1, reproduced as Xerox 3227, MFNAP, GCML.

74. Lewis B. Hershey, "Annual Report of the Director of Selective Service for the Fiscal Year 1952 to the Congress of the United States Pursuant to the Universal Military Training and Service Act as Amended," January 3, 1953, 2, 63, reproduced as Xerox 2610, MFNAP, GCML.

75. George C. Marshall, "Statement by General Marshall on Enactment of UMTS Law," June 19, 1951, 1, reproduced as Xerox 2610, MFNAP, GCML.

76. Quentin R. Mott, "UMT Outlook—Youth Can Rest Easy: It's a Long Road Ahead," *Star*, August 12, 1951, 1, reproduced as Xerox 2610, MFNAP, GCML.

77. On the UMT Experimental Unit, see William A. Taylor, "The Cavalcade of Universal Military Training: Training and Education within the Experimental Demonstration Unit," *Marine Corps University Journal* 9, no. 1 (Spring 2018): 97–119.

78. National Security Training Commission, "Universal Military Training: Foundation of Enduring National Strength, First Report to the Congress by the National Security Training Commission," October 1951, 6–7, 68, reproduced as Xerox 2610, MFNAP, GCML.

79. David Lawrence, "UMT Defeat Called Sign That U.S. Won't Face Facts," *New York Herald Tribune*, March 6, 1952, reproduced as Xerox 2610, MFNAP, GCML.

80. Marshall, "Obligation to Serve," 3.

2

TO MEDIATE CIVIL WAR

Marshall and the Mission to China

In 1945, after its eight-year struggle against Japan, China was also recognized as one of the Allies in the larger global conflict. But this conflict, added to the previous periods of turmoil in China, increased the disorganization and devastation of the country. The Nationalist Party (Guomindang, or GMD) government, led by Chiang Kai-shek (Jiang Jieshi) was isolated in the southwest of the country at Chongqing (Chungking), while the Chinese Communist Party (CCP), headquartered in Yan'an (Yenan), was expanding its control in north and central China. Meanwhile, more than 1 million Japanese troops remained in China.[1] They had been ordered to surrender, but would they? They had surrendered but had not been defeated. These troops needed to be disarmed and repatriated, but by whom? The GMD wished to deny the right to accept Japanese surrender to the CCP, or allow the Communists access to Japanese arms and supplies. The GMD refused to recognize the Communists' wartime role, describing them as "bandits."[2] The CCP was determined to gain access to Japanese arms and supplies, as they had not benefited from aid or assistance from the Allied powers. They wished to establish their postwar role as a recognized political and military force within the country. Both parties anticipated a resumption of the civil war that had been interrupted by Japanese aggression, and each jockeyed for advantage as the global war drew to a close. When the Japanese surrender on August 15, 1945, caught both sides by surprise, competition for aid and influence intensified.

China's 1912 revolution was its first attempt at a nontraditional and nonimperial government. The newly proclaimed Republic of China tried to elect officials and a parliament. The experiment failed when a military takeover ended the attempt, which shortly disintegrated into the Warlord Era from 1916 to 1927 and a divided territory ruled by militarists. During this period both the Guomindang and the Chinese Communist Party were formed with the advice and financial help of the Soviet Union through the 1923 Sun-Joffe Agreement. They formed a United Front from 1924 to 1927, because both parties were small, in order to unify and stabilize the country and to attempt to eliminate the concessions granted previously to the Western powers and Japan. The front dissolved when the larger Guomindang, under the direction of Chiang Kai-shek, attacked the members of the CCP, attempting to eliminate a rival for power. Mao Zedong (Mao Tse-tung) began to direct the Communists' policy from this time. The division lasted until Japan attacked, first in Manchuria in 1931, and then into north China. A second United Front was attempted with some success, at least for the first years of the war, from 1937 to 1939. Thus China was "never sufficiently peaceful to learn democracy, or politically mature enough to embrace it."[3] During the war, the Americans supplied materials to the internationally recognized Nationalist Government, isolated in the southwest, through Lend-Lease, much of it by air support over the "Hump." The American Volunteer Group, known as the Flying Tigers, was active in China prior to the attack on Pearl Harbor. For Chiang, however, the aid was never enough. Americans were also dispatched to Yan'an late in the war, both to assess the extent of Soviet influence on the CCP and to establish a rescue operation for downed American flyers in China. The Americans were present as joint trainers and advisers in Chiang's headquarters in the China theater. Gen. Joseph W. Stilwell, encouraged by President Roosevelt, had attempted to unify Chiang's and Mao's militaries into a more effective force in the war against Japan, without success.[4] The problem was, in part, the geographic distance between the two. In addition, the leaders of the parties had been in control of their organizations and militaries for many

Gen. George C. Marshall (*second from left*) and Chairman Mao Zedong have a final discussion prior to Marshall's departure from Yenan, China. Capt. E. K. H. Eng (*left*) is interpreting. March 5, 1946. Courtesy George C. Marshall Library, Lexington, Va.

years and did not trust each other. Furthermore, the GMD had four hundred thousand of its elite troops blockading the Communist stronghold in Yan'an.[5] In the later stages of the war the need for a Chinese base from which to invade Japan became unnecessary for the Americans, and with the Japanese ICHIGO campaign in 1944 the American Bomber Command had been withdrawn. The U.S. Headquarters at Chongqing under Gen. Alfred C. Wedemeyer was relocated to Shanghai in late 1945.[6]

An additional consideration was the presence of Soviet forces in Manchuria in accordance with the Yalta Agreements reached in February 1945 and the thirty-year Sino-Soviet Treaty of Friendship and Alliance signed on August 14, 1945.[7] Occupation by these troops of northeast China (i.e., Manchuria), with elements of the CCP in close proximity, complicated the immediate postwar relations between the GMD and CCP as well as between the United States and USSR, and the interrelations between any combination of them. The relationship has been described as an "unstable parallelogram of forces."[8] Assumptions were made as to the cooperation or control of the CCP by the Soviet Union and of the domination of the GMD by the United States. These assumptions were too simple. Neither party wished to be seen as dominated by a foreign power given China's history. To state that postwar China's situation was complex is the ultimate understatement.

In 1944 President Franklin D. Roosevelt sent Gen. Patrick J. Hurley to China to try to establish a coalition government and end skirmishes between the two major parties. Hurley was later made ambassador. On November 6, 1945, angry at the failure of his negotiations, Hurley resigned, while publicly blaming the Truman administration for the failure due to "communist sympathizers" in the State Department.[9] Many of Truman's political opponents, along with supporters of the Chinese Nationalist Government, criticized the administration. To carry out the announced U.S. policy toward China, the Marshall mission was authorized on December 15, 1945. Gen. George C. Marshall was recalled to duty after four decades of army service, having just retired as chief of staff. For this reason, and also to emphasize his nonpolitical role in negotiations as he envisioned it, he would appear in uniform in China.[10] He was directed to broker a cease-fire, prevent a civil war, and negotiate a coalition government and unified military, thereby uniting the country. These changes would allow China to be a strong, unified, and democratic example in East Asia, to offset the influence of Japan and the Soviet Union. China had been made one of the permanent members of the UN Security Council and therefore would be regarded as one of Roosevelt's "four policemen" to maintain stability in the world—the others being the United States, Great Britain, and the Soviet Union. Neither the British nor the Soviets agreed with this assessment.[11] Several commentators, then and subsequently, described this policy as "Mission Impossible."[12]

Marshall had an enviable reputation for integrity in office and competency in handling interservice and international negotiations; moreover, he had served as a field-grade officer in China in the 1920s. He had read reports from Stilwell and Hurley throughout their operations in the country. Furthermore, he had requested that U.S. government agencies not be included in the oversight of his efforts in order to prevent the Chinese from playing one organization against another.[13] But he was charged with a mission that had not been possible with the pressures of war. Would his postwar attempt be any more successful?

The Moscow Conference from December 16 to 27, 1945, preceded Marshall's arrival in China. Foreign ministers of Britain, the United States, and the Soviet

Union met in a friendly atmosphere to address some issues of concern. They
decided that the United States should demobilize and repatriate the Japanese
in China and that American forces should be stationed there. Given various
agreements and basically friendly interactions among the three powers, many
in China believed that Marshall represented this attitude of accord and that he
enjoyed the support of all three governments.[14] This assumption aided in the
initial meetings Marshall held with representatives of the Chinese parties and
persons of influence. The fact that, after arriving in China, Marshall called on the
Soviet ambassador and dined at the Soviet embassy reinforced this perception.[15]
In fact, Stalin did support the mission, already having troops in occupation in
Manchuria and a treaty with China, which gave the Soviets a naval base and a
warm-water port there. In addition, they shared control of infrastructure with
the Chinese, in particular that of two rail networks. Therefore, the Soviet borders were secure, and China's problems were not of immediate concern to him.

Meanwhile, more than fifty thousand U.S. Marines, the Third Amphibious
Corps, landed in China to accept the surrender of the Japanese (if, in fact, that
was their intention), control the ports through which they would be repatriated, and establish control over the major northern cities until the Nationalist
Government could relieve them. In addition, the American force would guard
key infrastructure such as railroads and essential coal mines in the area.[16] The
marines began to occupy major cities and communications hubs in north China.
The First Division occupied Dagu (Taku), Tianjin (Tientsin), Beijing (Peking),
Tangu (Tanku), and Qinhuangdao (Chinwangtao), while the Sixth Division
occupied Qingdao (Tsingtao). Both divisions met some resistance from Communist forces in their respective areas. The GMD hoped that the American presence would facilitate the control of these areas until its forces could be moved,
by American airpower and sealift, to relieve the marines. Thus an immediate
association of the U.S. forces with the GMD Party was established, even though
the Nationalists were the recognized government in China. The presence of the
marines was to facilitate the disarming and repatriation of Japanese soldiers and
their civilian counterparts. They were also to prevent the surrender of these
forces with their weapons to the CCP. This policy was a potential, and real,
source of conflict between the CCP and the marines, and indeed several inci-
dents occurred as the American forces remained in China. Meanwhile, Chiang
Kai-shek ordered the Japanese to retain their arms and control until relieved
by the Americans or the GMD.[17] With the Japanese and Americans controlling
much of north China, the GMD focused on its Communist opponents, not on

relieving friendly forces. Some Japanese would remain in China co-opted by the GMD as technical specialists or, according to the Communists, as garrison troops. A relatively smaller number joined the CCP.[18]

The presence of the marines placed them approximately two hundred miles from Soviet military personnel in Dalian (Dairen) and Lushunkou (Port Arthur). Therefore, one major focus of this period influencing the Marshall mission was the concern—or indeed expectation—that a potential World War III would begin in Manchuria between the forces of the United States and USSR as their relations deteriorated in the ensuing period.[19] The interplay of the superpowers elsewhere in Asia and in Europe sometimes overshadowed the situation in China. Winston Churchill's "Iron Curtain" speech on March 5, 1946, announced that six months after the end of one war, another—the Cold War—had begun.[20] Many analyses of the mission concentrate on this topic, which did have an effect on negotiations at any given time. For example, the Soviets were to remove their troops from Manchuria within three weeks of the war's conclusion. They changed their withdrawal date several times, however, not actually withdrawing until May 16, 1946.[21] They offered to return their troops to Soviet territory when the Americans removed their forces from China—perhaps simultaneously? This offer was rejected.

The Chinese Communists hoped to take advantage of the Soviet presence to expand and consolidate their control in the northeast. At first the Soviets did not cooperate with their Chinese comrades, but later as concerns changed and Stalin believed that he had achieved the maximum concessions possible from Chiang Kai-shek, he allowed the transfer of Japanese arms and supplies to the CCP. He also allowed the Communists to enter urban areas, enhancing their ability to defend themselves if they were attacked in force by the GMD. The Soviet presence in the area, including parts of north China and Inner Mongolia, a "cordon sanitaire," challenged the erstwhile goal of a unified country without undue foreign influence.[22]

Chiang Kai-shek was head of the recognized government of China, head of the Guomindang Party, and generalissimo of the army. Possessing control of the majority of resources, Chiang had no intention of sharing power in any but a cosmetic way, and, with American help, he was regaining control of much of Chinese territory. His military outnumbered the Communists by a five-to-one margin.[23] His goal, unchanged from his first attempts in the late 1920s and 1930s, was to eliminate the Communists and to be recognized as the only logical leader of a one-party government. This goal, rather than enacting economic and government reforms as territory was returned to Guomindang control, dominated his plans in the immediate postwar period. There were factions in his party, which Chiang had to keep in some measure of balance. Many of his forces were, in essence, independent warlord or puppet forces whose loyalty was opportunistic at best. That the war had ravaged the country, with inflation out of control and infrastructure in need of restoration, did not change his focus as he moved his wartime capital from Chongqing to the official capital, Nanjing (Nanking), in May 1946. First the Communists must be destroyed, then these problems could be resolved. Chiang, in time, came to look on Marshall as a holdover from the Franklin D. Roosevelt administration, because his goals echoed those of previous American military figures.[24] Chinese representatives in the United States developed other avenues of support for the Nationalist Government and lobbied for continued aid. Marshall was, on occasion, blunt in his talks with Chiang, which numbered more than sixty during his year in China.[25] Chiang was insulted by this lack of deference, to which he felt entitled.

Mao Zedong also headed a party that controlled an independent military. It was basically unified and, while smaller than its rival, had increased exponentially in numbers and territory controlled during the war. The CCP military, with an organized militia, was—unlike its rival—all-volunteer with good morale and popular support in the areas that it controlled. Mao's long-term goal was to install a Communist government in Beijing. But at the end of the war, with Soviet support limited at best, as the Soviets sought to squeeze as many concessions from the Nationalist Government as possible, Mao had to be flexible in his approach in order to survive. He had described possible cooperation with other political entities in his writings "On Coalition Government." This approach had been put into effect in some areas; local governments were to be one-third Communist, one-third Guomindang, and one-third other. He occasionally discussed the need for China to experience a bourgeois revolution before a socialist one was possible.[26] Meanwhile, he concentrated on practical matters and hoped for recognition of the party as legitimate, with a chance to participate in determining a new government and its policies. Mao hoped that a good relationship with Marshall might result in needed aid for the CCP. Therefore, Zhou Enlai, the CCP representative in negotiations, was instructed to appear cooperative.[27] Zhou had announced that he hoped to neutralize the American position in China through such cooperation. He used empathy, diplomacy, and rationality to maintain a cordial relationship with Marshall, at least until October 1946.

That these two parties had basically irreconcilable goals and had never been able to work together for any length of time—and given that the Guomindang considered the Communists to be "bandits," not a political or military force to be recognized—set the stage for the Marshall mission. Marshall, whose arrival in China had been delayed by congressional testimony, landed in Shanghai on December 20, 1945, and immediately met with General Wedemeyer, commander of U.S. Forces China Theater, and Walter S. Robertson, the chargé d'affaires at the U.S. Embassy, for a briefing.[28] Marshall's immediate desire for information and context would be characteristic of his tenure in China. He would meet with government leaders, officials and opponents, Communist leaders, nonaligned reporters, intellectuals, businessmen, missionaries, and other influential people. He returned to the United States only briefly from March 11 to April 18, 1946, to lobby for additional aid for China, always hoping that his mission would be brief and would lay the groundwork for the Chinese to solve their problems peacefully. At this time, the Soviet Union announced that it would withdraw from China, not waiting for the arrival of the Nationalist troops to relieve them. This announcement opened much of Manchuria to CCP expansion as the GMD scrambled to bring its troops into the territory, thus complicating an already complex situation.

Marshall's status as the personal representative of the president with the rank of unofficial ambassador made the previous success of the Nationalist Government in derailing the American government's pressure to unify the military and establish a coalition government questionable. Marshall was too famous, too influential, and too respected to ignore or obviously to push into the background.[29] While the goals of the Nationalists remained the same, the means they employed would have to change. Chiang Kai-shek was convinced that demonstrating to Marshall that the CCP was only the tool of the Soviet Union in its attempt to control Chinese territory, directly or indirectly, would bring him to understand Chiang's point of view. Meanwhile, Chiang would attempt to play the Soviets against the Americans to his benefit.[30]

Mao, caught between the interests of his party, his hope of Soviet aid, and the possibility of U.S. recognition, also attempted to play international powers against each other. Mao had hoped that as the Soviets occupied Manchuria, they would welcome the CCP and share with them the surrendered weapons of the Japanese forces there. Soviet policy swerved several times between, on the one hand, limiting the movement and access to weapons of their Communist brethren, a designation Stalin was unsure fit the organization, and on the other hand, permitting the CCP to take control of some rural areas and local governments and gain some degree of access to the arms and supplies of which it was in need.[31]

The Soviet Union, or rather Stalin, had gotten almost all that he wanted in the Yalta Agreements, which had not included China, although the accords would have a major impact on the country. The Soviets wanted all the privileges that the Imperial Government had acquired prior to the Russo-Japanese War.[32] Negotiations between China and the Soviets resulted in a Treaty of Friendship and Alliance, in which Stalin negotiated additional concessions, some of them joint and lasting for a specific time. Chiang at this time was trying to protect his northern border, and at the same time to prevent Soviet support of the CCP. Therefore, Soviet relations with the latter party were confused—sometimes favorable, sometimes less so—but never to the point that Stalin could not use their existence as a lever with the Nationalist Government.[33] When he believed that he had reached the maximum concessions from the Guomindang, the more he openly supported the CCP and increased the amount of "war booty" removed from Manchuria as war reparations. Factories, rolling stock, power-generating machinery, and anything else of value were sent to the Soviet Union on purloined trains, which were also retained. The estimated value of these "war reparations" was $2 billion.[34] Having by this point become more publicly supportive of the CCP, Stalin adjusted his relationship with the United States, partly in response to problems in Europe and partly due to the presence of the U.S. Marines in close proximity to his borders.

General accounts of the Marshall mission break it into three stages: first, from January through February 1946, a stage of cooperation while all parties tried to assess Marshall's purpose, support, and possible benefit for themselves; second, from March through June of that year, when increasing demands from both parties and failures of both to carry out the agreements already reached hampered further progress; and third, from June through December as Marshall's influence decreased and as proposed solutions were nitpicked and rejected. In this period the Guomindang felt assured of continuing American support regardless of its failures to reform and Marshall's threats to cut off aid. Meanwhile, the CCP began to receive improved support from the Soviets, coupled with the increasing success of the Communists' military campaigns and ideological efforts to win the hearts and minds of the people.[35]

Truman's statement of American policy on the eve of Marshall's departure for China on December 15, 1945, reiterated the need for a strong, unified, stable, and democratic China to establish a balance of power in East Asia. Therefore, a coalition government was to be formed and a National Assembly and constitution established. One problem, frequently discussed in arguments over the effectiveness of the mission, was that Marshall's idea of a democratic government and unified military were based solely on his experiences as an American: that is, a government with two opposing parties, which were freely elected and cooperating for the most part.[36] The U.S. military was not political—it had no party cadres, unlike in China—and was under civilian as opposed to party control. In negotiating these positions, Marshall found that a typical meeting consisted of tea, general discussions of the weather, sundry proclamations and justifications of position, and more tea.[37] Marshall tried to avoid these time-wasting exercises by preparing a proposal as a starting point, and then allowing only discussions related to the proposed items. Some problems developed with the perceptions of Marshall's role by the Chinese: he believed that he acted as a mediator and neutral entity, while others seemed to consider him as a referee.

A cease-fire was of initial importance, because negotiations on political and military unification could not begin until the military engagements ended. Since early on, both of the Chinese parties wanted to see what was proposed, how it would be negotiated, and when any agreements would, in theory, be implemented, an early cease-fire was agreed on January 10, 1946. The only caveat was that the movement of the Nationalist troops into central and north China would continue with the help of U.S. ships and planes. A cease-fire would also assist in the movement of surrendered Japanese troops and civilians from the interior to the port areas.[38] The early achievement of this agreement gave many hope that a peace could be achieved. Negotiated compromises had to be instituted, however, in order for the agreement to hold. Marshall therefore consented to participate in further discussions, which he had hoped to leave to the Chinese. The first agreement on January 7, 1946, was for a Committee of Three: one representative from the Guomindang, one from the CCP, and Marshall.[39] The committee was to iron out misunderstandings and proceed with proposals for government and military reorganization. While the Nationalist representatives varied over time, Zhou Enlai was the constant member for the Communists. Therefore, Marshall developed a closer relationship with Zhou, who was known for being personable. Chiang apparently sent one negotiator, Chen Chang, when events were favoring the Nationalists, and another, Zhang Zhizheng, when they were not; the latter was therefore more insistent in demanding conditions than otherwise.[40]

The second organization, which was established on January 14, 1946, was the Executive Headquarters in Beijing, whose members were to monitor the cease-fire and investigate any reported breaches. Headquarters teams consisted of one member from each of the Chinese parties and one American officer—army or marine—as chair, with the deciding vote.[41] They would be sent as required to areas of dispute, except Manchuria. This exception was to become a sticking point in negotiations: Marshall wanted Manchuria included once the Soviet forces had withdrawn. The Soviet presence was one complication in the establishment of the truce teams in the north. What if the Soviets demanded equal representation on the teams? There were diplomatic hints that this might happen, but events in Manchuria precluded that development. That argument was also used as justification to encourage the withdrawal of all U.S. forces from China once Japanese repatriation was achieved. Most Japanese were gone by July 13, 1946.

Negotiations began for a coalition government with a National Assembly, in which all recognized parties would be represented by elected delegates, and a constitution devised that recognized the rights of the minor parties, as well as general rights for the people. Since the two major parties were single-party governments, with similar organization but on different scales, these discussions were more problematic. Yet an agreement was reached in principle, with the promise of continuing U.S. aid when it was formalized. The Political Consultative Conference (PCC) had been agreed to in principle prior to Marshall's arrival.[42] A date for the conference, January 10, 1946, was accepted shortly thereafter. The delegates to the meeting, which lasted until January 31, consisted of thirty-eight appointees: eight from the GMD; seven from the CCP; nine from the Democratic League, which consisted of six small parties; five from the Youth Party; and nine prominent nonparty members—leaders in education, culture, and economics.[43] They were, under the leadership of Chiang Kai-shek, to construct the framework for a truly national government, with broad representation and a constitution with guarantees of individual rights. A National Assembly would be constituted, replacing the 1936 GMD organization, and would meet in May. To bring pressure on the GMD for change, the small-party groups frequently joined with the CCP in voting on the conference protocols.[44] After a week, the conference stalled into delivery of speeches. Marshall met with Chiang and delivered concrete proposals to move the process forward. Chiang resented this advice but reworked the proposals and presented them as his own to the conference.[45] These agreements in principle described a broad outline of reforms, which were published. A mechanism for government ratification and implementation, however, was not included. The results of the meetings raised some hopes, but little more than that.

While negotiations were under way, the CCP expressed concerns regarding its role in the proposed coalition government. News from Western Europe describing coalitions there reported the initial inclusion of socialist and communist parties. Shortly thereafter, however, news of these parties' electoral losses ended their participation in the government. The CCP was hesitant to agree to participate unless it received guarantees, including the recognition of its legitimacy as a party.[46] When the Communists refused to nominate delegates to the May National Assembly meeting, it was postponed until November, with the same result for the Communists: the Nationalists held their assembly and wrote their constitution, and basically nothing changed politically.

The third, and most controversial, proposal was to unite the two parties' militaries into a single Chinese National Army. To negotiate this coalition, a subcommittee of the Committee of Three was appointed, including Marshall, who had hoped to leave these negotiations to the Chinese but was overridden by the U.S. government.[47] The Guomindang Army was bloated with ill-trained and poorly equipped recruits. There were some effective divisions, trained and equipped by the United States during the war, but organization, communication, logistics, and standardization were lacking for many units. An American Military Advisory Group for China was requested to help train both forces; it was later authorized but allowed by the Chinese government to assist only the GMD Army.[48] Mao's forces were not oriented to basic training maneuvers, marching in formations, or other peacetime practices. To spare them any embarrassment when joined with the Nationalist units, the Americans offered a six-week separate training opportunity, with American advisers and weapons. This training was to begin on April 15, 1946. But Zhou asked that it be pushed back to July, by which time events overtook the offer.[49]

Chiang valued loyalty above ability, and many of those in command positions saw the opportunity to enrich their families and enhance their status without worrying about their troops or the enemy. Since the Nationalists had a numerical advantage and were gaining control of formerly occupied areas, they demanded that the Communists demobilize their army prior to the implementation of the political agreements. Mao had smaller forces and less-sophisticated weapons, until later aided by the Soviet Union, but was willing to consider the idea of a unified force—with American offers of training and supplies—but not until a political agreement was enacted. Mao was confident that he could win a political war, although not yet a military conflict. These opposing positions would constitute a major blockage in achieving military unification, but for the time, it was papered over. The accepted agreement, titled "The Basis for Military Reorganization for the Integration of the Communist Forces into the National Army," was an awkward compromise, but as with other aspects, it was finally agreed to, on February 25, 1946.[50]

Manchuria was the key to the hope of any success for the mission; it was also where all agreements foundered. Chiang planned to recover it—an area the size of France and Germany combined, with rich resources—as part of the unification of the country and to defeat and destroy the CCP. The Communists, who claimed that Chiang had abandoned the area to the Japanese in 1931, saw no justification for the GMD presence there after the war.[51] The CCP, which had more control of the area from its efforts during the war, could and did withdraw its forces from targeted areas when necessary but were not defeated—or even badly damaged—as conflicts between the two forces escalated. They could resort to guerrilla tactics and organize the rural population. There was some talk of a divided Manchuria, with the CCP in the north and the GMD in the south, but that was not in accordance with Chiang's plans for the unification of all China.[52] Since the GMD was successful for the most part in 1946, it found no reason to compromise or form a coalition.

With his early apparent success, Marshall returned to Washington in March to plead with Congress for additional aid for China. The postwar members were much less inclined to provide generous foreign aid, as there were too many problems at home and with more familiar countries. Marshall remained longer than he had anticipated but returned to China with the promise of substantial aid. He found on his return in early April that all the agreements had unraveled in his absence. Both Chinese parties maneuvered for position prior to the anticipated resumption of negotiations. This was especially true for the Nationalist Government, whose forces were attacking elements of the Communists in order to gain control of more territory and resources and to deny these to their opponents. The key issue, again, was Manchuria, where the truce teams were not engaged, the Soviets were leaving, and the Communists were expanding their hold. The Soviets had denied the Nationalists access to some Manchurian ports.[53] Chiang wanted the Americans to transport additional troops to emphasize his determination to enter and control the area in the name of national reunification. The Americans refused this request, because to aid one side in the ongoing civil war was against stated U.S. policy. Because the focus was in the northeast (Manchuria), the Guomindang Army did not relieve the U.S. Marines in the ports and coal mines, along the railroads, or those guarded by the Japanese who remained at the government's invitation.

During these months, Zhou Enlai continued to make suggestions more in line with Marshall's, seemingly more cooperative.[54] The focus, therefore, was on the Nationalists, who postponed negotiations or demanded conditions that they knew would not be accepted. Meanwhile, the impressive political agreements reached by the various representatives at the Political Consultative Conference were not instituted. With the constant clashes of the two parties' militaries, the prospect of Chinese unification dimmed. Chiang declined to allow the materials sent to train the Communist armies under the military agreement to leave the docks at Shanghai.[55] Chiang became more obviously frustrated that Marshall did not see his point of view and refused to postpone the destruction of his Communist foes any further.

Meanwhile, the Guomindang's reoccupation of areas formerly controlled by the Japanese was alienating many Chinese people. Officials from the capital claimed control of local governments, took over businesses and farms, limited or prevented press criticism of their actions, and attacked their printing presses and facilities. In addition, the government failed to control hyperinflation, which the ongoing conflict exacerbated.[56] Many who criticized the GMD represented minor parties or organizations composed of influential intellectuals, businessmen, bankers, and others elites. Marshall began to hope that these smaller organizations could be formed into an alliance; the Democratic League had already brought together a number of concerned individuals and groups.[57] In a coalition with others, this Third Party Group could act as a buffer between the larger opposing forces and, under the leadership of Chiang Kai-shek, develop a more representative system of government, as had been agreed during the PCC negotiations.[58] That Chiang had no intention of allowing any opposition was becoming obvious; token representatives would be allowed in the National Assembly so that a "democratic" government could be claimed. Mao was somewhat open to a temporary multiparty system, to include minority parties. Many of the members of these smaller organizations, however, preferred to philosophize about their political positions but not to accept responsibility for any actions.[59] These organizations split when the National Assembly convened on November 12, 1946, because the Communists refused to join, as the CCP had not been recognized as legitimate. They had been invited with the expectation of their refusal as the delegates had been appointed by the Nationalists in 1936.

While criticism of the Marshall mission was prevalent in China from the first announcement, the initial agreements had put a damper on the general anti-American sentiment. More extensive negative reporting increased during the second phase of the mission. Most of these accounts were directed at U.S. policy. From the summer of 1946, much criticism by both parties was aimed at Marshall personally. Chiang, for example, had announced that he would not allow the United States to save the CCP with negotiations if the Soviet Union was not supporting it.[60] The CCP's attacks focused on Marshall's support of the GMD with aid, transport, and military presence, which constituted foreign domination of China that was unacceptable. These condemnations were especially virulent after the signing of the China-U.S. Treaty of Friendship, Commerce, and Navigation in November.[61] Perhaps these denunciations were the reason that Marshall's focus was more frequently centered at this time on the third parties' potential role in government.

The third stage of the mission took place amid full-scale civil war; it involved the withdrawal of most of the American forces and Marshall's continuing search for a means of accomplishing his goals. He arranged for an arms embargo on China from July 1946 to May 1947 in hopes of pressuring Chiang into some concessions; as American supplies had been arriving steadily, however, this temporary interruption had little real effect.[62] Marshall frequently stated that he would withdraw completely and return home, but then a chance of achieving some small step forward would encourage him to postpone his return. By this time, Chiang believed that he would be backed no matter what actions he took or failed to take, encouraged by support from U.S. media, such as *Time* and *Life* magazines; and by former missionaries and businessmen with Chinese experience, some of whom were in Congress. His position improved as relations between the United States and the Soviet Union deteriorated.[63] Mao was beginning to benefit from Stalin's change of policy regarding the CCP, which made supplies of weapons available, including tens of thousands of Japanese weapons and ammunition, in addition to Soviet artillery and tanks.[64] Stalin did not believe that Mao could win but thought that he could control northern Manchuria and thus protect Soviet borders.[65] By this stage both Chiang and Zhou were frequently absent from the meetings, the former more often, but either's absence from the Committee of Three precluded it from meeting. Occasionally other representatives of the parties would be sent to meet with Marshall, but they did not have the authority to make decisions; they met to avoid being blamed for the cessation of the talks. Two further cease-fires were negotiated, in June and September, while territory was consolidated and supplies replenished, but both sides viewed them as good publicity, not as permanent agreements.[66]

Meanwhile, a new American ambassador was announced. Initially, when Marshall envisioned a short mission, he had favored Gen. Alfred C. Wedemeyer as his successor. As events unfolded, however, Marshall realized that he would need a more neutral figure, as Wedemeyer had been chief of staff to Chiang in the later part of World War II, and was considered his supporter. Marshall nominated Dr. John L. Stuart, a longtime China missionary who had been president of Yenching University (Yanjing Daxue) for years and had taught many of the leaders of the various political factions in China. Chiang's reaction to the announcement was dismissive, calling Stuart "an old man who was a mere professor."[67] Stuart attempted to institute a Committee of Five in August, consisting of two members of each contending party and himself as chair.[68] Events had developed a momentum, however, that negotiations could not influence, even if that had been the focus of either party's representatives.

In Marshall's statement on his departure on January 7, 1947, he reiterated that the major focus of his last months' efforts had been with the Third Party Group: he had hoped that these small parties could be brought under an umbrella organization and provide a buffer that would allow progress toward a unified government. Many small parties were in fact organized between 1945 and 1949. Their aim was generally to end one-party rule, though a few of these groups believed one-party organization was the only way to govern the country.[69] Therefore, inherent differences in the movement meant that an amalgamation into a sufficiently strong organization to act as a buffer between the two major parties was unlikely. The Democratic League, comprising six smaller parties, had been formed in 1941. It claimed to represent the middle class: journalists, teachers, businessmen, and other educated urban elements.[70] The GMD was supported by many landlords as well as militarists; the CCP recruited members from the rural populations who were tenant or small farmers. So the Third Party Group potentially filled a needed role.

The third parties had been represented in the Political Consultative Conference of January 1946. They, in alliance with moderate members of the GMD, had forged political agreements that would lead to a reformed government structure and a guarantee of individual rights proclaimed in the PCC Protocols.[71] These were announced but not enacted or enforced. It was this group toward whom

Marshall's efforts were directed in the last months, until in June a peace delegation from Shanghai, made up of intellectuals and other influential individuals,
was attacked and beaten at the rail station in Nanjing. Shortly thereafter, two
leaders of the Democratic League were assassinated.[72] The movement not only
split but lost any influence it had tried to exert. In part the small parties' lack of
authority was due to their failure to develop mass support or an alliance with
an independent military force. Nor were they well organized; their goal was
sway, not control.[73]

Marshall finally recognized that his clout in this matter was spent. Marshall
blamed those whom he described as the "irreconcilables" in both major parties
as the reason for his failure.[74] CCP and GMD hardliners refused to endorse any
compromise. He decided to accept the repeated offer from Truman to become
secretary of state, although he requested that the announcement be withheld
until he had left China.[75] Marshall's experiences in China influenced U.S. policy
toward that country and others during his tenure in that office. He had a close
relationship with President Truman, W. Averell Harriman, Dean Acheson, and
many other policy makers in the War Department, after forty years of army
service, as well as many years in nongovernmental organizations. He would
become a target of the "Who Lost China" movement and blamed for the loss,
when, as secretary of state, he refused to allow major U.S. military action in
China in support of the Nationalist Government.[76]

U.S. policy for China was inherently contradictory, as was frequently
pointed out by supporters and critics alike. The goal was a unified country in
which power was shared; yet American support of the Nationalist Government
was also expected, as evidenced in continuing aid, the transport of GMD
troops, and the presence of U.S. Marine Corps personnel guarding critical
infrastructure. That Marshall was to preside over negotiations as a "neutral"
mediator made the goals problematic from the first and fueled criticism of
American "meddling" in Chinese affairs. So Marshall "was to mediate, but
the U.S. was not neutral."[77]

The Marshall mission has been analyzed in news accounts, official papers,
biographical publications, and other scholarly books and articles. It is still controversial, although details of the reasons for its failure differ with the emphasis
of the author and level of access to sources. Part of the mission's problem was
its attempt to reconcile two different parties, each with definite and opposing
ideologies, to determine the composition of the government of China. Both

were determined on a single-party government, with perhaps some show of inclusion of small parties. Each major party was supported by an independent military, thereby leading to the possibility of a divided China. This development was occasionally suggested as an alternative to an ongoing, if originally sporadic, civil war.[78]

Assessments of the mission began at its inception and continue to the present. Recent access to official papers in Soviet and Chinese archives have added to various previous studies. Congressional hearings in the United States on the mission were sporadically held from 1945 to 1970. Many individuals, including Wedemeyer, Henry Luce, and other critics, changed their views of the mission as conditions in China changed, particularly with reference to increasing tensions between the Soviet Union and United States. The latter focused attention on areas of strategic importance to the United States; China was not of great strategic—only commercial and perhaps sentimental—concern. In addition, in the immediate postwar era, the domestic focus was on demobilization and economic stability. Opposition to the Truman administration intensified with Republicans gaining control of Congress in the 1946 midterm elections, and despite their subsequent losses in 1948, the attacks on the president and his appointees during the "Who Lost China" controversy definitely enhanced negative reviews of the mission. The defeat of the GMD in the Chinese Civil War, as one analyst wrote, "was not seen as the end of an unsuccessful government, but as the American loss of territory to an unfriendly regime."[79]

Marshall indirectly affected many of those in positions of power, whether they were supporters or opponents, including journalists, government officials in several departments, businessmen, former missionaries, or servicemen who had served in China. He influenced relations with the Soviet Union and American allies, as well as the ongoing conflict in China. Although many observers in China viewed his presence as American "meddling" in Chinese affairs, they could not fail to respect his attempts to reform aspects of Chinese governance. Marshall had hoped not to be directly involved in the various issues; he wished the Chinese to solve their problems themselves, perhaps with neutral advice. If he could have directed changes to benefit the Chinese people, then he would have basically succeeded in his view of his role. The Marshall mission officially ended on January 29, 1947.[80]

Marshall's experience in China informed his actions as secretary of state from 1947 to 1949 and as secretary of defense from 1950 to 1951. As Ernest R. May's

Marshall Lecture indicated, Marshall kept us out of war in China, when heavy domestic pressure was for "saving" China from a feared ideology and avoiding loss of anticipated markets.[81] He had, as a result of his China experience, a more informed idea as to what could be done with the resources available and what was imprudent to attempt. He made deals with Congress, as necessary, requesting support for China in order to receive aid for Europe, eventually referred to as the Marshall Plan. When the latter was announced, Chiang requested that a similar plan be developed for China.[82] As the GMD forces were being repeatedly defeated by this time, the request was as much for military intervention as economic aid, and it was refused. Marshall received in 1953 the Nobel Peace Prize for his recovery plan for Europe. Marshall had not only proven to be a capable secretary of state, but his policies were of benefit to the nation.

The problem with the Marshall China mission from the first was that it was a U.S. policy infused with elements of American political and military culture. It was not designed to fit the plans of the two adversarial Chinese leaders at the time, although both claimed to want a unified and democratic government in the future when the other had been eliminated. Therefore, Chiang Kai-shek's and Mao Zedong's relations with Marshall evolved from competition and cooperation to confrontation, which was always the end game for each, when American support was either expected or had been denied and further negotiations with him served no purpose.

NOTES

1. Except for the name Chiang Kai-shek, the author has used the Pinyin Romanization system for names and places, with the Wade-Giles spelling in parentheses following. Another exception is the Guomindang, or Nationalist Party, for which the alternate spelling, Kuomintang, is not included.

2. Department of State, *The China White Paper* (Stanford, Calif.: Stanford University Press, 1949), 44.

3. Wang Chen-main, "Marshall's Approaches to the Mediation Effort," in Larry I. Bland, ed., *George C. Marshall's Mediation Mission to China, December 1945–January 1947* (Lexington, Va.: George C. Marshall Foundation, 1998), 21–44.

4. In time Chiang and Zhou began to equate Marshall with Stilwell. John K. Fairbank, *The United States and China* (Cambridge, Mass.: Harvard University Press, 1980).

5. George C. Marshall, *Marshall's Mission to China, December 1945–January 1947: The Report and Appended Documents* (Arlington, Va.: University Publications of America, 1976), 1:xv.

6. Daniel Kurtz-Phelan, *The China Mission: George Marshall's Unfinished War, 1945–1947* (New York: W. W. Norton, 2018), 51–52.

7. Immanuel C. Y. Hsü, *The Rise of Modern China* (New York: Oxford University Press, 1995), 609.

8. Steven I. Levine, "International Mediation of Civil Wars: China (1945–1946) and Mozambique (1990–1992)," in Bland, *George C. Marshall's Mediation Mission*, 527–48.

9. Larry N. Shyu, "In Search of Peace in Postwar China: The Domestic Agenda," in Bland, *George C. Marshall's Mediation Mission*, 275–92.

10. Mark A. Stoler, "Why George Marshall? A Biographical Assessment," in Bland, *George C. Marshall's Mediation Mission*, 3–14.

11. Hsü, *Rise of Modern China*, 602; Kurtz-Phelan, *China Mission*, 28.

12. Edmund S. Wehrle, "Marshall in China: The Colonels' Stories," in Bland, *George C. Marshall's Mediation Mission*, 15–20; Harry C. Shallcross, "The Marshall Mission to China, December 1945–January 1947: A Study of U.S. Foreign Policy Decisions" (PhD diss., Florida State University, 1984).

13. Shallcross, "Marshall Mission to China," 284; Kurtz-Phelan, *China Mission*, 47; Forrest C. Pogue, *George C. Marshall*, vol. 4: *Statesman, 1945–1959* (New York: Viking, 1987), 70.

14. Edmund S. Wehrle, "Marshall, the Moscow Conference, and Harriman," in Bland, *George C. Marshall's Mediation Mission*, 67–68; Jay Taylor, *The Generalissimo: Chiang Kai-shek and the Struggle for Modern China* (Cambridge, Mass.: Belknap Press of Harvard University Press, 2009), 334.

15. Andrei M. Ledovsky, "Marshall's Mission in the Context of U.S.S.R.-China-U.S. Relations," in Bland, *George C. Marshall's Mediation Mission*, 423–44.

16. Kurtz-Phelan, *China Mission*, 39; Edward J. Marolda, "The U.S. Navy and the 'Loss of China,' 1945–1950," in Bland, *George C. Marshall's Mediation Mission*, 409–22.

17. Taylor, *Generalissimo*, 356; Kurtz-Phelan, *China Mission*, 241; Roger B. Jeans, *The Marshall Mission to China, 1945–1947: The Letters and Diary of Colonel John Hart Caughey* (Lanham, Md.: Rowman & Littlefield, 2011), 3.

18. Odd Arne Westad, "Could the Civil War Have Been Avoided? An Exercise in Alternatives," in Bland, *George C. Marshall's Mediation Mission*, 503.

19. Jeans, *Marshall Mission to China*, 301; Kurtz-Phelan, *China Mission*, 4; Odd Arne Westad, *Decisive Encounters: The Chinese Civil War, 1946–1950* (Stanford, Calif.: Stanford University Press, 2003), 9; Maochun Yu, *The Dragon's War: Allied Operations and the Fate of China, 1946–1950* (Annapolis, Md.: Naval Institute Press, 2006).

20. Kurtz-Phelan, *China Mission*, 1.

21. Ibid., 175; Robert Edwin Herzstein, "Henry Luce, George Marshall, and China: The Parting of the Ways in 1946," in Bland, *George C. Marshall's Mediation Mission*, 115–48.

22. Westad, *Decisive Encounters*, 31.

23. Wehrle, "Marshall, the Moscow Conference, and Harriman," 76.

24. Odd Arne Westad, *Cold War and Revolution: Soviet-American Rivalry and the Origins of the Chinese Civil War, 1944–1946* (New York: Columbia University Press, 1993), 44; He Di, "Mao Zedong and the Marshall Mission," in Bland, *George C. Marshall's Mediation Mission*, 173–200.

25. Ramon H. Meyers, "Frustration, Fortitude, and Friendship: Chiang Kai-shek's Reaction to the Marshall Mission," in Bland, *George C. Marshall's Mediation Mission*, 149–72.

26. Shyu, "In Search of Peace," 275–92; Joseph K. S. Yick, "The Communist-Nationalist Political Struggle in Beijing during the Marshall Mission Period," in Bland, *George C. Marshall's Mediation Mission*, 357–90; Zhang Baijia, "Zhou Enlai and the Marshall Mission," in Bland, *George C. Marshall's Mediation Mission*, 201–34.

27. Taylor, *Generalissimo*, 327.

28. Mark F. Wilkinson, "A Shanghai Perspective on the Marshall Mission," in Bland, *George C. Marshall's Mediation Mission*, 327–56; Kurtz-Phelan, *China Mission*, 52.

29. Stoler, "Why George Marshall?," 6.

30. Department of State, *China White Paper,* introduction; Shallcross, "Marshall Mission to China," 255; Kurtz-Phelan, *China Mission*, 71.

31. Westad, *Decisive Encounters*, 31.

32. Philip Short, *Mao: A Life* (New York: Henry Holt, 1999), 402.

33. Kurtz-Phelan, *China Mission*, 86.

34. Hsü, *Rise of Modern China*, 623; Department of State, *China White Paper*, introduction.

35. He, "Mao Zedong," 185; Shallcross, "Marshall Mission to China," 10.

36. Zhang, "Zhou Enlai," 233.

37. Kurtz-Phelan, *China Mission*, 122–23.

38. Wang, "Marshall's Approaches," 26.

39. Maochun Yu, *Dragon's War*, 190; Jeans, *Marshall Mission to China*, 2.

40. Shyu, "In Search of Peace," 289; Zhang, "Zhou Enlai," 54; Pogue, *Statesman*, 81.

41. Gen. Alvan C. Gillem Jr., U.S. Army (ret.), box 10, folder China Correspondence, 1941–1950, Alvan C. Gillem Jr. Papers, Military History Institute, Carlisle, Pa.; Jeans, *Marshall Mission to China*, 2; Maochun Yu, *Dragon's War*, 190.

42. Shyu, "In Search of Peace," 285.

43. Ibid.

44. Short, *Mao*, 404.

45. Kurtz-Phelan, *China Mission*, 110–11.

46. Ibid., 53.

47. Jeans, *Marshall Mission to China*, xx; Kurtz-Phelan, *China Mission*, 101.

48. Keith E. Eiler, "Devotion and Dissent: Albert Wedemeyer, George Marshall, and China," in Bland, *George C. Marshall's Mediation Mission*, 91–114; Taylor, *Generalissimo*, 325; Kurtz-Phelan, *China Mission*, 141.

49. Yick, "Communist-Nationalist Political Struggle in Beijing," 395; Marc Gallicchio, "About Face: General Marshall's Plans for the Amalgamation of Communist and Nationalist Armies in China," in Bland, *George C. Marshall's Mediation Mission*, 393–94; Kurtz-Phelan, *China Mission*, 124.

50. Yick, "Communist-Nationalist Political Struggle," 395; Gallicchio, "About Face," 393–94.

51. Kurtz-Phelan, *China Mission*, 180.

52. Taylor, *Generalissimo*, 328; Kurtz-Phelan, *China Mission*, 151.

53. Ledovsky, "Marshall's Mission," 424; Taylor, *Generalissimo*, 334; Hsü, *Rise of Modern China*, 624.

54. Shallcross, "Marshall Mission to China," 281.

55. Gallicchio, "About Face," 402; Wilkinson, "Shanghai Perspective," 342.

56. Westad, *Decisive Encounters*, 8; Hsü, *Rise of Modern China*, 613; Marshall, *Marshall's Mission to China*, xiii.

57. Pogue, *Statesman*, 77.

58. Kurtz-Phelan, *China Mission*, 107.

59. Jeans, *Marshall Mission to China*, 293.

60. Westad, "Could War Have Been Avoided?" 505.

61. Jeans, *Marshall Mission to China*, xxiii; Yick, "Communist-Nationalist Political Struggle," 377.

62. Jeans, *Marshall Mission to China*, 3; Wang, "Marshall's Approaches," 39; Taylor, *Generalissimo*, 557.

63. Luce initially praised Marshall, who was twice on the cover of *Time* magazine; he was critical later. Luce claimed that one hundred American businessmen and ten missionaries could solve China's problems. Herzstein, "Henry Luce, George Marshall, and China," 121; Kurtz-Phelan, *China Mission*, 149.

64. Kurtz-Phelan, *China Mission*, 176.

65. Zhang Suchu, "Why Marshall's Mission Failed," in Bland, *George C. Marshall's Mediation Mission*, 57.

66. Wang, "Marshall's Approaches," 36.

67. Herzstein, "Henry Luce, George Marshall, and China," 133; Eiler, "Devotion and Dissent," 104.

68. Wang, "Marshall's Approaches," 37; Kurtz-Phelan, *China Mission*, 254.

69. Pogue, *Statesman*, 96.

70. Jeans, *Marshall Mission to China*, 296; Kurtz-Phelan, *China Mission*, 108.

71. Short, *Mao*, 404; Kurtz-Phelan, *China Mission*, 287.

72. Meyers, "Frustration, Fortitude, and Friendship," 164; Taylor, *Generalissimo*, 355.

73. Ledovsky, "Marshall's Mission," 428.

74. Wang, "Marshall's Approaches," 28; Kurtz-Phelan, *China Mission*, 253.

75. Taylor, *Generalissimo*, 365.

76. Congressional hearings on this topic were held through 1970. Shallcross, "Marshall Mission to China," 13.

77. Herzstein, "Henry Luce, George Marshall, and China," 124.

78. Jeans, *Marshall Mission to China*, 301.

79. Shallcross, "Marshall Mission to China," 2.

80. Taylor, *Generalissimo*, 365; Jeans, *Marshall Mission to China*, 6; Marshall, *Marshall's Mission to China*, 2:522.

81. Ernest R. May, "1947–1948: When Marshall Kept the U.S. Out of War in China," *Journal of Military History* 66, no. 4 (October 2002): 1001–10.

82. Kurtz-Phelan, *China Mission*, 338.

3

THE ADVOCATE OF AIRPOWER

Marshall and an Independent U.S. Air Force

Following the decisive victories of World War II and holding a monopoly on atomic weapons, the United States emerged as the single most powerful nation on earth. The Allied victory over the Axis powers came about not from a single approach but from a combined-arms effort that leveraged air, land, and sea forces in a concerted global campaign. Cutting off enemy sea lines of communication in the Pacific and grinding Axis ground forces down through an attritional fight while bombing industrial centers in both Germany and Japan, the Allies rid the world of the fascist threat. What was more impressive was that the United States carried the fight to the enemy by force-projection capabilities that no other nation on earth could match. By either strategic shipping or airlift, these achievements came about only through a national effort of mass mobilization of personnel, industrial might, and effective strategic planning.

While most Americans know the names of operational commanders and combat heroes of World War II, many overlook the contribution of the planners, staffers, and leaders who worked behind the scenes to support the personnel engaged in combat. Overseeing much of this complex and expansive planning effort during the war was George C. Marshall. A strategic visionary, Marshall not only built a ground force to defeat the Axis powers, but also oversaw the construction of an air fleet capable of global reach. In his role as army chief of staff, he not only directed the ground war but facilitated the development and employment of both strategic and tactical airpower in multiple theaters of war. Seeing this new medium of air as an important aspect of modern warfare, Marshall contributed significantly to the development of the U.S. Army Air Forces and the rise of American airpower. One of his lasting legacies was his subsequent endorsement of an independent U.S. Air Force on an equal footing with the other armed services.

Since the very beginning of powered flight, the utility of airplanes as a battlefield application had been questioned by military professionals. In the early years, airplanes were largely unreliable, flimsily constructed machines that looked to be of limited value in the increasingly lethal environment of modern warfare. In March 1913, little more than a year before World War I broke out, French Marshal Ferdinand Foch, the Supreme Allied Commander during that conflict, argued that "aviation is fine as a sport, but as an instrument of war it is worth zero." British Expeditionary Force Commander Sir Douglas Haig expressed this same sentiment when in 1912 he espoused that learning to fly was "a waste of time" and could "never be of any use to the army." As a result, aviation had much to prove when the "Great War" broke out in August 1914.

Despite these dismissive views of aviation, most European powers had some form of an air fleet when World War I opened. While these fledgling air forces were composed of differing kinds of aircraft, there was no precedent regarding the use of this new technology. As early as the opening moves of the Schlieffen Plan in August 1914, however, the airplane proved its value by spotting the German First Army's southeast movement heading toward the Marne. The use of the airplane for observation became a key mission in the early years of the war as ground forces used it for intelligence gathering. As the war progressed with the advent of long-range artillery, gunners needed airplanes and in some cases balloons to observe where their rounds impacted. In order to counter this observation mission, armies developed fighter aircraft to deny enemy aircraft access to friendly airspace. Later, larger aircraft were used to bomb enemy assets and infrastructure behind the front lines. By 1916, military air services began defining distinct roles for airplanes along with other airframes designed for specific missions established in specially constructed squadrons. As a result, the first fighter squadrons were organized along with bomber wings and reconnaissance groups. By the end of World War I, airpower had matured significantly. After four grueling years it was obvious that airplanes had a place on the modern battlefield. It would also be fair to say, however, that the war shaped airpower more than airpower shaped the war.

During the interwar years, aircraft technology and capabilities grew by leaps and bounds. Designers and engineers built airframes that flew higher, faster, and carried bigger payloads. In concert with these technological improvements, theorists began formulating concepts and ideas for the use of airpower in future conflict. Hoping to avoid the kind of quagmire that characterized the ground warfare of World War I, some military theorists looked to aviation to solve the problem. Men like Giulio Douhet, Billy Mitchell, Hugh Trenchard, and the faculty of the Air Corps Tactical School (ACTS) framed ideas that would serve as the doctrinal foundations for the potential use of airpower in the next conflict. While many of the ideas they espoused were based on observations from World War I, experiments during the interwar years combined with the promise of growing aviation technology led them to believe that airplanes would be decisive in future military operations.

One of the key concepts developed during the intervening years that held promise was the idea of strategic bombing. Attacking an enemy's industrial cities and their associated populations seemed like a way to avoid the catastrophe of a long slog in the trenches reminiscent of much of World War I. Airpower appeared to offer a potential quick victory as fleets of aircraft would attack all corners of the enemy state. Decimating enemy populations, destroying infrastructure, and reducing cities to rubble would be too much for the targeted nation to endure, some theorists claimed. As a result, those who survived the aerial onslaught would force their governments to sue for peace after only a few weeks of such horror. While the killing of women and children was abhorrent for most analysts, the deaths of thousands of civilians for a few weeks was much better than millions of soldiers over the course of many years.

Despite the macabre math that justified early ideas on strategic bombing and the hope of quick victories, airplanes had another attractive benefit. A few squadrons of aircraft were relatively inexpensive compared to large standing armies or vast naval fleets. Aircraft promised a way to build both offensive and defensive combat power without the large price tag of dozens of divisions of soldiers or several squadrons of naval warships. Furthermore, given the austere budgets following the war for all the major powers—especially during the Great Depression—airpower looked like a good way to spend a nation's defense dollars. Not everyone, however, was sold on these early concepts of airpower. After the debacle of the army's assumption of airmail routes from 1933 to 1934, a review of military air policy was ordered. Headed by former Secretary of War Newton D. Baker, and thus known as the Baker Board, it rejected the idea of an independent air force, and its findings became de facto policy.[1] Admirals and army ground commanders believed that airpower would serve a support role in any future combat operation. They viewed airpower as merely one of many combat arms used in conventional military operations. With this kind of thinking, many believed that an independent air force was a waste of time and resources. With this mind-set and existing policies, aviators stopped their push for an independent air force for a time but remained hopeful that airpower would indeed come of age eventually.

In the case of the United States, the rise of American airpower can be directly attributed to Gen. Henry H. "Hap" Arnold. No individual worked harder, politicked more bureaucrats, hectored more defense officials, and drove the civilian aviation industry more aggressively in the cause of the U.S. Army Air Corps than Hap Arnold. As one of the first army aviators, Arnold was an unrepentant advocate of airplanes and airpower. He not only facilitated the growth of army aviation by working with ground-force commanders in his early years but was also a pioneer in the new technology. Rated as an army aviator in 1912 after taking classes at the Wright brothers' factory in Dayton, Ohio, he won the first Mackay Trophy for the most meritorious military flight that same year. In this endeavor, he proved the observation value of aircraft by locating "enemy" forces during war games in northern Virginia. Years later in 1934, he led a formation of all-metal monoplane B-10 bombers to Alaska, photographing some 20,000 miles of wilderness to include Mount McKinley (Denali). For this operation Arnold earned yet another Mackay Trophy and a Distinguished Flying Cross. Eventually, he became chief of the U.S. Army Air Corps (USAAC) in 1938 and was one of its fiercest advocates. For all his individual efforts and advocacy on the part of airpower, however, one of his biggest contributions toward the establishment of an independent air force was his professional relationship and personal friendship with George C. Marshall. The relationship between these two men not only saw to the effective defeat of the Axis powers but also created a lasting legacy in the U.S. military with the prominent role that airpower had come to play.

Gen. George C. Marshall (*center*), U.S. Army chief of staff, and Gen. Henry H.
Arnold, commanding general, U.S. Army Air Forces, during the Potsdam
Conference. July 23, 1945. U.S. Army Signal Corps. Courtesy Harry S. Truman
Library, Independence, Mo.

The two men first met in 1913 on the Philippine Islands at Fort McKinley in
Manila. With his wife, Bee, Arnold found himself assigned base quarters next
to George and Lily Marshall. By this time, Marshall had already established a
reputation as an outstanding officer, even at this early point of his career. As
a first lieutenant, the future army chief of staff had already been an instructor
at the U.S. Army's Command and General Staff School at Fort Leavenworth,
Kansas, and was able to lead and direct complex military operations. When his
unit was directed to serve as the "offense" in war games and seize Manila after
an amphibious assault at Batangas, Marshall proved his professional mettle.
Working as an adjutant for an elderly colonel who was unable effectively to lead
the unit, and after the chief of staff also fell ill and required hospitalization, the
offensive unit was left without leadership.[2] After learning that the aggressors
had "lost" their leadership for the exercise, an officer on the staff of Maj. Gen.

Hunter Liggett, the commanding general of the exercise, suggested that First Lieutenant Marshall was clearly capable of taking charge.

With Liggett's approval, Marshall led the "assault" from the beaches north to Manila over dense and unforgiving terrain. During this operation, Arnold happened upon Marshall under the shade of bamboo trees giving orders and organizing for the unit's final assault.[3] Observing Marshall's manner and command presence, Arnold made note and in a letter to his wife wrote: "Marshall still holds the job as main guy for the detachment and tells colonels where to take their regiments and what to do with them. However, everyone agrees that he has the ability to handle the situation so there is no bad feelings."[4] Despite his junior rank, Marshall's demeanor, professionalism, and competence were more than enough to earn the respect of those officers much senior to him. After the exercise was over, Arnold held Marshall in the highest esteem, telling Bee, prophetically, "That man will one day be the Army Chief of Staff."[5] While the two men's paths would not officially cross again for some years, the foundation of an excellent working relationship, with Arnold as the subordinate, was laid in the jungles of the Philippines.

As the years passed, Marshall's abilities became known to a wider audience, and with war clouds looming on the horizon, his candor, frankness, and intellect paid dividends not just for himself, but for the nation as a whole. Years later both men were stationed together in Washington, D.C. After Marshall was assigned in July 1938 as the assistant chief of staff, War Plans Division, Arnold made a concerted effort to educate him about the value of airpower and convince him as to its virtues.[6] The future chief of staff visited air bases and talked to aviators while learning about the nature, capabilities, as well as limitations of airpower. Arnold, who had been appointed assistant chief of the Army Air Corps in 1936, marveled at Marshall's ability to absorb and appreciate aviators' concerns.[7] While many senior leaders paid lip service to supporting the corps, Marshall made himself available to aviators to understand better how airpower could serve as an important element in a future conflict.[8] A subordinate air corps officer who observed these two men regularly described their relationship quite accurately: "Without question, Arnold had great respect for Marshall. I suspect that Marshall had a lot of respect for Arnold. I never heard them argue though they may have done so in private, Marshall was always senior but I never heard of his pulling rank over Arnold. Arnold was free to announce his intentions and plans. I never heard his asking Marshall's permission. Theirs was a unique topside relationship."[9] While no aviator himself, with Arnold's assistance Marshall became appreciative of the fact that airpower consisted not just of airplanes and pilots, but required mechanics, infrastructure, and, more importantly, an aviation industry capable of producing both airframes and engines. No doubt the professional relationship between Arnold and Marshall led the latter, in writing to Army Chief of Staff Malin Craig, to endorse Arnold's recommendation to be chief of the air corps in November 1938.

The education provided by Arnold regarding airpower came into play well before the entry of the United States into World War II. Looking to limit defense expenditures, many in the War Department continued to push for the procurement of cheaper, existing aircraft designs rather than newer, more capable, yet increasingly expensive airframes.[10] With an open mind and a new appreciation of airpower, Marshall in October 1938 took Arnold's advice and argued that the current fleet of twin-engine B-12 and B-18 bombers was obsolete when compared to newer, more capable European designs. In this effort Marshall pushed for the acquisition of the innovative and far more capable four-engine Boeing B-17 "Flying Fortress" bomber.[11] Initially designed in 1935, the B-17 would eventually become the mainstay of the Combined Bomber Offensive (CBO) in the European Theater of Operations (ETO) and gained a worthy reputation as a rugged, reliable aircraft. In his argument for the bomber, Marshall wrote that the plane's safety features, ability to provide maritime patrol, and capability to reinforce the nation's overseas possessions were a clear progression in American airpower and were in concert with President Roosevelt's envisioned plan of expanding the Army Air Corps.[12] By January 1939, even Roosevelt made a special request for the new bomber and demanded that special appropriations be made to accommodate its acquisition.[13] In his argument, Roosevelt articulated what many aviators already knew: "Increased range, increased speed, increased capacity of airplanes abroad have changed our requirements for defensive aviation."[14]

At that time, however, USAAC's strength was paltry at best. With only 1,650 officers, 16,000 enlisted personnel, roughly 750 cadets in the pilot-training pipeline, and slightly more in the mechanic and ground crew schools, the air corps was minimally staffed. Furthermore, the branch had only a few obsolete P-26 "Peashooter" and Seversky P-35 fighters, and a handful of B-10 and B-12 bombers, with about a dozen B-17s.[15] In the autumn of 1938, with the security situation in Europe worsening, President Roosevelt looked to help the nation's allies threatened by a resurgent Germany. Many Americans hoped to remain neutral if another war broke out, and Roosevelt knew that he had to be careful with any overt assistance to the potential Allied belligerents. In order to avoid any appearance of engagement in a coming conflict, the president suggested that American airplane manufacturers start producing ten thousand aircraft a year in an effort to build up the USAAC. While the number of aircraft that the USAAC required and its plan for employment still needed development, Marshall understood that America needed to start ramping up both procurement and production of aircraft in case of war. Both of these functions could not occur overnight and required a dedicated, detailed plan.[16]

While the chief executive framed the request claiming that it was for the air corps, what Roosevelt really intended was to send many of the airframes to Great Britain and France in anticipation of a European war. Marshall was present at the meeting and immediately realized what the president's request meant and what effect it would have on the USAAC. Understanding the limitation of the American aviation industry at the time, and disinclined to give European air forces priority over the USAAC, Marshall knew that the proposed plan would leave the United States in a precarious position regarding airframes. When the president asked for his opinion, the general replied, "I am sorry, Mr. President, I don't agree with you at all."[17] In his dissension, Marshall was looking out for the USAAC and was concerned that the United States was giving away aviation assets that would be needed if and when the nation became involved militarily in the impending conflict. While aircraft manufacturing did increase during this period, many airframes and engines were indeed shipped to the Allies, leaving the USAAC wanting. Marshall's concern regarding the lack of airframes in the USAAC was finally illustrated to Roosevelt after the war started. As a result of Roosevelt's support of the Allies, Marshall informed the president that the USAAC had only forty-nine such bombers in its inventory. According to an eyewitness, Roosevelt's "head shot back as if someone had hit him in the chest."[18]

When Marshall assumed his duties as army chief of staff on September 1, 1939, he also witnessed the opening salvo of the global war they had all expected.[19] While it would be more than two years before the United States was fully engaged, Marshall clearly had his work cut out for him. One of the changes he instituted was to create positions on the army staff for aviators and representatives from the air corps. While serving under his predecessor, Malin Craig, Marshall found most army general staff officers indifferent or ignorant of the capabilities of airpower.[20] On the eve of the war, many army officers still adhered to the idea that the only function of airpower was to further the mission of the ground army. In this role, aviation was a mere adjunct to ground operations, providing observation, reconnaissance, close air support, and transport.[21] The idea that airpower could play an independent and decisive role was a foreign concept. In fact, the curriculum at the U.S. Army Command and General Staff College at Fort Leavenworth, Kansas, where most officers went for intermediate-level education, dedicated few hours to the study of airpower and focused largely on ground-combat operations and functions.[22] Any appreciation for the study of airplanes and their use in war required assignment to the Air Corps Tactical School, which was largely reserved for aviators themselves with little involvement from the other branches of the army. As a result, the larger body of army officers had little familiarity with aviation concepts or consideration of airpower in operational planning. The motto of the ACTS illustrated its unique nature: *"Proficimus More Irretenti"* (meaning "We Make Progress Unhindered by Custom").[23] With this in mind, USAAC officers were heading in new theoretical directions by themselves, without influencing or educating the army at large.

Reminiscing about his indoctrination to the army staff, Marshall told his official biographer, Forrest Pogue: "I found everyone on the Staff hostile to air, the young air officers were going to Congress and stirring up everything—and the situation was in a general muddle. They had something to complain about because they weren't getting any recognition."[24] In order to address this deficiency, Marshall ordered Gen. Frank Andrews, a well-known aviator, to the General Staff to serve as chief of staff for operations and training. Given the current global war footing, this was a key position in preparing the army for future conflict.[25] Appointing an aviator to this important position was an unpopular decision among the civilian leadership in the War Department and with outgoing Army Chief of Staff Craig. Regardless of their displeasure and the words exchanged over the appointment, Marshall not only defended his choice but also brought in Maj. Larry Kuter to help draft a plan for the expansion of the USAAC.[26] Standing his ground and including aviators in key positions helped to raise awareness of airpower and its acceptance as a key component of the larger army.

By early 1940, the Army Air Corps put the finishing touches on its planned expansion and presented it to Marshall. With Kuter taking the lead on the brief, the plan called for the USAAC to grow to fifty-four groups. Included in the brief was not just a recommendation for more airplanes, but a detailed analysis for personnel, matériel, and supporting infrastructure. When the brief was finished, Marshall asked why Kuter recommended only fifty-four groups and not more.[27] Kuter replied that the proposed structure was based on feasibility in the near future and that the number of groups could be expanded at a later time. With this one question, Marshall showed that he expected officers to be able to articulate with specificity how and why they generated numbers. Without further questioning and giving carte blanche approval, Marshall replied: "The Program is approved . . . let's get on with it."[28] By the time the war was over, from 25 to 35 percent of the entire American industrial effort for the war was geared toward the building of more than 325,000 aircraft.[29] This figure was well beyond the 10,000 airframes a year that Roosevelt had requested just a few years before the war.

Once America began to ramp up industrially for the war, the nation had to prioritize and harbor its strategic resources. Various kinds of materials, ores, metals, and other natural resources were needed to build the military force required to defeat the Axis powers. The War Production Board served as the body that monitored and controlled these required resources. When Glenn Martin's aircraft company, maker of the B-26 medium bomber, had production lines standing still due to a lack of aluminum, Marshall stepped in.[30] Making calls to those who controlled resource allocation, Marshall freed up the production of aluminum not for just Martin, but for all aircraft manufacturers so they would have an ample supply of the metal for aircraft construction.[31] While not having a direct hand in the production of aircraft, Marshall's advocacy of their production was a key element in the growth of American airpower.

While helping to spur the growth of the Army Air Corps, Marshall also had a hand in the planned application of airpower for the coming conflict. In August 1941, a small team of army aviators over the course of nine days drafted what became known as Air War Plan Document-1 (AWPD-1). Housed in the old Munitions Building located on the National Mall, four men worked in the oppressively hot spaces of the War Plans Division to develop the concept for employment of American airpower. This document served as the blueprint for America's air war in the European theater and called for some 68,000 aircraft and over 2 million men, including 135,000 pilots, navigators, bombardiers, and other flight personnel with another 850,000 technicians.[32] In addition to outlining the requirements for the air war, AWPD-1 also specified the target methodology for the American bomber offensive, identifying some 154 individual German targets. Planned for a six-month strategic bombing campaign, the effort focused exclusively on German industry and infrastructure leading to the capitulation of the Nazi state.[33]

Only a few weeks later on August 30, 1941, the aviators briefed their plan to senior army officers and civilian leaders, including Marshall and Arnold, as well as Averill Harriman, the president's representative. Presented by Kuter and Haywood Hansell, another framer of the precision-bombing concept, the briefing lasted for two hours. Given Marshall's position and range of authorization, he easily could have dismissed the concept and in a single decision derailed the entire strategic plan. According to Hansell, "Marshall was the one man in the War Department who could with a gesture, dismiss the entire effort. If the plan did not have his endorsement . . . it had no chance whatever of acceptance."[34] After the presentation and discussion of various issues and questions, Marshall replied rather simply: "Gentlemen, I think the plan has merit. I would like the Secretary [Secretary of War Henry L. Stimson] and assistant secretaries to hear it."[35] What was more important in Marshall's response than his approval was his decision to bypass the Joint Board—where the brief would probably be rejected by the navy and groundcentric officers—and instead proceed directly to the secretary of war. Two weeks later, Stimson received the briefing with Marshall present and echoed the same sentiment claiming, "I like the plan . . . be prepared to present it to the president."[36] What the plan laid out was uncannily accurate regarding the size of the force required, but it had a number of major flaws and assumptions that were unforeseen in 1941.[37] Regardless of these oversights, the American strategic air effort now had official sponsorship.

In June 1941, the U.S. Army Air Corps was reorganized and renamed the U.S. Army Air Forces (USAAF) in an effort to provide more autonomy and facilitate unity of command. Furthermore, this change also created a staff to oversee and manage specific aircentric issues.[38] In this move, the chief of the USAAF, Hap Arnold, was given his own set of staffs and created an Air Council, which was to review and coordinate major aviation projects of the army. By 1942, Arnold sat as the chief for a policy staff and operating staff and held sway over eight separate specified commands. Furthermore, he held quite a bit of influence over the hiring and firing of air commanders. While directed by Secretary of War Stimson, Marshall too concurred with the reorganization and endorsed the need for a more streamlined structure regarding aviation matters. Bit by bit during Marshall's tenure, significant steps toward air force autonomy allowed unified control of military aviation by aviators themselves.[39]

Simultaneously, after the United States entered the war, the American public also began to see the need for an independent air force. Newspaper articles fostered much of this sentiment. Indicative of its growing independence, in February 1942 the *Washington Star* reported that "the air force is given what amounts to an independent status. Lt. Gen. H. H. Arnold, as head of the force, reports only to Gen. George C. Marshall. General Arnold has picked a group of officers to operate the air force who are not afraid of new ideas or new techniques and who are making ambitious plans for the use of the airplane."[40] A month later the *Washington Post* ran an article entitled "Air Force Will Gain in Army Shakeup," reporting that the airmen would play a larger role in the war with Stimson saying that "this is very largely an air war . . . [and] that it will give the Air Force its proper place."[41]

With America in the war, Marshall was not, at least at this time, pushing for a completely independent air force. In September 1941, he feared that full autonomy might threaten unity of command for combatant commanders. In observing the early German successes of blitzkrieg, he attributed part of the German Wehrmacht's accomplishment to its ground commanders' ability to leverage air support. In his own words, Marshall thought that much of the German tactical success came from "[their] subordination of airpower to the supreme command of the armed forces."[42] In this regard, he saw the synergy provided by combined arms and ability to mass fire, both ground and air, at the decisive point on the battlefield and the flexibility that aviation possessed for dynamic tasking. While most army brass rejected the idea of a separate air service on par with the army and navy, Marshall was open to the idea but believed it was still a rash move at the time given the number of challenges that the U.S. military faced with the impending conflict.[43]

Furthermore, Marshall's support of aviation and airpower was not necessarily a blank check that the air corps could write for itself. While indeed an advocate, he did not necessarily buy in to the idea of the capitulation of the Axis powers by strategic bombing alone and did not see aviation as being the single decisive factor that many aviators did. Marshall still adhered to the idea that ground-based operations were paramount and believed that amphibious assaults would be required.[44] As one biographer noted, Marshall "emphasized the fact that airpower was not a panacea or substitute for balanced forces."[45] While the AWPD planners believed that they could cause German capitulation in a relatively short period of time, Marshall was not as optimistic and remained confident that an amphibious assault followed by a ground campaign was an imperative. In the European Theater of Operations, he would be a major advocate in the planning for a cross-channel invasion as articulated in the plans entitled ROUND-UP and SLEDGEHAMMER as early as 1942 or 1943. These plans eventually morphed into the OVERLORD plan executed on D-Day, June 6, 1944.

In the Pacific, even as late as the summer of 1945, Marshall still thought an invasion of the Japanese home islands was required. While the B-29 firebombing efforts in the Pacific were razing dozens of square miles of Japanese urban landscape and before the dropping of the atomic bombs, Marshall still planned for the execution of a November 1 Allied assault code-named OLYMPIC on the island Kyushu. Additionally OLYMPIC was only a precursor for another assault code-named CORONET scheduled for the spring of 1946 on the island of Honshu. His envisioned need for these possible invasions became a point of consternation for many policy makers. Air leaders like Gen. Curtis LeMay, commander of the XXI Bomber Command in the Marianas, believed that bombing alone eventually would end the war. With Victory-in-Europe Day freeing up troops in the ETO, many veterans looked to return home in the summer of 1945. Marshall was not convinced, however, that the Japanese would capitulate pressed by airpower alone. Contrary to Marshall's concerns, Harold Ickes, secretary of the interior, warned of labor shortages and economic concerns on the home front. If the army did not discharge soldiers, Ickes argued that there would be a lack of personnel for the coal industry, leading to a shortage for the upcoming winter.[46] Keeping troops in the army was Marshall's way of planning for these Japanese assaults. Congressman Edwin Johnson called the military's measured demobilization plan "blind, stupid, and criminal" and charged that the army was unnecessarily holding men.[47] Despite these criticisms, Marshall still saw amphibious assaults as the main focus of effort.

At a June 18, 1945, meeting with the war and navy secretaries, as well as Generals Marshall and Eaker and Admiral King, President Truman authorized the invasion of Kyushu. At the meeting, discussion ensued regarding the efficacy of the aerial bombardment campaign as opposed to the amphibious invasion. Marshall briefed that the Kyushu amphibious assault "was a necessity" and that the arrangements for that operation should still continue.[48] Marshall went on further to point out that he did not believe that airpower alone could force the Japanese to quit. Eaker, who was attending at the behest of Arnold, agreed with Marshall's statement. Despite Eaker's agreement regarding the inability of airpower alone to knock Japan out of the war, the naval blockade combined with a strategic air assault was seen by many in the USAAF as the best way to force a Japanese surrender without an amphibious assault. LeMay was a proponent of such a strategy, but he fully believed that airpower alone could force Japan's surrender.[49] In order to make his point, LeMay traveled to Washington and briefed the Joint Chiefs of Staff, which included Marshall. The briefing was poorly received; according to LeMay, General Marshall slept through most of it.[50] In defense of his ideas, LeMay later stated:

> Most of us in the Army Air Force had been convinced for a long time that it would be possible to defeat Japan without invading their home islands. We needed to establish bases within reasonable range; then we could bomb and burn them until they quit. That was our theory, and history had proven that we were right. The ground gripping Army, and the Navy, didn't agree. They discounted the whole idea.[51]

Countering LeMay, Marshall eventually quipped, "Despite what generals with cigars in their mouths had to say about bombing the Japanese into submission . . . we killed 100,000 Japanese . . . but it didn't mean a thing insofar as actually beating them."[52] Arnold, while a believer in the potential of the strategic air effort, paradoxically favored a land invasion of at least one home island. Despite LeMay's ideas, Arnold accepted the need to capture the southern home island of Kyushu, code-named Operation OLYMPIC, and using it as a base for B-17s and B-24s to attack the main island of Honshu. In this effort, the seizure of Kyushu would allow the Eighth Air Force to transfer from Europe to the Pacific, thereby increasing offensive strategic airpower in the latter theater. These aircraft could then be used against the main island of Honshu and possibly make unnecessary the invasion of the larger island.[53]

Arnold's official concurrence via Eaker, however, had possible implications for the future of an independent air force. His submitted recommendation was worded possibly in order to avoid the potential alienation of Marshall, who advocated the use of ground forces for an invasion but who was also an advocate of an autonomous U.S. Air Force. As Hansell wrote in his memoirs, Marshall stood "in loco parentis" for an independent air force and his relationship with Arnold was a key factor.[54] In Arnold's quest for an independent air arm, however, the USAAF chief had to be diplomatic and could not risk the alienation of Marshall in a JCS decision.[55]

While the USAAF went through a number of organizational changes and adjusted responsibilities as the war progressed, one important assignment that illustrated that airpower had come of age was Arnold's inclusion as a member of the Joint Chiefs of Staff. From the beginning of America's entry in the war, Marshall gave Arnold a "seat at the table" with the Joint Chiefs. As a result, the USAAF chief sat on par with the chief of naval operations and army chief of staff—although Arnold always understood his subordinate position vis-à-vis

Marshall.[56] This position not only allowed the USAAF chief to participate in the development of grand strategy for the United States, but also made Arnold a participant in the discussions and decisions of the Combined Chiefs of Staff (CCS), which included the British. Not everyone was happy with this arrangement, however, especially the U.S. Navy. When the JCS conferred about American policy, Chief of Naval Operations Adm. Ernest King was alone whereas two army generals, Marshall and Arnold, were always present. Much to King's chagrin, his heads of the navy's Bureau of Aeronautics—Admirals John Tower, John McCain, and Dewitt Ramsey, successively—were not afforded a seat at the JCS or CCS tables on an equal footing with Arnold.[57] While naval representation at the White House included Adm. William D. Leahy, thus equaling the balance of representation, this placement of the USAAF at the table was also lauded by President Roosevelt, who wrote: "My recognition of the growing importance of air power is made obvious by the fact that the Commanding General of the Army Air Forces is a member of the Joint and Combined Chiefs of Staff."[58]

While Marshall was indeed head of the army, he gave Arnold great latitude in the day-to-day execution of air activities. While Arnold kept his boss informed of actions taken by the USAAF throughout the globe, Arnold was given free rein to exercise his authority as he deemed necessary.[59] According to Larry Kuter, Marshall never "pulled rank" on Arnold when it came to matters regarding airpower.[60] There was a mutual respect and trust between the two men that resulted in greater autonomy for the USAAF. After 1944, the conduct of the strategic air war was largely overseen by the USAAF alone, apart from the larger army or the JCS. For most of the CBO, target selection, methodology, and execution was done primarily by USAAF personnel with little input from other branches. In fact, in some applications the air staff was enabled to circumvent the regular army bureaucracy and report directly to the JCS. In this method, the USAAF indeed was operating as if it were an independent entity. Marshall decided early on to treat Arnold "as nearly as I could Chief of Staff of the Air without restraint."[61] He recognized Arnold's abilities, work ethic, and leadership skills and felt comfortable placing his faith in Arnold. Concurrently, while Marshall granted Arnold much autonomy, the air chief knew implicitly his place in the chain of command and understood that he was indeed the subordinate. Arnold clearly acquiesced not only to Marshall's position and rank, but to his intellect, acumen, and leadership, as he told Ira Eaker: "If George Marshall took a position contrary to mine, I would know I was wrong."[62]

Another factor that assisted in the growing autonomy of the USAAF was the amount of talent placed with the air staff. Marshall marveled at the intellectual acumen of the men that Arnold had elected to surround himself. Larry Kuter, Haywood Hansell, Lauris Norstad, Barney Giles, and others were not only excellent aviators, but superb staff officers able to operate effectively within the byzantine and multifarious bureaucracy that was the Pentagon. Smart, capable officers who believed in the promise of airpower, Arnold's acolytes proved a formidable force in pushing the cause. According to Kuter, Marshall facilitated the idea of leveraging junior officers not encumbered by precedent or archaic thinking. He urged Arnold to promote young energetic officers over "antique staff officers and passé fliers" in order to grow a core nucleus of competent, innovative air leaders.[63]

As the war unfolded, the American experiment with daylight precision bombing failed to live up to its full promise. Weather and technical limitations, a determined enemy, lack of long-range fighter escorts, and poor strategic intelligence were among the many factors that precluded the success of the envisioned campaign. The U.S. Strategic Bombing Survey (USSBS), conducted after the war to measure the effectiveness of the CBO, found that in 1943 only 20 percent of bombs landed within 1,000 feet of their designated targets, with the same statistic improving to only 60 percent by April 1945.[64] These were hardly the accuracy figures that USAAF planners expected. Furthermore, the USSBS found that German industrial output skyrocketed during a large part of the strategic bombing effort counter to the predictions of ACTS theorists. Additionally, casualty rates for bomber aircrews were horrific. Loss rates on some raids were as high as 20 percent with the overall average hovering around 10 percent.[65] Consequently, an aircrew statistically would not live long enough to complete its required tour of twenty-five missions.[66] In one study of just six bombardment groups, only 559 airmen survived out of an original group of 2,051.[67] In this survey's sample, 1,195 men were either killed or became prisoners, with the average loss rate per mission of 3.9 percent.[68] The bloody years of 1943 and 1944 caused American leadership to question the efficacy and worth of the entire effort. Over the course of the CBO, the Eighth Air Force alone suffered some 18,000 airmen killed, 6,500 wounded, and 33,500 missing.[69] For all the European theater alone, strategic and tactical air forces suffered some 33,000 killed.[70]

Despite these losses, Marshall still believed airpower could have a decisive effect on the enemy's will to fight. In late 1944, Allied air planners devised an operation code-named CLARION. The plan envisioned using groups of Allied aircraft to attack transportation assets, infrastructure, or any useful equipment in smaller towns and villages all over Germany.[71] While first devised in the summer of 1944, the executed plan was in partial response to the German winter offensive that culminated in the Battle of the Bulge in December 1944. Fearing that the Allied forces were losing momentum, Marshall pushed for this massive use of airpower to facilitate the end of hostilities by destroying equipment and affecting German morale. The hope was that such damage inflicted solely by airpower would also overwhelm the Reichsbahn repair teams tasked with keeping railroad transportation networks functioning.[72] While many airmen objected to the idea for various reasons, Marshall on January 31, 1945, directed the JCS to conduct CLARION to coincide with a Soviet offensive in February.[73]

Furthermore, Marshall advocated another massive air operation code-named THUNDERCLAP. This plan targeted specific areas of German cities and road networks used by the retreating Wehrmacht while also affecting fleeing refugee populations.[74] The initial proposal also included a planned daylight raid on the administrative section of Berlin that might be "sufficient to devastate completely an area two and one half square miles . . . with the [targeted] population [experiencing] 100 percent destruction of all personnel and equipment in the affected areas."[75] Again, this operation met with some resistance by USAAF leadership in theater. Gen. Jimmy Doolittle, commander of the U.S. Eighth Air Force, rejected the idea: "There are no basically important strictly military targets in the designated area."[76] In this rebuttal, Doolittle tried to argue that the USAAF only targeted military personnel and not civilians. This was a central tenet of America's prewar doctrine of precision bombardment. By this time in the war, however, such distinctions were largely semantic and hardly practical. Regardless of the arguments regarding the wanton destruction that both operations caused, they were indeed advocated by Marshall as a way that airpower might hasten an end to the conflict. While neither operation lived up to its billing as a culminating blow, the endorsement of these plans by the army chief of staff indicated that he still placed great faith in the promise of airpower.

No event introduced the world to the effect of airpower more than the dropping of the atomic bombs in August 1945. One aircraft with a single bomb now had the power to destroy a whole city and kill many tens of thousands in a single strike. With even more atomic weapons and a large air fleet, military planners believed it was now possible to actually "kill a nation."[77] With the destruction of Hiroshima and Nagasaki, many military theorists believed that the nature of warfare had indeed changed forever. This vision supposed that wars would no longer be fought with ground forces in protracted campaigns or on the high seas with warships engaged in a crescendo engagement. In an article published in *Collier's* magazine in December 1945, Gen. Carl A. Spaatz, the first air force chief of staff, argued, "War in the future would be aimed and smashing the enemy's whole organism and would counter his offensive incidentally in the process. . . . Immediate blows against [enemy] means of civilization and support, his industrial and economic area would make his continuance of the struggle pointless and bring about quick surrender."[78] Much like Douhet envisioned in the 1920s, airpower enthusiasts embraced these new technical advances as watershed events in the history of warfare. The capabilities of nuclear fission combined with long-range intercontinental bombers appeared to make both armies and navies largely irrelevant—or at least place them in subordinate roles.

While many events and perceptions during the war encouraged the reorganization of the American military, perhaps the biggest was the coming of the age of airpower.[79] Airpower's contribution to the overall war effort was also reflected in the highest echelons of the U.S. government. With Marshall's support, Hap Arnold became one of the president's principal military advisers and helped raise the awareness of this increasingly important dimension of war. In the summer of 1947, as unification of the armed services was taking place under the title "National Military Establishment" (NME), President Truman directed a study of airpower and its utility for the future of the nation. Eventually known as the Finletter Commission, the chief executive wanted "an evaluation of the course which the United States should follow in order to obtain . . . the greatest benefits from aviation."[80] In a six-month study, one of the main conclusions of the commission determined, "In our opinion the Military Establishment must be built around the air arm. Of course an adequate Navy and Ground Force must be maintained. But it is the Air Force and naval aviation on which we must rely. Our military must be based upon airpower. . . . For a second best air force, when war takes place, is almost as bad as none."[81] With these findings, along with others, it was clear that airpower had indeed proven its worth. After the war, airmen were even more convinced of the relevance of airpower as a military tool. Combined with its monopoly on atomic weapons, the United States looked forward to an American "Pax Atomica" able to check any aggression on a global basis.

While George Marshall retired as the army chief of staff in November 1945 and then quickly departed for his ill-fated mission to China, one of his lasting legacies was his support and enthusiasm for airpower. While he did not endorse the idea of an independent air force during the exigencies of wartime, he did see the need for a separate air service in the future. His relationship with Hap Arnold was a key component of airpower's growth in the United States, and their mutual respect set a tone in the halls of the War Department and the White House conducive to an independent air force. He was the first army chief of staff to give airmen a venue in the army staff, fought for procurement of the B-17 and air fleet modernization, was a driving force in the expansion of the Army Air Corps in anticipation of a forthcoming war, allowed the USAAF to operate independently during the war, and envisioned airpower having a culminating effect on the Axis powers and in the future. Through his cumulative efforts, he helped paved the way for the birth of the U.S. Air Force and the reorganization of the American military.

NOTES

1. Wesley Craven and James Lea Cate, *The Army Air Forces in World War II*, vol. 6: *Men and Planes* (Washington, D.C.: Office of Air Force History, 1983), vi.

2. Thomas Coffey, *Hap: The Story of the US Air Force and the Man Who Built It* (New York: Viking, 1982), 78.

3. Mark A. Stoler, *George C. Marshall: Soldier-Statesman of the American Century* (Boston: Twayne, 1989), 27, 79–80.

4. Coffey, *Hap*, 80.

5. John W. Huston, *American Air Power Comes of Age: General Henry H. Arnold's World War II Diaries* (Montgomery, Ala.: Air University Press, 2002), 7; Coffey, *Hap*, 80; Stoler, *George C. Marshall*, 27.

6. Coffey, *Hap*, 180.

7. Henry H. Arnold, *Global Mission* (New York: Harper and Row, 1949), 163–64; Coffey, *Hap*, 180.

8. Michael Sherry, *The Rise of American Airpower* (New Haven, Conn.: Yale University Press, 1987), 86.

9. Laurence S. Kuter, "George C. Marshall, Architect of Air Power," *Air Force Magazine* 61, no. 8 (August 1978), as referenced in Coffey, *Hap*, 209–10.

10. Arnold, *Global Mission*, 167.

11. Coffey, *Hap*, 188; Arnold, *Global Mission*, 180.

12. Thomas H. Greer, *The Development of Air Doctrine in the Army Air Arm, 1917–1941* (Washington, D.C.: Office of Air Force History, 1985), 101.

13. Ibid.

14. Ibid.

15. Arnold, *Global Mission*, 165; Coffey, *Hap*, 181; Kuter, "George C. Marshall," 65.

16. Coffey, *Hap*, 188.

17. Leonard Mosely, *Marshall, Hero for Our Times* (New York: Hearst, 1982), 121; Stoler, *George C. Marshall*, 65.

18. Stoler, *George C. Marshall*, 75.

19. On the same date, Marshall ironically assumed his duties while airborne in a U.S. Army Air Corps aircraft when the announcement was made (as referenced in Arnold, *Global Mission*, 190–91).

20. Coffey, *Hap*, 205.

21. Haywood Hansell, *The Strategic Air War against Germany and Japan: A Memoir* (Washington, D.C.: Office of Air Force History, 1986), 33.

22. Peter J. Schifferle, *America's School for War: Fort Leavenworth, Officer Education, and Victory in World War II* (Lawrence: University Press of Kansas, 2010), 193.

23. Robert T. Finney, *History of the Air Corps Tactical School, 1920–1940* (Washington, D.C.: Office of Air Force History, 1992), v.

24. Coffey, *Hap*, 205.

25. Charles Griffith, *The Quest: Haywood Hansell and American Strategic Bombing in World War II* (Montgomery, Ala.: Air University Press, 1999), 81; Kuter, "George C. Marshall," 66.

26. Kuter, "George C. Marshall," 66.

27. Ibid., 65.

28. Ibid.; Coffey, *Hap*, 209.

29. Stephen L. McFarland and Wesley P. Newton, "The American Strategic Air Offensive against Germany in World War II," in *Case Studies in Strategic Bombardment*, ed. R. Cargill Hall (Washington, D.C.: Air Force History and Museums Program, 1998), 233.

30. Arnold, *Global Mission*, 205. The B-26 was a twin-engine design that was considered a "hot" plane by its pilots. High landing speeds, wing loading, and performance characteristics earned it the nicknames "Widow Maker" and "The Baltimore Whore." The latter nickname resulted from Baltimore being the location of the Martin Aircraft Company, and with short, stubby wings the plane had no visible means of "support."

31. Arnold, *Global Mission*, 205.

32. Griffith, *Quest*, 69.

33. Ibid., 71.

34. Haywood Hansell, *The Air Plan That Defeated Hitler* (Atlanta: Higgins-McArthur, 1972), 94.

35. James C. Gaston, *Planning the American Air War: Four Men and Nine Days in 1941* (Washington, D.C.: National Defense University Press, 1982), 91–92; Griffith, *Quest*, 80; Hansell, *Air Plan That Defeated Hitler*, 94.

36. Hansell, *Air Plan That Defeated Hitler*, 96.

37. The original AWPD plan called for 239 air groups. In 1945, the USAAF had 243 fully equipped groups. The total number of air groups was 269, including groups not fully equipped.

38. Craven and Cate, *The Army Air Forces in World War II*, vol. 1: *Plans and Early Operations, January 1939 to August 1942* (Chicago: University of Chicago Press, 1948), 115; Greer, *Development of Air Doctrine*, 127.

39. Craven and Cate, *Army Air Forces*, 1:115; Greer, *Development of Air Doctrine*, 127.

40. Newspaper clipping: Owen Scott, "US Creating Air Force Equal to Its Need," *Washington Star*, February 8, 1942, box 1, folder Scrapbook File vol. 2 [2 of 3], Robert A. Lovett Papers, Harry S. Truman Library.

41. Newspaper clipping: John C. Norris, "Air Force Will Gain in Army Shakeup," *Washington Post*, March 6, 1942, box 1, folder Scrapbook File vol. 2 [2 of 3], Robert A. Lovett Papers, Harry S. Truman Library.

42. Craven and Cate, *Army Air Forces*, 6:25.

43. Kuter, "George C. Marshall," 67.

44. Griffith, *Quest*, 251.

45. Stoler, *George C. Marshall*, 116.

46. "Stimson Refuses Earlier Releases," *New York Times*, August 3, 1945.

47. Ibid.

48. J. Samuel Walker, *Prompt and Utter Destruction: Truman and the Use of the Atomic Bombs against Japan* (Chapel Hill: University of North Carolina Press, 1997), 36–37.

49. Ibid., 39.

50. Curtis E. LeMay in Richard H. Kohn and Joseph P. Harahan, eds., *Strategic Air Warfare: An Interview with Generals Curtis E. Lemay, Leon W. Johnson, David A. Burchinal, and Jack J. Catton* (Washington, D.C.: Office of Air Force History, 1988), 65.

51. Curtis E. LeMay and MacKinlay Kantor, *Mission with LeMay: My Story* (New York: Doubleday, 1965), 381.

52. John P. Sutherland, "The Story General Marshall Told Me," *U.S. News and World Report* 47 (November 2, 1959): 50–56, as cited in Walker, *Prompt and Utter Destruction*, 3.

53. Hansell, *Strategic Air War*, 251.

54. Ibid.

55. Ibid.

56. Craven and Cate, *Army Air Forces*, 6:49.

57. Ibid.; Kuter, "George C. Marshall," 67.

58. Craven and Cate, *Army Air Forces*, 6:50.

59. Sherry, *Rise of American Airpower*, 221.

60. Coffey, *Hap*, 346.

61. Sherry, *Rise of American Airpower*, 221; Coffey, *Hap*, 232.

62. Coffey, *Hap*, 346.

63. Kuter, "George C. Marshall," 67.

64. U.S. Strategic Bombing Survey, *Overall Report (European War)* (Washington, D.C.: Government Printing Office, 1945), 5.

65. Richard G. Davis, *Bombing the European Axis Powers: A Historical Digest of the Combined Bomber Offensive, 1939–1945* (Montgomery, Ala.: Air University Press, 2006), 121–25.

66. Ibid.

67. Mark K. Wells, *Courage and Air Warfare: The Allied Aircrew Experience in the Second World War* (London: Frank Cass, 1995), 46.

68. Ibid.

69. Davis, *Bombing the European Axis Powers*, 585.

70. Ibid.

71. Ronald Schaffer, *Wings of Judgment: American Bombing in World War II* (Oxford: Oxford University Press, 1985), 91.

72. Davis, *Bombing the European Axis Powers*, 494.

73. Staff Meeting Notes, December 23, 1944, box 16, Carl A. Spaatz Papers, Manuscript Division, Library of Congress; Schaffer, *Wings of Judgment*, 94.

74. Schaffer, *Wings of Judgment*, 96.

75. Annex I, box 153, folder Operation Thunderclap, Carl A. Spaatz Papers, Manuscript Division, Library of Congress.

76. Richard G. Davis, *Carl A. Spaatz and the Air War in Europe* (Washington, D.C.: Center for Air Force History, 1993), 495.

77. Col. Grover Brown, "Concepts of Strategic Air War," 1951, as cited in Edward Kaplan, *To Kill Nations: American Strategy in the Air Atomic Age and the Rise of Mutually Assured Destruction* (Ithaca, N.Y.: Cornell University Press, 2015), 3.

78. Carl A. Spaatz, "Air Power in the Atomic Age," *Collier's Magazine*, December 8, 1945, box 268, Carl A. Spaatz Papers, Speeches and Article File, Manuscript Division, Library of Congress.

79. Alfred Goldberg, ed., *History of the Office of the Secretary of Defense*, vol. 1: *The Formative Years, 1947–1950*, ed. Steven L. Rearden (Washington, D.C.: Office of the Secretary of Defense, Historical Office, 1984), 18.

80. Air Policy Commission, *Survival in the Air Age* (Washington, D.C.: Government Printing Office, 1948), v.

81. Ibid., 8.

SEAN N. KALIC

4

MILITARY POSTURE FOR PEACE

Marshall and the National Security Act

Gen. George C. Marshall is well known as U.S. Army Chief of Staff during World War II, yet his role in the Allied victory was much more complicated as he fulfilled duties beyond just leading the army. Marshall was the U.S. Army's "overall director of global operations," which meant that he also advised President Franklin D. Roosevelt on strategic matters, in addition to serving as the primary representative to the Allied coalition.[1] Historians have lauded him as one of America's greatest heroes based on his abilities as a soldier and statesman.[2] After his success during World War II, Marshall transitioned to civilian government positions as secretary of state from January 1947 to January 1949 and secretary of defense from September 1950 to September 1951.[3] Marshall's service at the most senior levels of government from 1939 to 1951 represented a period of significant change for the world, and especially for the United States. The experience of leading the U.S. Army in its global fight to defeat the Axis powers provided Marshall with keen insights into how the U.S. military and indeed the nation needed to prepare and organize to fight on such a grand scale. This experience proved valuable as the United States adjusted to the seismic shifts happening in the international security environment between 1945 and 1955.

In the immediate aftermath of World War II, Marshall and Dwight D. Eisenhower, as well as President Harry S. Truman, made an argument for the unification of the military services of the United States based on their experiences during the war.[4] The argument in favor of unification held that "victory required a single commander with absolute authority to harness the power of ground, air, and naval forces in a way that brought the strength of each to maximum effectiveness."[5] In addition to the debates about the unification of the military, the Truman administration also wrestled with the rapidly changing Cold War security environment. Concerns over the encroachment of communism in Western Europe, especially in France and Italy, demanded the attention of Truman and Marshall. Striving to stabilize the post–World War II security environment in Europe, the United States worked on a series of policy measures designed to contain and confront the spread of communism. From the announcement of the Truman Doctrine to the development of the European Recovery Act to the support of the Berlin Airlift, the United States embraced the onset of a new security paradigm, which directly identified the Soviet Union as the primary adversary in this tumultuous era.

Despite the beginning of the Cold War, Truman still worked to demobilize the large wartime U.S. Army Ground Forces and Army Air Forces, Navy, and Marine Corps of World War II, as he also attempted to shift the economy of the United States back to a civilian footing. The confluence of strategic, political, and economic issues drove yet another debate within the U.S. government as to how the United States should "rearm itself" in the opening period of this epoch.[6] The underlying recognition in this period was the perceived military power of the Soviet Union and the potential for a war with a former U.S. ally in World War II. These tensions were the backdrop during which George C. Marshall served as secretary of state and later as secretary of defense.

The National Security Act of 1947 and its amendments in 1949 were a major effort designed to reorganize the U.S. defense establishment into the Department of Defense (DOD), from its predecessor, the Department of War. This significant piece of policy evolved from the debate over military unification and came as the Truman administration began to solidify its policies for the early Cold War. The overall justification was based on the need for the United States to be prepared to fight the Soviet Union in either a conventional or

Gen. George C. Marshall (*right*) rides with Gen. Dwight D. Eisenhower in a
motorcade leaving National Airport. June 18, 1945. Courtesy George C. Marshall
Library, Lexington, Va.

atomic war. The emerging belief was that the next war would not allow time
for the United States "to mobilize" its military and industrial base; therefore,
the United States needed a perpetual state of readiness and mobilization.[7]
Secretary of State Marshall had little direct input into the overall legislation,
but his experience during World War II led him to believe that readiness and
efficiency were two major traits that the United States needed to maintain into
the Cold War. As such, he believed that the United States required a long-range
strategy that focused on maximizing and mobilizing its strengths to maintain
Western vigilance against the encroachment of communism supported by
the Soviet Union.[8]

Marshall, therefore, was an important figure in the development of the early
Cold War military reorganization because he demanded that the United States
remain focused and militarily ready to combat advances made by the Soviet
Union. His work toward unification of the military services as well as the reorga-

nization of the Department of State provided the foundation that would endure for the entirety of the Cold War. In addition to serving as secretary of defense, Marshall oversaw reform efforts that emerged from the National Security Act of 1947 and its follow-on adjustments in 1949. As such, George C. Marshall was a vital architect of the national security policy of the United States that persisted for the duration of the Cold War.

To better understand this claim, it is necessary to look at three periods associated with the early Cold War. The first section of this chapter details Marshall's position in the unification debates and outlines the evolution of the National Security Act of 1947. Next, Marshall's role in shaping national security and foreign policy associated with the early Cold War during his tenure as secretary of state and later as secretary of defense demonstrates how he enacted and applied these critical measures as a trusted member of Truman's administration. The final section of this chapter places Marshall's actions within the greater context of the Cold War as the Truman administration solidified its national security policies during the Korean War.

In the immediate aftermath of World War II, President Truman in his message to Congress on December 19, 1945, outlined his support of a unified military. Truman stated:

> One of the lessons which have most clearly come from the costly and dangerous experience of this war is that there must be unified direction of land, sea and air forces at home as well as in all other parts of the world where our Armed Forces are serving. . . . But we never had comparable unified direction or command in Washington. And even in the field, our unity of operations was greatly impaired by the differences in training, in doctrine, in communication systems, and in supply and distribution systems, that stemmed from the division of leadership in Washington.[9]

The core elements of unification, which was heavily opposed by the U.S. Navy, centered on five primary points that had been distilled from the ad hoc efforts of Franklin D. Roosevelt, Marshall, Adm. Ernest King, and Gen. Henry H. "Hap" Arnold during World War II. These points were:

a. A single executive Department headed by a civilian Secretary, a civilian Under Secretary, and civilian Assistant Secretaries.
b. A Chief of Staff of the Armed Forces who is the senior military advisor to the President and Secretary.

    c. Three coequal arms—Army, Navy, and Air—with their own commanders, with their armies, fleets, and air forces, each charged with operations in its own sphere.

    d. A Navy includes Naval Aviation and the Marine Corps.

    e. A Chiefs of Staff organization makes recommendations on Military Policy, Strategy, and the Budget.[10]

A major adjustment in this proposal to restructure and unify the Department of the Navy and the Department of War was to elevate the U.S. Army Air Forces (USAAF) to an independent service status and provide it with a coequal importance to the U.S. Navy and U.S. Army. To advocate further for these significant bureaucratic changes, Truman used the recent experience of U.S. forces fighting in the Pacific theater to highlight the need for adjustment. He stated:

> Whatever the form of future war may take, we know that the men of our separate services will have to work together in many kinds of combinations for many purposes. The Pacific campaign of the recent war is an outstanding example of common and joint effort among land, sea, and air forces. Despite its success, that campaign proved that there is not adequate understanding among the officers and men of any Service of the capabilities, the uses, the procedure, and the limitations of the other services.[11]

Based on his extensive experience, Marshall shared President Truman's sentiments about unification. As part of his testimony before the Senate Military Affairs Committee, Marshall declared:

> The national security is measured by the sum, or rather the combination of the three great arms, the land, air, and naval forces. The urgent need is for an over-all, not a piecemeal, appraisal of what is required to solve the single problem of national security with the greatest economy compatible with requirements. I am strongly convinced that unless there is a single department for the armed forces, within which the difficult and numerous complexities can be ironed out prior to a presentation of requirements to the President and the Congress, there can be little hope that we will be able to maintain through the years a military posture that will secure for us a lasting peace.[12]

Also during his testimony, Marshall outlined how the unification process would better assist in building more effective and efficient defense budgets that would ultimately be in the best interest of the United States.[13] Based on his position during the war, Marshall believed that the U.S. armed services needed to unify to ensure that they were not squandering the nation's precious and limited economic resources. Marshall argued that unification would allow the three services to better synchronize their budgets, rather than fight over them. Furthermore, he believed that unification focused on the long-term strategic needs of the United States, which in turn allowed Congress to "wisely appropriate" the budget for defense.[14]

The essence of the unification debate focused on how to keep the chief of staff arrangement, which worked well for the most part during World War II, while suppressing the tension between the Department of the Navy and the War Department. Beyond just providing a more coordinated military structure, the proposal also included the elevation of the USAAF into an independent service. Furthermore, policy advisers such as Ferdinand Eberstadt, chair of the Army-Navy Munitions Board, believed that "linking strategic plans with their conversion into natural resources was among the very desirable objectives" for a postwar defense structure.[15] Based on Eberstadt's experience and his review of the best practices incorporated during the war, which was written up as an official government document for the Truman administration, he recommended a National Security Resources Board as a necessary and primary element of the reorganized defense infrastructure.[16] He envisioned that this new entity would coordinate civilian and military demands on U.S. natural resources as the country prepared to make adjustments to the emerging Cold War. In essence, the various proposals from within the military and from within the executive branch sought more coordination and focus on strategic issues relating to the allocation of natural resources as they applied to rebuilding and sustaining the U.S. armed services.

Furthermore, the unification debates centered on maintaining individual service capabilities within the departments of the U.S. Air Force, Army, and Navy, but coordinating these efforts with a chief of staff of the armed forces that reported directly to a civilian undersecretary and a civilian secretary.[17] The president, who resided at the top of the organization, would also receive advice and policy recommendations from a body called the "U.S. Chiefs of Staff," composed of "Chief of Staff to the Commander in Chief, the Chief of Staff of

Armed Forces, as well as individual Chiefs of Staff for Air, Navy, and Army."[18] The argument behind this arrangement was that it kept the elements of the Joint Chiefs of Staff that worked during the war to advise President Roosevelt but also brought the military services into a much more centralized command-and-control structure as a means to build and synchronize U.S. strategy for the early Cold War. Despite the direction of these political debates, the attempts to unify the services did not succeed. This did not mean, however, that the process was dead. In fact, out of the ashes arose the National Security Act of 1947, which took many of the elements of the debates outlined above and added additional structures as a way to build a comprehensive Department of Defense that could handle the coordination and demands of the early Cold War.

Marshall, who had supported the unification of the services and had since gone on to represent the United States in China as a means to assist in averting civil war there, was sworn in as secretary of state on January 21, 1947, in the presence of President Truman.[19] Therefore, his input into the National Security Act of 1947 was minimal, save for the elements of the unification debates that were incorporated into the defense reorganization. Despite not having a direct influence on this specific and important piece of legislation, however, Marshall's testimony and ideas about how best to order the U.S. government for a new strategic era were reflected in the monumental changes to the national security structure of the United States. Specifically, during the unification debates Marshall stated that during World War II he quickly learned that minor issues could easily transform into major issues. He outlined the following in his briefing:

> . . . the organization of the forces, the allotment of personnel, of material; in the settlement of priorities, what should be built and when, in matters of that kind we had tremendous difficulties, protracted discussions, and in many cases unsatisfactory solutions. When there are no longer operations, when strategy is not the great factor of the day, you [Congress] will then be confronted almost entirely by the questions of financing, or the question of the military posture that we will have in terms of personnel, what service it is to be in, in terms of equipment, whether we have this type of equipment or that, the large or the small, the ship or the plane, the tank, all the various affairs, and particularly in the matter of special developments that we now see indicated through our scientific progress. Those will be our daily battles in time of peace and the matters regarding which we have had the least satisfactory experience.[20]

These were the exact issues that the Truman administration wrestled with when Marshall become secretary of state. The administration was in a serious debate with Congress and the military over the force structure, global presence, and budgets of the military services as they focused on a restructuring process that made sense for the looming crisis with the Soviet Union. The National Security Act of 1947 assisted to provide a structure as well as a process by which a strategy could be developed to shepherd the United States into this new international security environment. Marshall's words in 1945 about the need to focus on priorities and budget allocations were a major part of the background when President Truman signed the National Security Act on July 26, 1947.[21]

The U.S. Congress formulated the National Security Act "to provide a more manageable and better managed military machine."[22] This was not just a push from civilians in the executive and legislative branches of the U.S. government to get more control over the armed services; the demand also came from Marshall and other high-ranking commanders who believed that the new peacetime security environment demanded a higher degree of flexibility.[23] From the military's perspective, the uncertainty of the new international security environment left a wide range of possibilities open for which the U.S. military had to prepare. Not having perfect awareness of the demands of the future meant that the services had to be dynamic in their warfighting capabilities to meet a whole host of prospects that encompassed everything from short-term peace and stability operations to full mobilization for total war against the Communists.[24] These demands also had to be considered within the post–World War II context of demobilizing the huge military infrastructure that evolved to fight and eventually win World War II. Recognizing that the Cold War was quickly becoming a reality of the late 1940s, President Truman, Marshall, Congress, and the leadership of the military services all wrestled with the proper balance between postwar civilian demands and the military requirements to ensure American security in the new atomic era. The National Security Act of 1947, also known as Public Law 253, was the first major attempt to rebuild the security and defense structure of the United States for the early Cold War.

The advocates of the national security act designed it to maintain and enhance key tenets of the U.S. defense establishment and national security structure. The first and primary element was civilian control of the military, which would also be coordinated with additional new agencies within the executive branch.[25] Under the structure of the new system, the secretary of defense became the head of the reorganized defense bureaucracy and operated as the president's "full time representative" over military matters.[26] Furthermore, with the development of a secretary of defense, Congress had a single individual it could call to answer questions and points of inquiry over national security and defense matters.[27]

Recognizing that the wartime structure of a Joint Chiefs of Staff (JCS) needed to be maintained, Congress kept the JCS and aligned them under the secretary of defense. The duties of the JCS outlined by the 1947 act were:

1. To prepare strategic plans and to provide for strategic directions of the military forces;
2. To prepare joint logistic plans and to assign the military services logistic responsibilities in accordance with such plans;
3. To establish unified commands in strategic areas when such a unified command is in the interest of the United States;
4. To formulate policies for joint training of military forces;
5. To formulate policies coordinating the education of members of the military forces;
6. To review major materiel and personnel requirements of the military forces, in accordance with strategic and logistic plans; and
7. To provide United States representation on the Military Staff Committee of the United Nations in accordance with the provisions of the Charter of the United Nations.[28]

Furthermore, the JCS also served as the principal military advisers to the secretary of defense and also to the president of the United States. The composition of the JCS was the Chief of Staff, U.S. Army; Chief of Naval Operations; and Chief of Staff, U.S. Air Force. The legislation also allowed for a chief of staff to the commander-in-chief based on presidential preference.[29] A glaring new addition to the JCS structure was the addition of the chief of staff of the U.S. Air Force. This new billet replaced the previous chief of staff of air forces, which Gen. Hap Arnold had filled during World War II. With Truman's signature on the act, the U.S. Air Force become a separate and independent branch within the new defense bureaucracy.[30]

Staying focused on the military structure and borrowing ideas from the debate over unification, Congress maintained the Department of the Army; continued the Department of the Navy, which included the U.S. Marine Corps; and established the Department of the Air Force. Each of these armed service departments had a cabinet-level civilian secretary appointed by the president of the United States, as well as a military chief of staff who served as the head of the individual service component.[31] The service department secretaries reported directly to the secretary of defense but could appeal to the president if there was a disagreement. Furthermore, the individual service component chiefs of staff also reported to the secretary of defense. This structure provided each service with both representation and access to the secretary of defense, as the three service departments individually controlled their own budgets, war plans, and force structure. This function was kept separate and distinct from the JCS structure, which served as an advisory body focused on more strategic and national-coordination matters.

In addition to the major effects that the National Security Act had on the newly created secretary of defense and defense bureaucracy, it also inaugurated three additional agencies that were designed to synchronize elements of national security as the United States struggled to outline and define a strategy for the early Cold War. These agencies were the National Security Council (NSC), the Central Intelligence Agency (CIA), and the National Security Resources Board (NSRB). As with the reforms to the defense structure within the U.S. government, wartime experience confirmed that the U.S. president needed additional agencies that could assist with coordinating matters of strategy, intelligence, and industry within the broader context of U.S. national security.

Marshall in his testimony supporting unification before Congress had argued that this coordinating function was vital if the United States wanted to maintain and perpetuate its international position, especially during times of peace.[32] Likewise, Ferdinand Eberstadt came to see the importance of "linking strategic plans with national resources as a very desirable objective of a postwar defense structure."[33] Eberstadt envisioned the Office of War Mobilization, run during the war by James F. Byrnes, as a model of effective synchronization between industry, national resources, and military strategy.[34] Much like Marshall, Eberstadt believed that Cold War national security demanded an apparatus that coordinated policy among civilian and defense organizations with an aim toward maintaining "plans, programs, and structures" necessary to "translate military plans into industrial and civilian mobilization."[35]

Between 1945 and 1947, the Truman administration spent a considerable amount of energy striving to balance an extensive set of demands. First and foremost was the transition of the United States from wartime back to a peacetime footing. Although Truman was fixated on a deliberate yet quick process of demobilization, he still acknowledged that the wartime alliance with the Soviet

Union had evaporated and had been replaced with significant ideological and geopolitical tensions. He and many policy makers within his administration were well aware of the rapidly increasing demands to maintain a more robust military force. In addition to trying to balance demobilization and the possibility of rebuilding another conventional military force to confront the expansion of communism, Truman had to assist in stabilizing Western Europe. In short, all these issues demanded agencies and bureaucratic structures that supported the president in unifying the elements of national power toward a defined strategic objective. The creation of the NSC, CIA, and NSRB by the National Security Act of 1947 provided the president with the assistance he needed in the early Cold War and beyond.

To highlight the mutable security environment Clark M. Clifford, White House counsel, wrote a policy paper for Truman, in which he stated "that the expansion of Communism was 'the gravest problem facing the United States,' as the Soviet Leadership appeared to be on a course for aggrandizement designed to lead to eventual world domination."[36] Clifford's assessment of the strategic objective of the Soviet Union was not the first instance of a member of Truman's administration making this evaluation. In February 1946, George F. Kennan, a diplomat and foreign service officer, wrote a seven-thousand-word telegram in which he outlined the political objectives and methods used by the Soviet Union and its government to obtain its goals and control its people.[37] A year later, Kennan became the first director of the new Policy Planning Staff in the U.S. State Department, an organization that Marshall established when he was confirmed as secretary of state. Kennan's telegram and article in *Foreign Policy* magazine entitled "Sources of Soviet Conduct" highlighted and outlined the dynamic and turbulent political security environment of the new Cold War and focused on the expansionist tendencies of the Soviet Union and communism.[38] As these internal debates evolved within the administration, forces drove Truman and the U.S. Congress to focus on building government agencies to combat the spread of communism within the context of the Cold War. The Truman administration and Congress saw the creation of the NSC, CIA, and NSRB as critical means for harnessing and synchronizing the political, the military, the economic, the industrial, and the diplomatic capabilities of the United States to contain the forces of communism while also ensuring that the United States was prepared to fight if it had to.

The concept for the National Security Council evolved from Eberstadt's ideas in 1945 about the need for the U.S. president to have a "board of directors to provide overall guidance and policy direction."[39] James V. Forrestal, secretary of the navy at that time and later the first secretary of defense, also endorsed the idea. Specifically, Forrestal stated that the new international security environment drove the need for the United States to "create a future mechanism within the Government which will guarantee that the Nation shall be able to act as a unit in terms of its diplomacy, military policy, its use of scientific knowledge, and of course its moral and political leadership."[40] These ideas were a major component as the senior political and military leaders debated unification and the way ahead for the United States in the opening years of the Cold War. Marshall had advocated in a similar fashion during his extensive testimony.

The National Security Act of 1947 implemented these ideas in the creation of the National Security Council (NSC). Specifically, Congress designated that the NSC "advise the President with respect to the integration of domestic, foreign and military policies relating to the national security."[41] Furthermore, the NSC was to "assess and appraise the objectives, commitments, and risks of the United States in relation to our actual and potential military power and to make recommendations to the President on these matters."[42] The authors of the act outlined membership on the NSC in 1947 as the president; secretary of state; secretary of defense; secretaries of the three military services—army, navy, and air force; and chair of the National Security Resources Board.[43] The director of the Central Intelligence Agency would "advise and make recommendations to the NSC on intelligence matters."[44] Truman appointed retired Rear Adm. Sidney W. Souers as the first executive secretary of the NSC. Souers had a staff of military and foreign service officers that focused on the day-to-day operations of the NSC, which primarily directed its efforts to build and offer options for "U.S. policy relating to a country or a geographic area; policy relating to broad functional areas such as foreign trade, mobilization, or atomic energy; questions of organization and procedure pertaining to NSC operations, foreign intelligence, and internal security; and basic national security policy."[45] The structure, focus, and objective of the NSC provided President Truman and future U.S. presidents an executive-level agency that provided informed and professional advice and policy options. As Eberstadt originated in 1945, the NSC was not charged with making, coordinating, or implementing policy; rather, its function was to think strategically and to provide advice and recommendations to the president.

Furthermore, the National Security Act outlined that the Director of Central Intelligence (DCI) would advise the NSC. The DCI's primary job, however, was to head the newly created Central Intelligence Agency. The CIA was a Cold War evolution of the Office of Strategic Service (OSS) that President

Franklin D. Roosevelt had used throughout World War II to conduct covert operations behind enemy lines. Truman disbanded the OSS at the end of the war and created in 1946 a Central Intelligence Group (CIG), which was designed to provide intelligence to the president on matters of national security and strategic importance. In the midst of the early Cold War, members of the defense and political communities believed that the United States could not afford to be caught unaware of significant events, such as had happened with the Japanese surprise attack on Pearl Harbor, Hawaii. As a result, the need to have an intelligence agency with the primary duty of collecting and disseminating strategic, political, diplomatic, and industrial intelligence was of the utmost importance. Therefore, Truman created the CIG.[46] This short-lived half-step, however, evolved further in 1947 with the creation of the Central Intelligence Agency, as outlined by the National Security Act. The agency, which was originally subordinate to the NSC, was charged with "making recommendations for the coordination of intelligence; to correlate and evaluate intelligence from all quarters relating to national security; to perform services of common concern to all the government's intelligence organizations as determined by the National Security Council."[47] Knowing that the new international security environment was constantly shifting, Congress stipulated that the CIA also had to be prepared to "perform such other functions and duties related to intelligence affecting national security as the National Security Council may from time to time direct."[48] One can see how the duties and responsibilities outlined for the CIA in the 1947 act aligned with the way Truman, Marshall, Forrestal, and Eberstadt envisioned the need to have mutually supportive agencies that could provide the president of the United States with a wide range of strategic information necessary to make and enact national security policy in the opening years of the Cold War.

It is important to note that the architects of the National Security Act designed the CIA as an intelligence-collecting organization and that its covert-operations functions, which came to characterize the CIA, were largely developed and spearheaded by the NSC.[49] These functions become of increased significance as Truman and Marshall worried about the political situation in France and Italy. Concern over increased communist activity in Europe, overt and covert, led the NSC to focus on developing two "streams of U.S. countermeasures" to keep communism at bay in Europe.[50] The first stream used "overt foreign information activities," while the second stream focused on designing and proliferating covert propaganda and psychological warfare.[51] Marshall approved of these actions.[52] On December 17, 1947, the National Security Council approved NSC 4/A, which paved the way for the CIA to start operating covertly in Europe. Within NSC 4/A, the NSC provided the DCI with $20 million to "initiate and conduct covert psychological operations designed to counteract the Soviet and Soviet inspired activities which constituted a threat to world peace and security."[53] The specific operations authorized in NSC 4/A included "propaganda, sabotage, demolitions, subversion of adversary states, and assistance to indigenous and anticommunist underground movements."[54] By the end of 1947, therefore, the Truman administration had established the foundations of a robust espionage system that worked to counter the political influence of the Communist Party in France, as well as in other European countries, particularly Italy. Hence, within a year of its origin, the Truman administration expanded the CIA's responsibilities and powers based on the rapidly changing security environment in Western Europe. Both Truman and Marshall played critical roles in solidifying and expanding the national security infrastructure of the United States to meet the increased demands of the Cold War. Moving beyond intelligence, the Truman administration supported the National Security Resources Board as the third major agency that evolved from the National Security Act of 1947. Much like the previous structural changes to the defense bureaucracy, the NSRB was directly linked to the ideas advocated by Marshall, Eberstadt, and Forrestal during the unification hearings.

Based on his experience during World War II, Eberstadt extracted lessons for the U.S. government in the immediate postwar period. Eberstadt believed that industrial and economic mobilization had to be planned and coordinated prior to wartime by a body composed of military and civilian members.[55] The authors of the 1947 act created the NSRB as a board of advisers to provide the president with information, intelligence, and policies focused on "the coordination of military, industrial, and civilian mobilization in the event of war."[56] From Eberstadt's perspective, the NSRB should function like the NSC, with the major difference being that that Resources Board focus on subjects linked to mobilization of the U.S. economy and industry.[57] The real objective of the NSRB beyond advising the president of the United States was to build long-range planning documents that concentrated on mobilizing the U.S. economy for war. Specifically, the NSRB focused on:

> Identification of potential shortages in resources, manpower, and pro-
> ductive facilities to meet potential wartime requirements; policies for

ensuring the most effective wartime mobilization and utilization of U.S. civilian manpower; policies for wartime unification of the activities of all federal agencies involved in the mobilization effort and for the establishment and conservation of adequate reserves of strategic and critical materials; programs for the effective use of the nation's natural and industrial resources to meet military and civilian needs, for the maintenance and stabilization of the civilian economy, and for the adjustment of the economy to war needs and conditions; and the strategic relocation of industries, services, government, and economic activities essential to the nation's security.[58]

The first chair of the NSRB was Arthur M. Hill, former president of Greyhound Corporation.[59] Throughout its short existence, the NSRB had a difficult time asserting its authority within an already established defense infrastructure. The idea of an agency specifically designed to deal with issues of mobilization was initially welcomed, but quickly ran into operational challenges with respect to the Departments of Commerce, Labor, Agriculture, and the Interior as the United States demobilized and adjusted to the Cold War.[60] Although the NSRB was a statutory organization outlined in the National Security Act of 1947, President Truman remained deeply skeptical of the dynamic alterations that were creating competing agencies charged with diffused portions of long-range strategic planning for the United States.[61] With his wariness of such agencies, Truman influenced the 1949 amendments to the National Security Act, which resulted in a 1950 adjustment that created the Office of Defense Mobilization and engineered the slow demise of the NSRB by 1953.[62]

Although the NSRB had the shortest-lived existence of all the major components of the National Security Act, it did provide a deliberative function that remained housed within the executive branch: to conduct long-range planning and coordination of government agencies, both military and civilian, in order to advise the president on mobilization plans for wartime. The original work done on the NSRB transferred easily into the Office of Defense Mobilization and solidified as a critical, necessary component of long-range strategic planning, which Truman and Marshall saw of vital importance to guide U.S. policy in the early years of the Cold War.

Marshall's influence on the National Security Act of 1947 was indirect and largely based on his comments and testimony in the unification debates that took place in 1945. His comments before Congress on unification of the armed services emphasized many of the ideas and structural arrangements found in the final draft of the legislation for the National Security Act. Marshall had moved on from assignments with the U.S. Army, however. When Truman selected Marshall as his secretary of state, Marshall maintained many of his same ideas and in fact brought some major changes to the State Department that reflected the emphasis on making sure the United States prepared itself for the possibility of future conflict. His lessons learned from World War II assisted in providing guidance and direction to the United States in the opening years of the early Cold War.

Marshall's influence and interaction with the National Security Act of 1947, therefore, was minor during his tenure as secretary of state. Marshall also served one year as secretary of defense, from 1950 to 1951, which provided him with the opportunity to work with the modifications of the defense establishment engendered by the 1947 act, as well as the amendments passed in 1949. In fact, many historians have credited Marshall as the force behind making sure that the newly created Department of Defense worked as intended.[63]

As secretary of state from 1947 to 1949, Marshall had a tremendous and lasting impact not just on the State Department, but also on how the U.S. government planned for and waged the overall Cold War. Though short in duration, his tenure was extraordinary.[64] Marshall saw the need to make immediate and substantial reforms within the State Department, much like those aimed at unifying the armed services. Based on his previous wartime experience, Marshall strove to "impart greater coherence to American diplomacy" by creating an organization within the U.S. State Department that would be in charge of planning and developing policy options for the president.[65] The Policy Planning Staff was the organization that Marshall built, which he believed would provide the United States the necessary long-range planning needed for the ideological battle against the Soviet Union.

The need for an organization within the State Department that could concentrate on long-range issues, strategies, and policy options was a common theme in Marshall's thinking from World War II onward.[66] His efforts first to establish and then to rely on the Policy Planning Staff during his tenure as secretary of state had a profound and lasting influence on the way the United States prepared to contain the Soviet Union during the Cold War. The first director of the Policy Planning Staff was the long-serving foreign service officer and expert on the Soviet Union, George F. Kennan. Marshall selected Kennan for his intellect and vast experience with matters pertaining to Russia and the USSR.[67]

In accordance with Marshall's vision, Kennan organized the Policy Planning Staff to begin working on a long-term strategy, eventually known as containment, to combat the Soviet Union. Kennan had asserted in his "long telegram" and later in his thinly veiled anonymous article in *Foreign Affairs* magazine entitled "Sources of Soviet Conduct" that the Soviet Union had expansionist tendencies.[68] Furthermore, based on his enduring analysis of the political, economic, diplomatic, and social structure of the Soviet Union, Kennan argued that the system had inherent flaws that over time would erode the fabric of the Communist system. From the position of the United States, Kennan believed that an integrated and lasting strategy needed to be outlined with an overall objective of counterbalancing the perceived growing power of the Soviet Union and its Communist satellites.[69] To stand fast against the forces of communism, Kennan and the Policy Planning Staff outlined a strategy that leveraged political, diplomatic, economic, and military strengths of the United States into a single durable strategy.

From Kennan's perspective, containment maintained consistent pressure on the Soviet Union in a way that allowed the United States and its allies to check the expansion of worldwide communism, while allowing the Soviet system to wither from within. Kennan advocated a slow and deliberate approach that was cautious about not weakening the economic, diplomatic, and political power of the United States. Mindful of these issues, Kennan advocated for a "strong point" strategy whereby the United States intensified pressure on the Soviet Union in Europe and East Asia.[70] For Kennan, containment was a global strategy that applied soft and hard power instruments in symmetrical and asymmetrical ways to eventually wither the Communists' power in the Soviet Union. The Policy Planning Staff's work on the basic outline of the containment policy was the exact type of effort that Marshall had envisioned when he created the organization within his first days at the Department of State.

For Marshall, Kennan's work to synchronize and coordinate the elements of national power of the United States had been a hallmark of his goals since the opening days of World War II. National strength for Marshall came not from one single source but in reality from the combination of elements that needed to be aimed effectively toward a defined objective. Therefore, Marshall's changes to the State Department empowered Kennan and the Policy Planning Staff to begin the process of outlining the key tenets of a containment policy that served as the basic national security strategy of the United States for the duration of the Cold War.[71] Marshall's ideas about the need for the United States to plan, synchronize, and apply national power toward a defined end state not only pertained to the National Security Act of 1947 but also included his tenure as secretary of defense.

As Marshall finished his term as secretary of state, the growing pains of the U.S. defense establishment were still being felt within the soon to be organized Department of Defense, as well as in the executive and legislative branches of government. Though the original act had made significant changes, there was still work to be done within the system by James Forrestal, secretary of defense from 1947 to 1949, as well as by his successor, Louis A. Johnson, from 1949 to 1950. The major elements of the 1949 act (Public Law 216) included an increase in the power and authority of the secretary of defense and the establishment of the Department of Defense as an executive-level agency. As a result, the civilian service secretaries lost power; and although the Joint Chiefs of Staff retained their advisory role to the president of the United States, they were provided with a chairman (CJCS) who would advise the president, as well as the secretary of defense.[72] In essence, the 1949 amendments to the National Security Act moved toward greater centralization of the Department of Defense under the direction of the secretary of defense, which had not been a major tenet of the original 1947 act.[73]

With the departure of Louis Johnson and with the United States involved in a new limited war in Korea beginning in June 1950, Truman needed an individual who could leverage the adjustments made to the Department of Defense and coordinate interdepartmental and interservice issues, as the United States mobilized to fight the first limited war of the broader Cold War.[74] Naturally, Truman selected Marshall. Marshall's goal beyond just synchronizing the U.S. defense bureaucracies was also to expand U.S. military forces to meet wartime requirements, as well as rebuild the military services to meet the demands of the Cold War. Marshall was on familiar ground in both cases, as he had done similar jobs during World War II.

Marshall served as secretary of defense until September 1951, during which time he provided steady leadership as the Truman administration tried to stabilize the situation in Korea, control Gen. Douglas MacArthur, and build up militarily for the larger Cold War.[75] On September 12, 1951, Marshall retired as secretary of defense, but prior to his departure he had supported and solidified civilian control of the military and ensured that the intent of the National Security Act of 1947 and its 1949 amendments had been implemented. In short, Marshall had greatly assisted in organizing and coordinating the United States to be in a strong position in its struggle with the Soviet Union and its Communist allies. The planning, resourcing, and execution of policies within both the State Department and the Defense Department under Marshall's tenures demonstrated his profound influence during the opening years of the Cold War.

Beyond his success as a leader of the U.S. Army during World War II, the history of the early Cold War demonstrates that Marshall deserves credit as one of the primary actors who shaped the strategic policy of the United States during this critical epoch. To appreciate fully the significance of George C. Marshall, however, it is necessary to look at the entire period from 1945 to 1955 as his influence was monumental. Coming out of the war, Marshall strove to apply the lessons that he and his commanders had learned as a direct result of building and fighting a global war on air, land, and sea. The importance of synchronizing not just the military services but also the means for mobilizing and sustaining the armed forces to fight across the globe drove Marshall to advocate in 1945 for the unification of the armed services. This was not an attempt to subvert the power or mission of the U.S. Navy, as some critics charged, but rather was a necessary task to ensure that the military services were organized and managed in the most effective way possible based upon the foreign policy objectives of the United States. Furthermore, in his quest to ensure that the United States remained vigilant, Marshall also sought to incorporate the necessary civilian elements into his overall plan so that the United States had the appropriate economic and industrial capability to sustain its readiness in a global struggle. Though the unification effort failed to reach the ultimate position that Marshall supported, the ideas that he established and explained in his testimony before Congress had a profound impact.

The National Security Act of 1947 incorporated many of the coordinating efforts that Marshall believed were critical during World War II. He also believed that as the United States entered a new era in the Cold War, these same elements needed to be combined into a single coherent strategy. The National Security Act of 1947 was an attempt by Congress to begin to organize the national security establishment toward the ultimate end state outlined by Marshall during his testimony on unification. Although Marshall had little direct involvement in the writing and passage of the legislation, the parallel points between his positions on unification and the National Security Act cannot be denied. Therefore, through indirect inspiration Marshall deserves recognition for providing elements of the intellectual underpinnings for the efforts to reform and reorganize the national security structure of the United States.

During the initial period of adapting to the new legislation, Truman nominated Marshall to be secretary of state. Marshall brought to his new position the same emphasis on building organizations that could deliberate enduring issues and strategy. To carry out his ideas, Marshall established the Policy Planning Staff within the State Department as an organization designed to think about and suggest long-range strategies to the president of the United States. The first and second directors of the Policy Planning Staff, George F. Kennan and Paul H. Nitze, respectively, fulfilled Marshall's vision as they both contributed to the policy of containment, which served throughout the Cold War as the basic national security policy of the United States. The Policy Planning Staff has remained a major institution within the State Department in the twenty-first century and still takes "a long-term strategic view of global trends" with an aim to developing and proposing policy options for the secretary of state and the president.[76] As such, Marshall's creation has continued to serve as a vital component of the national security structure for the United States since its inception in 1947.

In addition to infusing continuous strategic planning into the State Department, Marshall served one year as secretary of defense from 1950 to 1951. With his appointment, he was charged with ensuring that the Department of Defense ran smoothly as the United States fought a war in Korea, while also rebuilding its military for the ongoing containment of the Soviet Union and its Communist allies. Marshall succeeded in solidifying and entrenching the spirit and intent of the National Security Act of 1947 and its 1949 amendments. The coordinated and unified structure built in the late 1940s served the United States for the Cold War and continues to exist today with many of the same key elements that were established in 1947 and 1949. Marshall's short tenure as secretary of defense cannot be overlooked, as it came at a critical time when the United States needed a "soldier, administrator, and statesman" to organize the nation's defense establishment—for both peace and war.[77]

In short, Marshall's contributions to the national security structure of the United States were most impressive. His thoughts on unification of the military services and the need for long-range planning and coordination among them, as well as between the civilian and military bureaucracies, as manifested in the National Security Act of 1947 and its amendments, remain foundational to many U.S. foreign policy and national security strategies. The seismic transformations during the early years of the Cold War, indirectly and directly influenced by

George C. Marshall, are still felt as the United States faces the dynamic international security environment of the twenty-first century.

NOTES

1. Christopher R. Gabel, "George Catlett Marshall," in *Generals of the Army: Marshall, MacArthur, Eisenhower, Arnold, Bradley*, ed. James H. Willbanks (Lexington: University Press of Kentucky, 2013), 19, 53.

2. Mark A. Stoler, *George C. Marshall: Soldier-Statesman of the American Century* (Boston: Twayne, 1989), ix.

3. Sean N. Kalic, "Honoring the Marshall Legacy," *Command and General Staff College Foundation News*, no. 4 (Spring 2008): 11.

4. Sean N. Kalic, "Dwight D. Eisenhower," in Willbanks, *Generals of the Army*, 135.

5. Geoffrey Perret, *Eisenhower* (New York: Random House, 1999), 363.

6. Robert Jervis, "The Impact of the Korean War on the Cold War," *Journal of Conflict Resolution* 24, no. 4 (December 1980): 565.

7. David Jablonsky, "The State of the National Security State," *Parameters: U.S. Army War College Quarterly* 32, no. 4 (Winter 2002–3): 5.

8. Stoler, *George C. Marshall*, 158.

9. Harry S. Truman, "President Truman's Address to Congress," in *Unification of the Armed Services: An Analytical Digest of Testimony before the Senate Military Affairs Committee, 17 October to 17 December, 1945, and of The President's Message to the Congress* (Washington, D.C.: Government Printing Office, 1946), 13.

10. Foreword, in *Unification of the Armed Services*, 9.

11. Truman, "President Truman's Address to Congress," 16.

12. George C. Marshall, "Unification Is Necessary for the Development of a Comprehensive Military Plan and Program," in *Unification of the Armed Services*, 33.

13. George C. Marshall, "Unification Provides for the Overall Presentation and Consideration of the Budget," in *Unification of the Armed Services*, 35.

14. Ibid., 36.

15. Robert Cuff, "Ferdinand Eberstadt, the National Security Resources Board, and the Search for Integrated Mobilization Planning, 1947–1948," *Public Historian* 7, no. 4 (Fall 1985): 39.

16. Ibid., 41.

17. Foreword, in *Unification of the Armed Services*, 8.

18. Ibid.

19. Forrest C. Pogue, *George C. Marshall*, vol. 4: *Statesman, 1945–1959* (New York: Viking, 1987), 144.

20. George C. Marshall, "Voluntary Cooperation," in *Unification of the Armed Services*, 117.

21. Kenneth W. Condit, *History of the Joint Chiefs of Staff*, vol. 2: *The Joint Chiefs of Staff and National Policy, 1947–1949* (Washington, D.C.: Office of the Chairman of the Joint Chiefs of Staff, Office of Joint History, 1996), 1.

22. Elias Huzar, "Reorganization for National Security," *Journal of Politics* 12, no. 1 (February 1950): 130.

23. Alfred Goldberg, ed., *History of the Office of the Secretary of Defense*, vol. 1: *The Formative Years, 1947–1950*, ed. Steven L. Rearden (Washington, D.C.: Office of the Secretary of Defense, Historical Office, 1984), 15.

24. Ibid.

25. Huzar, "Reorganization for National Security," 130.

26. Condit, *Joint Chiefs of Staff and National Policy*, 3; Huzar, "Reorganization for National Security," 130.

27. Huzar, "Reorganization for National Security," 130.

28. Condit, *Joint Chiefs of Staff and National Policy*, 2.

29. Ibid. In later adjustments to the original act, the chairman of the Joint Chiefs of Staff replaced the chief to the commander-in-chief but maintained the same primary functions.

30. Although this development was a significant alteration to the military structure of the United States, a detailed discussion is beyond the scope of this chapter; John M. Curatola examines Marshall's influence on the independent status of the U.S. Air Force in Chapter 3 of this volume.

31. Condit, *Joint Chiefs of Staff and National Policy*, 26–27.

32. Marshall, "Voluntary Cooperation," 117.

33. Cuff, "Ferdinand Eberstadt," 39.

34. Ibid.

35. Ibid., 41.

36. William J. Daugherty, *Executive Secrets: Covert Action and the Presidency* (Lexington: University Press of Kentucky, 2004), 114.

37. George F. Kennan, "The Long Telegram," Moscow Embassy Telegram no. 511, February 22, 1946, in *Containment: Documents on American Policy and Strategy, 1945–1950*, ed. Thomas H. Etzold and John Lewis Gaddis (New York: Columbia University Press, 1978), 50–63.

38. George F. Kennan (X), "The Sources of Soviet Conduct," *Foreign Affairs* 25, no. 4 (July 1947): 855. The Policy Planning Staff, especially during the early Cold War, was a department created by George C. Marshall within the State Department that worked on building national security policy and strategy within other executive-level agencies. See the detailed discussion of the Policy Planning Staff in this chapter.

39. Rearden, *Formative Years, 1947–1950*, 19.

40. Ibid.

41. Ibid., 118.

42. Ibid.

43. Ibid. The 1949 amendments to the National Security Act removed the civilian military service secretaries from the NSC and replaced them with the Joint Chiefs of Staff, as well as adding the vice president as a standing member of the NSC.

44. Ibid., 118–19.

45. Ibid., 119–20.

46. John Ranelagh, *The Agency: The Rise and Decline of the CIA* (New York: Touchstone, 1987), 106–9.

47. Ibid., 111.

48. Ibid.

49. Rearden, *Formative Years, 1947–1950*, 143.

50. Daugherty, *Executive Secrets*, 118.

51. Ibid.

52. Rearden, *Formative Years, 1947–1950*, 143.

53. Daugherty, *Executive Secrets*, 118–19.

54. Ibid., 119.

55. Cuff, "Ferdinand Eberstadt," 40.

56. Rearden, *Formative Years, 1947–1950*, 129; Cuff, "Ferdinand Eberstadt," 41.

57. Cuff, "Ferdinand Eberstadt," 41.

58. Rearden, *Formative Years, 1947–1950*, 129.

59. Ibid., 130.

60. Cuff, "Ferdinand Eberstadt," 45.

61. Ibid., 46.

62. Ibid., 51.

63. Doris M. Condit, *History of the Office of the Secretary of Defense*, vol. 2: *The Test of War, 1950–1953* (Washington, D.C.: Office of the Secretary of Defense, Historical Office, 1988), 481–95.

64. Stoler, *George C. Marshall*, 152.

65. John Lewis Gaddis, *Strategies of Containment: A Critical Appraisal of Postwar American National Security Policy* (Oxford: Oxford University Press, 1982), 25.

66. Pogue, *Statesman*, 150.

67. Gaddis, *Strategies of Containment*, 25.

68. George F. Kennan, "The Long Telegram," Moscow Embassy Telegram no. 511, February 22, 1946, https://nsarchive2.gwu.edu/coldwar/documents/episode-1/kennan .htm; Kennan, "Sources of Soviet Conduct," 858–59.

69. Gaddis, *Strategies of Containment*, 36.

70. Ibid., 58–61.

71. The containment policy outlined by Kennan was unsustainable based on the late 1949 international security environment, as well as the onset of the Second Red Scare within the United States. After a falling out with Dean Acheson, Marshall's deputy secretary of state and his successor as secretary of state, Kennan left the Policy Planning Staff. Paul H. Nitze replaced Kennan as director of the Policy Planning Staff and proceeded to adjust and evolve Kennan's ideas on a containment policy. The result of the Policy Planning Staff's work was the signing of NSC-68 by President Truman in September 1950. With Truman's signature, the United States had a long-term strategy to contain the Soviet Union for the duration of the Cold War. The success of containment was linked back to the original work done by Kennan and Nitze, who built a robust policy framework that allowed each subsequent U.S. president to alter and adjust the

elements of national power to meet the changing needs of the Cold War struggle against the forces of communism.

72. Rearden, *Formative Years, 1947–1950*, 54.

73. Ibid., 55.

74. Stoler, *George C. Marshall*, 181.

75. Ibid., 190.

76. U.S. Department of State, Policy Planning Staff, "Mission Statement," https://www.state.gov/about-us-policy-planning-staff/.

77. Stoler, *George C. Marshall*, 190.

FRANK A. SETTLE JR.

5

TO HARNESS ATOMIC POWER

Marshall and Nuclear Weapons

Gen. George C. Marshall was one of the few senior-level officials who partici-pated in or witnessed all the major decisions involving nuclear weapons during the first decade of the atomic age. As army chief of staff during World War II, he oversaw the Manhattan Project, which produced the first atomic bombs, and commanded the U.S. Army Air Forces, which delivered them to their targets in Japan. As secretary of state from 1947 to 1949, he dealt with nuclear issues in the emerging Cold War. Finally, as secretary of defense from 1950 to 1951, he continued to confront the control of the U.S. nuclear arsenal, as the Cold War became a "hot" war in Korea.

The use of the atomic bomb on Japan dramatically changed the nature of warfare and diplomacy in the postwar world. This chapter explores how Mar-shall's views of the bomb evolved as America's nuclear monopoly vanished and the nation confronted a nuclear-armed Soviet Union. His involvement with the development, use, and management of nuclear weapons provides valuable lessons for current U.S. policy. In the period between Japan's surrender and his retirement as army chief of staff in November 1945, Marshall warned against a drastic reduction in the size of the army in favor of a reliance on nuclear weapons. During this time, he also advised the president on sharing the secrets of the atomic bomb with America's allies.

On September 25, 1945, members of the House Appropriations Committee asked Marshall how the bomb might affect the size of the military establishment. He responded: "The fundamental requirements of conducting successful war have not changed any more than they were altered by the discovery of gunpowder, the submarine, gas, tanks, or planes. The techniques changed but never as much as first anticipated, and almost invariably with each development, the number of men required is increased."[1]

Marshall recognized that the new weapon would require that the military train and maintain a technically skilled fighting force. In an article published in the November 1945 issue of the *Army and Navy Journal*, he emphasized the bomb's influence on the size of the armed forces:

> The new weapons—atomic explosive, supersonic rockets and those even more devastating that unquestionably will come in the years immediately ahead—make the careful preparatory training of all personnel the more imperative. And now the atomic age has arrived. It is clearly the lesson of history that the more complicated the techniques of war the more intensive must be the training. It also seems clear to me that the more sudden, far-reaching and devastating the weapons, the greater the necessity for highly trained units ready to react with speed and power. If universal military training is approved by the people of this country, for the first time in our existence this country will be the real master of its own destiny. Together with an active body of scientific research, a substantial trained civilian reserve behind our permanent establishments will guarantee our security in case of attack by an aggressor state. But in my opinion it will do far more than that. It will present to the world an available power that will discourage any plans to upset the peace of the world.[2]

Marshall's call for universal military training reflected the citizen-soldier tradition of his alma mater, the Virginia Military Institute.

In the elation that followed the defeat of Japan, Marshall counseled against overconfidence. He appreciated the critical roles that science and technology played in defeating the Axis powers and stressed their continued importance in the postwar world. An excerpt from his June 30, 1945, biennial report to the secretary of war, reprinted in the October issue of *Yank* magazine as an article entitled "Our Weapons," reveals his concerns:

> Overshadowing all other technological advances of the war was the Allied development of the atomic explosive. The tremendous military advantage of this terrifying weapon fell to us through a combination of good luck, good management, and prodigious effort. The harnessing of atomic power should give Americans confidence in their destiny but at the same time we must be extremely careful not to fall victim to overconfidence. The fact that we overtook Germany's head start on the atomic explosive is comforting but certainly should not lull us into complacent inertia.[3]

Addressing the *New York Herald Tribune* forum "Responsible Victory," Marshall reflected on his experience with the atomic bomb and its impact on military planning. He stressed that the nation's current mood favoring significant reductions in the size of the armed forces placed too much reliance on the new weapon:

> In the current emotionalism of the hour we turn for relief from positive action to new theories, new discoveries—the supersonic rocket, of atomic power or explosion. If these remarkable products of our science are merely to turn us from action to inaction on one plea, one theory or another they may well have a more tragic influence on the destiny of the United States than the most pessimistic fear they will have on civilization. I have been considering the military ramifications of atomic explosion for more than two years since my job placed me in the grim race towards this scientific power. I think I have—if only because of my head start—spent much more time than most Americans, thinking about such bombs and what they will mean to military operations as well as civilization at large.
>
> I cannot escape the conclusion that the possibilities of atomic explosion make it more imperative than ever before that the United States keep itself militarily strong and use this strength to promote world order. No one can foresee unerringly into the future but it is not hard to predict that supersonic atomic rockets will have a profound influence on any war that ever again has to be fought. But, rather than decrease the necessity for our

preparation both in manpower and material, this terrible new weapon will tremendously increase it.[4]

The "supersonic rockets" were a reference to the German V-2 missiles used to attack Britain near the end of the war in Europe.

Marshall also supported universal military training as a means of demonstrating America's resistance to the spread of communism. Congress failed to heed his appeals for a strong conventional military and in 1947 allowed the draft to expire. The armed forces shrank from 12 million American men and women to 1.5 million by the time Marshall became secretary of state. "It was no demobilization. It was a rout," he quipped.[5] Later reflecting on his experience in dealing with the results of the dramatic downsizing, he said:

> I remember when I was secretary of state, I was being pressed constantly, particularly when in Moscow, by radio message after radio message to give the Russians hell. When I got back I was getting the same appeal in relation to the Far East and China. At the time my facilities for giving them hell—and I am a soldier and know something about the ability to give hell—was one and one-third divisions over the entire United States. That is quite a proposition when you deal with somebody with over 260 divisions and you have one and a third.[6]

Marshall exaggerated the Soviets' strength. Nevertheless, Soviet forces indeed far outnumbered those of the United States.

President Truman was well aware of the disparity but believed along with the majority of Americans that the nation's possession of the atomic bomb leveled the global balance of forces, offsetting any advantage that potential adversaries might have through larger conventional forces. This illusion evaporated in June 1950 when the country's army could not provide a rapid response to North Korea's invasion of South Korea and the use of the atomic bomb was not practical. Marshall's use of "atomic explosive" in the preceding testimony indicated an effort to link his experience with traditional ordnance to the new, more powerful nuclear weapons that he appeared to view simply as larger conventional bombs. He seemed largely unaware of the effects of radioactivity associated with their detonations. This was due in part to an August 24, 1945, memorandum from Gen. Leslie Groves, head of the Manhattan Project, that stated:

> Teams of investigators headed by General Farrell are moving into Japan with our occupying forces. Their mission is to make absolutely sure that

there can be no possible ill effects to American troops from radioactive materials at either Hiroshima or Nagasaki as well as to ascertain the damage at these places. Although we feel that Japanese casualties from radioactivity were unlikely, it is most important for the future of the atomic bomb work as well as for historical reasons, that we determine the facts.[7]

Groves and Gen. Douglas MacArthur, through his occupation authority, successfully suppressed any public discussion of radiation effects. The authority censored any reference to radiation in the Japanese press or scientific reports. The U.S. War Department concealed some reports of radiation, and Groves employed Manhattan Project scientists to refute public concerns about the effects of radiation.[8]

Shortly after the Japanese surrender, Marshall, realizing the momentous impact of two nuclear attacks, asked the Joint Chiefs of Staff to address the implications of the atomic bomb for the military and for warfare:

The development of the atomic bomb presents far-reaching implications and problems. What the potentialities of this weapon are and what effect it will have on warfare are problems whose solution must be in the future. At the present time discussion is going on in press, scientific, political and public circles generally on this subject. It is desirable that a concerted viewpoint of the military on the overall effect of this new weapon on warfare and military organization be developed as soon as possible in the light of the information now available and to the extent practical.[9]

The JCS assigned to the Joint Strategic Survey Committee (JSSC) the task of analyzing the impact of nuclear weapons on the military organization and warfare. The JSSC had been one of the most important planning groups for the wartime armed forces. The October 30 committee report stated that the United States had a five-year technological advantage in nuclear weapons and that for the foreseeable future only a limited number of atomic bombs would be available to industrialized nations. It recommended a hard line consisting of (1) U.S. control of all uranium sources, (2) maximum acceleration of research and development, (3) maintenance of the highest degree of secrecy, and (4) accumulation of a weapons stockpile sufficient to implement strategic war plans. The committee viewed the atomic bomb as a strategic weapon rather than a tactical one.

The report also reinforced Marshall's position, calling for action to counter the popular misconception that the atomic bomb made conventional forces obsolete:

> The ground forces will still have to be equipped to attack, occupy, and defend territory. The air forces will still have the same roles, which they had in this war. New weapons, new planes, and new defenses may change their methods, but almost certainly in the direction of greater complexity and hence, greater personnel and material requirements. The Navy will still have to control the sea, transport and land amphibious forces, and furnish air defense and air attacks.[10]

In early December, Gen. Dwight D. Eisenhower, the new army chief of staff, criticized the report, arguing that it did not address the transitory nature of the U.S. nuclear monopoly. He also opposed the policy of maximum secrecy, citing the U.S.-UK-Canadian agreement to share information. The Joint Chiefs of Staff approved a revised JSSC report on December 28. General Eisenhower continued his opposition to the revision in part because of its emphasis on conventional forces and marginalization of the role of nuclear weapons, a position opposite to that of Marshall's.[11] In March 1946, the Joint Chiefs of Staff, guided by Eisenhower, approved a final revision from the JSSC that included the need for diplomacy to achieve an effective worldwide prohibition of atomic weapons. In the meantime, the JCS stressed the need for the United States to maintain a large conventional force to meet any contingency.[12]

On October 3, 1945, President Truman called for legislation to set up a domestic Atomic Energy Commission to control all aspects of nuclear energy in the United States. He defined the goals of the commission as "promotion of the national welfare, securing the national defense, safeguarding world peace and the acquisition of further knowledge concerning atomic energy."[13] He also addressed the international implications of atomic energy: "The hope of civilization lies in international arrangements looking, if possible, to the renunciation of the use and development of the atomic bomb, and directing and encouraging the use of atomic energy, and all future scientific information toward peaceful and humanitarian ends."[14]

Two weeks later, Adm. William Leahy told the Joint Chiefs of Staff that the president wanted their advice as he prepared for a meeting with the prime ministers of Great Britain and Canada. He requested recommendations on military policies regarding keeping secrets associated with the atomic bomb

Robert A. Lovett (*right*) receives the oath of office as deputy secretary of defense from Felix E. Larkin (*left*), general counsel, and Secretary of Defense George C. Marshall (*second from left*). Mr. and Mrs. David S. Brown, daughter and son-in-law of Lovett, look on. October 4, 1950. U.S. Army. Courtesy Harry S. Truman Library, Independence, Mo.

from other nations. The JCS directed the JSSC to prepare a draft letter to the president for their approval. The committee presented three options: make nuclear information available to all nations, entrust control of the bomb to the United Nations, or keep the atomic bomb secret insofar as possible.

Marshall received a copy of the JSSC draft from Robert A. Lovett, assistant secretary of war, who attached a memorandum criticizing the committee conclusions. Lovett believed that the draft emphasized the Soviet threat and did not address issues of arms control. He suggested that "the period during which secrecy will be effective should be utilized with the utmost diligence to devise sound methods for control of this great new force."[15] Lovett recommended to Marshall that the JSSC revise the draft to include his ideas.

Marshall agreed with Lovett's suggestions and directed the JSSC to prepare an alternative draft. Upon receiving this draft, Marshall recommended that the

Joint Chiefs of Staff send the president the alternative draft. He argued that the JSSC's original focus on the Soviet Union was "politically undesirable." He also claimed the committee's view of the United Nations was pessimistic and defeatist with regard to nuclear arms control. Marshall believed that the Joint Chiefs of Staff should express an interest in discussions to prevent a nuclear arms race, which would expose the United States to "a form of attack against which there is no adequate defense."[16]

On October 23, the JCS sent Truman a letter in which they recommended that the United States maintain, for the present, "all existing secrets with respect to atomic weapons." The letter provided insights into Marshall's position on nuclear weapons at the time. It provided the following advice:

a. Other countries could not build atomic bombs for several years. This interval was especially valuable, due to the uncertainty of East-West relationships and the opportunity afforded to consummate an arms control agreement.

b. In the absence of great-power accords upon fundamental political problems, release of information would probably precipitate an arms race.

c. Since the United States was particularly vulnerable to atomic attack because of the country's urban concentrations, it seemed imprudent voluntarily to place such devastating weapons in other nations' hands.

d. At present, no adequate international control system existed.

e. If the UN Security Council wished to employ atomic weapons for the maintenance of peace, the United States would undoubtedly cooperate.

f. Unilateral disclosures [by the United States] could be regarded as a sign of weakness by other nations, and might not lessen suspicion and distrust so long as secrecy and censorship persisted elsewhere on the globe.

g. Since the United States was developing other advanced weapons (long-range bombers, rocket projectiles, and guided missiles) related to the techniques of atomic warfare, it would be unwise to set precedent for sharing secrets before adequate international controls were established.[17]

The Joint Chiefs of Staff emphasized that in order to prevent an arms race and reduce the prospect of atomic warfare, diplomatic negotiations "should be promptly and vigorously pressed during the limited period of American monopoly." Marshall, who was an influential member of the group, expressed the view that the United States should retain its control of its nuclear secrets while working toward international regulations to control nuclear weapons and develop atomic energy.[18]

In October 1945, Marshall's resignation as chief of staff of the army was accepted by Truman, who agreed to release him from active duty as soon as General Eisenhower could return from Germany to assume this position. Marshall's wife, Katherine, observed, "A great load seemed to roll off my husband's shoulders. At breakfast he was carefree, the heavy lines between his eyes began to disappear, he laughed once more."[19] On November 18, 1945, Marshall received orders relieving him of his duty as army chief of staff. In Marshall's subsequent citation for the Distinguished Service Medal, President Truman highlighted his contribution to the Manhattan Project among his many achievements: "He obtained from Congress the stupendous sums that made possible the atomic bomb, knowing that failure would be his full responsibility."[20]

On May 24, 1946, while in China as Truman's special presidential envoy, Marshall received a letter from his friend Bernard Baruch, who was the U.S. representative to the United Nations Atomic Energy Commission (UNAEC). Baruch wanted Marshall's advice on the control of nuclear weapons by the UNAEC. The commission was to draft a treaty to outlaw the use of nuclear weapons, facilitate inspections, and prescribe penalties for enforcement. Baruch asked if Marshall could "offer any suggestions for creating in the minds of men the desire to comply with the Treaty" and "how he would set up in the Treaty a plan for the automatic punishment of violators." Baruch added a postscript addressing the broader issue of eliminating war: "Have you any immediate suggestions as to how our present attitude could be expanded into a movement toward the elimination of war itself? I recognize, in posing this question, that the main purpose of the United Nations is the same objective—elimination of war. But I ask because you may have discovered some shortcuts."[21]

Marshall, occupied with his China mission, did not provide a written response until August 21. When he replied, he wrote that Baruch's proposals to the UNAEC were "sound and that he has heard of no alternative procedures which seem more practical or desirable." Marshall went on to give his view of the broader international situation and on the faint likelihood that there could be an end to war:

> After explaining above my own difficulty in giving clear thinking to the atomic question, I might say that the turbulence in which I am involved

and its tragic consequences to almost five hundred million people leads all my thinking to the urgency in this period of our civilization for finding a development without further delay of a positive means to put a stop to the probability of wars. My own experience here has led me to a few conclusions which of themselves might seem rather small factors. It grows more clearly evident to me every day out here that suspicion of the other fellow's motives, lack of understanding of his conception of your motives are the greatest stumbling blocks to peaceful adjustments. When trade factors and the pursuit of the dollar are added to the plot the problem grows even more complicated in time of peace.[22]

Marshall closed with an apology for not being more helpful. Baruch respected Marshall as a global strategist and supporter of international efforts to ban the use of nuclear weapons and eliminate war. Marshall realized that the atomic bomb had taken warfare to an even more unacceptable level. The UNAEC treaty to ban nuclear weapons did not materialize, and the nuclear arms race between the United States and Soviet Union continued unabated.

In the spring of 1946, Truman decided to replace James Byrnes, his secretary of state, and asked Marshall if he would accept this position. The president "highly valued his [Marshall's] political and diplomatic as well as his military skills. . . . He also knew how effective Marshall could be with Congress and how capable he was of removing issues away from the arena of partisan debate."[23] The ever dutiful but now sixty-six-year-old soldier, Marshall accepted and succeeded Byrnes as secretary of state on January 21, 1947. Learning of Marshall's appointment, former Secretary of State Henry L. Stimson wrote, "Your appointment as secretary of state has filled me with a great sense of security so far as our country is concerned. Mr. Truman made a wise as well as a very shrewd appointment." His wartime partner warned Marshall that the environment of the State Department would be quite different from the disciplined atmosphere of the military:

You will not find it an easy task. You will miss the support of an organized and loyal staff which is always behind the leaders of the War Department and the spirit of whose influence runs far down the lower echelons. To a certain extent that lack of organization is necessarily inherent in the kind of work which the State Department is called upon to do and it would be a great mistake to think that by the imposition of strict discipline you can remedy its deficiencies. In the State Department you will feel yourself far more often standing alone than you did as head of the General Staff.

Surprise bombshells from the outside world will drop upon you with much greater frequency than in the War Department even in time of war and the variety and unpredictability of these bombshells are greater than anything we experienced during the war in the War Department.[24]

Buoyed by Marshall's acceptance, Truman noted, "The more I see of him the more certain I am he is the great one of the age."[25] Dean Acheson, Marshall's undersecretary of state, observed, "The moment General Marshall entered a room everyone in it felt his presence. It was a striking and communicated force. His figure conveyed intensity, which his voice, low, staccato, and incisive, reinforced. It compelled respect. It spread a sense of authority and of calm. There was no military glamour about him and nothing of the martinet."[26]

As secretary of state from January 1947 to early 1949, Marshall confronted a variety of issues involving nuclear power. He facilitated the procurement of uranium ore for nuclear weapons from Great Britain and Canada. He advised the president on sharing of nuclear information with Britain and other allies. In 1947, the Berlin crisis involved him with the possible use of nuclear weapons. From then on, the threat of Communist expansion kept the atomic bomb in the forefront of every predicament. Marshall consulted his subordinates, many of whom advocated taking a hard line in dealing with the Soviets.

The issue of international control of nuclear weapons and atomic energy was one of the first "bombshells" dropped on Marshall. At a meeting of the UN Atomic Energy Commission on June 14, 1946, Bernard Baruch, the U.S. commissioner, presented the American plan for control of nuclear energy. It included an exchange of basic scientific information between all countries for peaceful ends and control of nuclear power to the extent necessary to ensure its use only for peaceful purposes. The plan also called for elimination of atomic weapons and all other major weapons adaptable to mass destruction. It stipulated the establishment of effective safeguards, including inspections to protect complying states against the hazards of violations and evasions by noncompliant actors. An International Atomic Development Authority (IADA) would manage the implementation of the proposed objectives.[27] Baruch's proposal immediately ran into trouble with the Soviets. It called for a survey of each nation's raw materials before implementation of international controls; punishment for violators, including atomic attack; and eliminating the UN Security Council's veto in IADA matters.[28]

The Soviets countered with a plan calling for the nuclear disarmament of the United States and for the United States to share atomic secrets before establishing international controls. Andrei Gromyko, Baruch's Soviet counterpart, also stated that the Soviet Union would accept no revision of the veto power as it applied to atomic energy issues. After months of failed negotiations, on December 30, 1946, the ten-member UNAEC voted on Baruch's plan. It passed with two abstentions—the Soviet Union and Poland. With this vote, the commission placed the issue of disarmament and atomic energy before the UN Security Council. Baruch resigned his position on January 4, 1947, concluding that he had carried out the U.S. administration's orders.[29]

In June 1946, Truman had appointed Vermont Sen. Warren F. Austin as the American representative to the United Nations. The Senate confirmed Austin as the first U.S. ambassador to the United Nations on January 13, 1947. Austin's initial task was to oppose the Soviet demand that the UN Security Council combine the issues of international nuclear disarmament and control of nuclear energy for deliberation. The United States considered that combining these issues could undermine the work of the UNAEC.

Marshall believed that the UN Security Council should address nuclear disarmament and international control of atomic energy as separate issues. On January 29, Marshall in consultation with Robert P. Patterson, secretary of war, and James V. Forrestal, secretary of the navy, formulated a strategy for Austin to present to the UN Security Council. Marshall "saw no hope of avoiding a discussion on disarmament, and any American move to do so would draw fire from other Security Council members."[30] The strategy included the creation of a new commission to handle arms regulation and a committee drawn from members of the UN Security Council to distinguish the roles of the new commission and the existing UNAEC.

On March 9, as the United Nations debated these nuclear issues, Marshall formed an executive committee to recommend U.S. policy regarding international control of atomic energy and regulation of nuclear weapons. It included representatives from the State, War, and Navy Departments, as well as the U.S. Atomic Energy Commission (AEC). Once again, Marshall approached complex problems by bringing together the various competent players required to address them. He chose George F. Kennan, a foreign service officer who had been stationed in Moscow, to chair the committee. Kennan became one of the primary architects of U.S. Cold War policy. Marshall told Kennan that the European situation was so bad that congressional representatives would soon be coming up with all kinds of unworkable schemes. The new secretary wanted a sound program, and he wanted it within two weeks. Upon leaving, Kennan asked the secretary if he had any further instructions. Marshall replied, "Avoid trivia."[31]

On June 12, Marshall confronted another nuclear issue when David Lilienthal, the chair of the AEC, informed him of nuclear tests to be conducted in the South Pacific. Lilienthal explained that the tests would have international ramifications because they would be conducted outside the United States. Lilienthal noted in his diary that Marshall appeared much different from the general he had met during the war: "For one thing, now quite relaxed, very free and with a twinkle in his eye, even when we were going to the point of the matter we were there to discuss. Youthful-looking in color and demeanor. And with not one sign of tension or worry. I am not sure whether this is a good thing or not, considering how much there is to worry about."[32]

On June 27, Lilienthal, Marshall, the armed services secretaries, and members of the JCS met with President Truman to discuss the tests. After Lilienthal recommended testing, the president turned to Marshall for his opinion. According to Lilienthal, Marshall, who was sitting in a large chair away from the conference table, remarked, "The only reason I have is the time. It would be awkward if this test occurred right before or right after the [foreign ministers] meeting in London in November. That may be our last meeting. (Marshall said this with the one-sided half-smile he has)."[33] Although Marshall thought it preferable to conduct the tests within the continental United States, the group approved a remote location in the Pacific. All present agreed plans for the 1948 tests should be kept top secret.

As the UN debates on the control of nuclear arms and energy dragged on with no tangible results, members of the U.S. government became increasingly uneasy with the situation. On August 21, 1947, Kennan completed his study of American policy. Historians Richard Hewlett and Francis Duncan summarized the report:

The analysis dismissed the fourteen months of talks at the United Nations as fruitless. The United States could not agree to destroy its atomic bombs without the guarantee of security, while the Russians would accept only the immediate destruction of the weapons, leaving security for later negotiation. Yet it was wrong to consider both positions as equally balanced for time favored the Soviets. As a sponsor of the majority plan, the Americans were committed, while the Russians were free to obstruct and delay, to confuse and obscure, as they gained time to develop their own atomic weapons.[34]

Despite this pessimistic assessment, Kennan recommended that the United States continue negotiations within the UN commission. If the negotiations broke down, then the United States should make sure that the Soviets understood the causes of the conflict.

On September 8, 1947, Marshall met with Kenneth C. Royall, secretary of war; John Sullivan, undersecretary of the navy; and Robert Bacher, AEC commissioner. Royall asked why the United States should approve the UN documents regarding international control of arms and atomic energy when the Soviet Union would veto them. Why not admit negotiations were hopeless? Members of the State Department argued that abandoning negotiations would only worsen the situation and forsake the nations that were supporting the U.S. positions.[35]

Three days later, Marshall, Forrestal, and Royall met with Kennan to consider the U.S. recommendations on control of nuclear weapons and atomic energy. After Marshall cited the critical shortage of uranium for the production of U.S. weapons, all agreed to negotiations with the British and Canadians, who controlled large quantities of uranium ore. Forrestal wanted clarification of the wartime agreement with the British on the use of the atomic bomb. He also raised the question of what the United States would do if the Soviets accepted the U.S. recommendations to the United Nations. Marshall's pragmatic response was that the USSR would reveal its position in the required follow-up negotiations.

The same day, the Soviet Union vetoed the recommendation of the UN Atomic Energy Commission to the UN Security Council for controlling nuclear weapons and atomic energy. Marshall expressed his frustration with this situation in an address to the UN General Assembly on September 17:

> For the achievement of international security, and the well-being of the peoples of the world, it is necessary that the United Nations press forward on many fronts. Among these the control of atomic and other weapons of mass destruction have perhaps the highest priority if we are to remove the specter of a war of annihilation. If the minority persists in refusing

to join the majority, the [UN] Atomic Energy Commission may soon be unable to complete the task assigned to it.[36]

This speech demonstrates Marshall's global perspective on the danger posed by the atomic bomb, and his recognition of difficulties in achieving agreements on nuclear issues. The United Nations continued to struggle with these issues even after another report from the commission in May 1948 stated that negotiations were deadlocked.

McGeorge Bundy's biography of Henry Stimson—*On Active Service in Peace and War*—provides useful insights into Marshall's views on dealing with the Soviets. Marshall and George Kennan agreed

> that some "American statesmen" were anxious to use the bomb as a diplomatic weapon against the Soviet Union. Kennan doubted their veracity and feared their publication "would play squarely into the hands of the Communists, who so frequently speak of our atomic diplomacy and accuse us of trying to intimidate the world in general by our possession of the bomb." He also objected to Bundy's statement that the policy of trying to reach accommodation with the Russians that Stimson had recommended in September 1945 "was not adopted, even partially, until the passage of several months in which an exactly contrary course was pursued with resulting changes in the whole international atmosphere."[37]

As would be revealed later, Marshall had the vision to see that economic aid to Europe would be more effective in combating the Communist threat there than the menace of nuclear weapons.

In the fall of 1947, the United States was dependent on uranium ore from the Belgian Congo, half of which was destined for the United Kingdom. The United States also obtained some ore from Canada. The British, aware of this critical shortage, were not willing to concede their stockpile and sources of uranium to either the United States or Canada. Marshall orchestrated an agreement with Britain and Canada for obtaining uranium ore. Signed on January 7, 1948, it stated:

1. All wartime [nuclear] agreements were null and void, except those articles that related to raw materials. There was no further need to get the "consent" of the United Kingdom before using the bomb.
2. All supplies of uranium produced in the Congo were allocated to the United States in 1948 and 1949.

3. If the United States needed additional raw materials to maintain its minimum program, they would be provided from the British stockpile.
4. The exchange of information would be shared.[38]

The British were less than pleased with the agreement but feared losing Marshall Plan aid and U.S. support for an intended Western European defense alliance. The agreement, known as a modus vivendi, described the relations between nations in an adversarial situation driven by circumstances to cooperate.

As secretary of state, Marshall approached the issue by first consulting the heads of involved departments and agencies to develop reasonable objectives and then assigning qualified, competent personnel to implement them. In the end, the agreement encompassed the Department of Defense, Department of State, U.S. Atomic Energy Commission, congressional Joint Committee on Atomic Energy, Combined Policy Committee, and British cabinet. Once again, Marshall demonstrated his aptitude for achieving consensus among groups with conflicting interests. Dean Acheson observed Marshall's exceptional ability to deal with nonmilitary issues, view all aspects of a problem, and "hold them in his mind until he was ready to precipitate a decision." Acheson saw this skill as "the essence and the method—or rather the art—of judgment in its highest form. Not merely military judgment, but judgment in the great affairs of state, which requires both mastery of precise information and apprehension of imponderables."[39]

In testimony before the Senate Armed Services Committee in March 1948, Marshall expressed the reservations of the U.S. military concerning the use of atomic bombs, even in clear case of need. He pointed out that strategic bombing meant the killing of many noncombatants. The United States had countenanced such actions in the war because of prior actions by Japan and Germany. For a nuclear-armed nation, he believed that "it was a terrible thing to have to use that type of power. If you are confronted with the use of that type of power in the beginning of the war you are also confronted with a very certain reaction of the American people. They have to be driven very hard before they will agree to such a drastic use of force."[40]

The Berlin crisis, resulting from differences between the Anglo-Americans and the Soviet Union on the future of Germany, tested Marshall's judgment. On June 24, the Soviet Union severed all land and water communications between Berlin and the Western Allies' zones of occupation. The next day the Soviets stated that they would not supply food or electricity to the civilians in the western sections of the city. As the crisis worsened and some in Washington counseled military action, a composed Marshall stated, "The policy of this country was based on the assumption that there would not be war and that we should not plunge into war preparations which would bring about the very thing we are taking these steps to prevent."[41] The State Department's assessments indicated that the Soviets would not take military action against the Western powers. Marshall held this position throughout the crisis. When Lt. Gen. Lucius Clay, commander of U.S. occupation forces, proposed to break the blockade with an armored convoy, Marshall advised Truman to deny the action, which the president did.

On June 25, Clay initiated the Berlin Airlift with Truman's approval. That evening Marshall received a cable from Robert Murphy, Clay's political adviser, recommending that the Western Allied forces remain in Berlin and suggesting that a withdrawal "would be the Munich of 1948." Murphy suggested positioning a force of nuclear-capable B-29 bombers in Europe to emphasize the U.S. commitment to remaining in the former German capital. Marshall sent the following strong message to the Soviet ambassador in Washington:

> The United States government categorically asserts that it is in the occupation of its sector of Berlin with free access thereto as a matter of established right deriving from the defeat and surrender of Germany and confirmed by formal agreement among the principal Allies. It further declares that it will not be induced by threats, pressures, or other actions to abandon these rights. It is hoped that the Soviet government entertains no doubts whatsoever on this point.[42]

During the next week, Marshall considered Murphy's idea of moving B-29s to Europe. Movement of these planes, which had delivered the atomic bombs on Japan, to within range of Moscow, would send a powerful message to the Soviets. It also might elevate the crisis. Marshall and others in the administration agreed on July 5 to the recommendations of the National Security Council to transfer sixty bombers to the United Kingdom and thirty to Germany on the condition that they were sent without atomic bombs. This was a moot point since none of the bombers even had the special fittings required to carry nuclear weapons.

When Marshall and Secretary of Defense Forrestal met with Truman to report the National Security Council's recommendations, Forrestal brought up the issue of control of the atomic bomb. He favored the air force request to assume control of the atomic bomb. Marshall opposed the appeal and supported Truman's decision to keep the decision to use the atomic bomb in civilian hands. Truman commented that he did not wish "to have some lieutenant colonel decide when would be the proper time to drop one."[43]

In a confrontation with one of his aides, Gordon Arneson, Marshall demonstrated his attitude on the use of nuclear weapons. When Arneson proposed the use of the atomic bomb to lift the Berlin Blockade, Marshall asked, "If we were to atomic bomb the Soviet Union, what targets would you choose? Would you bomb Leningrad with the Hermitage?" Arneson acknowledged that he might spare Leningrad, to which Marshall replied, "But if you are really serious about this, why is there a question? Go home and think about it."[44] Marshall's measured stance on the potential use of the atomic bomb did not keep him from adopting a tough stance during the crisis. On July 18, he insisted that the alternative to a hard line with the Soviets was "accepting the consequences of failure of the rest of our European policy." At a July 21 press conference, Marshall responded to a question concerning the "pretty widespread fears of war":

I can say at this time that our position I think is well understood. We will not be coerced or intimidated in any way in our procedures under the rights and responsibilities that we have in Berlin and generally in Germany. At the same time, we will proceed to invoke every possible resource of negotiation and diplomatic procedure to reach an acceptable solution to avoid the tragedy of war for the world. But I repeat again, we are not going to be coerced.[45]

An October 10 memo to the JCS and secretary of defense presented Marshall's position

that he considers the present situation [in Berlin] as one involving an attempt to purchase time. Two methods are involved: (1) the airlift and (2) our monopoly of the atomic bomb. Secretary Marshall believes that the Soviets are beginning to realize for the first time that the United States would really use the atomic bomb against them in time of war. In that connection he was interested to learn that Mr. Dulles accepted the use of the bomb as a foregone conclusion stating, "Why the American people would execute you if you did not use the bomb in the event of war."[46]

Marshall, visiting the pope on October 19 in Paris, "referred directly to the atomic bomb, the fact I thought the fear of it made it somewhat improbable Soviet resort to military action."[47] Marshall believed that the Soviets' perception of the U.S. possession of the atomic bomb and a bomber force capable of delivering it was one reason for their not escalating the crisis and finally lifting the blockade on May 12, 1949. It also accelerated the nuclear arms race by demonstrating to Stalin the need for nuclear weapons to offset the U.S. advantage.

In dealing with the crisis, Marshall remained calm but firm. He supported avoiding actions that would worsen the situation while advocating the application of indirect pressure on the Soviets. In addition to the Marshall Plan, the move included repositioning the bombers, creating a West German government, and supporting the formation of a Western European alliance, which was effected by the 1949 North Atlantic Treaty. He also facilitated cooperation with Britain and France, which was critical in the negotiations with the Soviets to resolve the crisis. Historian Avi Shlaim observed that of the key U.S. leaders, "Marshall was the least affected by rigid and distorting images during the Berlin crisis. His approach was pragmatic, low-key, and finely balanced. His awareness that America's entire European policy was at stake persuaded him that a determined attempt had to be made to defend the exposed outpost of the Western alliance."[48]

Marshall addressed the issue of nuclear energy in an address to the UN General Assembly in Paris on September 23, 1948. He emphasized "the early adoption of an international system for the control of atomic energy, providing the elimination of atomic weapons from national armaments, for development of atomic energy for peaceful purposes only, and for safeguards to insure compliance by all nations with the necessary international measures for control."[49] Meeting with foreign leaders after the Paris meeting, Marshall struck a firm tone concerning the U.S. use of its nuclear weapons to prevent Soviet aggression. He told Belgian diplomat Paul-Henri Spaak that as a soldier he knew that the Allies' buildup of military forces in Western Europe would take time. He said the United States was willing to use the threat of the atomic bomb as a deterrent to cover the expansion of these forces.[50] Speaking with the foreign ministers of France and Britain concerning the response to the Soviet threat to Europe, he said:

> I felt that there would be a gradual strengthening of Western countries toward the eventual situation where we could rest on the strength of our position and the problem would be the Soviets'. In presenting this

conception, I stated that I felt reasonably certain that the fear of the atom bomb at the present time discounted the probability of armed action by the Soviets; that they had evidently changed their opinion from feeling that the American public would never support the use of the bomb to recognition of the fact that the American public would be in favor of using the bomb.[51]

In October 1948, Marshall learned that he would need an operation to remove an enlarged kidney. Meeting with the president, he explained the need for the operation and his desire to resign as secretary of state. Ever loyal to the president, he delayed his resignation until after the November presidential election. On January 9, 1949, he stepped down from the position that he had held for two tumultuous years.

On September 23, 1949, President Truman stunned the nation with a brief announcement: "We have evidence that within recent weeks an atomic explosion occurred in the Soviet Union."[52] With the detonation of "Joe-1" on August 29, 1949, the USSR became the second nation on earth to possess an atomic bomb. On March 10, 1950, Truman approved a crash program to develop the hydrogen bomb, escalating the nuclear arms race. Marshall was not pleased with this rush to larger nuclear weapons. In a 1950 Memorial Day address at the Tomb of the Unknown Soldier in Arlington National Cemetery, he cautioned, "We should not place complete dependence on military and material power." Recognizing the destructive potential of nuclear weapons, he went on to say, "War is no longer just an evil. In this age, it seems intolerable. The victorious power will stand amidst its own ruins." He recommended that the United States support the United Nations, "where words can be used instead of bullets."[53]

In June 1950, North Korea invaded South Korea, and the Cold War suddenly became a "hot" war. Faced with this crisis and the need to unify his cabinet to accelerate rearmament, Truman once again called for Marshall's assistance. On September 6, 1950, Marshall met with Truman, who asked him if he would "act as Secretary of Defense through the crisis if I could get Congressional approval."[54] Marshall warned him to consider his request carefully: "I'll do it but I want you to think about the fact that my appointment may reflect upon you and your administration. They are still charging me with the downfall of Chiang's government in China. I want to help, not hurt you."[55]

On September 21, 1950, Marshall became secretary of defense, a position that he would hold for approximately one year. During this period, he confronted issues including the Soviets' possession of the atomic bomb, expanding U.S. military forces, developing strategy and objectives for the Korean War, and dealing with Gen. Douglas MacArthur's failure to adhere to the principle of civilian control of the military. As secretary of defense, Marshall again confronted challenges involving nuclear weapons. He dealt with major questions of nuclear policy as a member of both the National Security Council and its Special Committee on Atomic Energy. The committee included the secretary of state and the chair of the AEC. On the international front, the secretary of defense was a member of the Combined Policy Committee that coordinated nuclear policy among the United States, Britain, and Canada.

As a member of the president's cabinet and the National Security Council, Marshall knew that the president and Joint Chiefs of Staff had considered the use of atomic bombs in Korea during the summer of 1950. On a broader issue, he became familiar with the role of nuclear weapons in the seminal April 1950 National Security Council Report 68 (NSC-68).[56] This document included the role of nuclear weapons in the U.S. strategy and objectives for the Cold War. The subject of using tactical nuclear weapons surfaced during President Truman's meeting on the day of the North Korean invasion. Truman asked Air Force Chief of Staff Hoyt S. Vandenberg if U.S. planes could destroy Soviet bases near Korea. Vandenberg replied yes, but atomic bombs would be required. Hearing this, Truman ordered preparations for an atomic attack if the Soviets entered the war. In July, the administration flexed the U.S. nuclear muscle to show its resolve to prevail in Korea. Gen. Curtis LeMay, commander of Strategic Air Command, was ordered to position nuclear-capable B-29 bombers on Guam and in Britain, repeating the ruse used in breaking the Berlin Blockade.

In November 1950, when Chinese troops routed the allies in North Korea, the possibility of the use of nuclear weapons surfaced again. On November 30, Gen. Douglas MacArthur, commander-in-chief of United Nations Command, warned the JCS, "Everything leads to the conclusion the Chinese have as their objective the complete destruction of the United Nations forces and the securing of all Korea." At a news conference on the same day, Truman responded to a question concerning the possible use of the atomic bomb stating, "There has always been active consideration of its use, though I don't want to see it used."[57] The following day, the president requested funds to produce more plutonium and atomic weapons.

Once again, the Joint Chiefs of Staff considered the use of atomic weapons in Korea and concluded that their employment would be ineffective in the mountainous terrain on the peninsula. CJCS Gen. Omar Bradley reacted strongly to the idea of using nuclear weapons in Korea: "I've never heard anything so preposterous in my life."[58] Maj. Gen. Kenneth Nichols, Manhattan Project assistant to Gen. Leslie Groves and chair of the AEC's Military Liaison Committee in 1950, also saw the use of nuclear weapons as ineffective and possibly counterproductive. Although he was an outspoken proponent of military custody of nuclear weapons, he acknowledged that there were no suitable targets for the atomic bomb in Korea.[59]

General MacArthur did propose a plan to blanket the Chinese–North Korean border with radioactive material but did not send it to the JCS. He never directly proposed using the atomic bomb to the JCS, but given MacArthur's record the chiefs were uncertain of their ability to control his actions. Two of the reasons presented to the president and Marshall by the JCS for relieving MacArthur of his command reflected their concern: "it was difficult to coordinate plans with him as they never knew if he would follow orders and failure to relieve him would damage civilian control."[60] Marshall had been reluctant to relieve MacArthur, but these arguments resonated with his strong views on the chain of command and civilian control of the military. Neither Marshall nor the president wanted a rogue commander in control of the atomic bomb. Shortly after receiving the JCS recommendation, Truman relieved MacArthur of his command on April 11, 1951.

In January 1951, Marshall, not wishing to increase the specter of a nuclear war in Korea or Europe, stated his opposition to revealing U.S. testing of tactical nuclear weapons. Truman ignored Marshall's counsel, and the tests were conducted later that winter. In a February 1951 speech to the American Association of School Administrators, Marshall commented on the adverse influence of nuclear weapons on the Korean War:

It is generally conceded that the fear of our present great atomic power is the principal deterrent to Communistic Soviet aggressions. It is generally admitted, I think, that our well-known military weakness encouraged Communist aggression in Korea. If we had had immediately available a trained reserve that could have quickly been brought into action, that Korean attack would never have been made. But if made, it would have been suppressed, I think, long before this time.[61]

In a March 13 interview for *U.S. News and World Report,* Marshall continued to stress the need for ground troops despite the possession of nuclear weapons:

> I was very much struck with the public reactions to the atomic bomb on its first appearance. I had been thinking about its effect on warfare for about two years and a half, and yet the decision on its effect seemed to be settled in the press in about 24 hours. What we had to do in ground warfare in order to be in the position to use the bomb was completely overlooked. There was a reaction in favor of a sort of push-button warfare. People overlooked the tremendous number of men that would be involved before we could get the necessary fields from which to use the bomb. Take Saipan, for example—or Guam—those were gained in big, costly battles. And they were preceded by Tarawas and Kwajaleins—all necessary to acquire the fields from which we launched the bombs. There were many people involved in those operations.[62]

As a result of the Korean War, the military requested the deployment of nonnuclear components of nuclear weapons to forward areas where they could be quickly married to nuclear components. This led the Truman administration to reconsider the procedures for the use of nuclear weapons. Gordon Dean, chair of the AEC, worried that the civilian commission would lose control of these weapons granted to it by the Atomic Energy Act of 1946. Marshall recognized the military, political, and moral concerns surrounding the atomic bomb, and he maintained a firm belief in the preeminence of civilian authority in addressing these vital issues.

On April 16, the president met with Marshall and Secretary of State Acheson to consider the civilian control of nuclear weapons. As a result of the meeting, the president asked the National Security Council's Special Committee to study the matter. The committee recommended that the final decision to use nuclear weapons should rest with the president in consultation with the secretary of defense, secretary of state, and chair of the AEC. The AEC commissioners approved the recommendation, but the JCS balked at the idea that a civilian agency would intervene between the military and the president.[63] They asked Marshall to oppose any study on the procedures to be followed in deciding the use of nuclear weapons. Marshall sided with those who insisted that ultimate control of nuclear weapons should lie with the president rather than with military leaders. Nonetheless, he agreed with the JCS that a military representative should be among those advising the president on the use of the atomic bomb.

As secretary of defense, Marshall inherited policies regarding nuclear weapons outlined in NSC-68, which included increasing the production of fission weapons and the development of the more powerful hydrogen bomb. The Soviet detonation of an atomic bomb in August 1949 and the onset of the Korean War in June 1950 resulted in congressional demands for increasing the number of nuclear weapons, which were led by Sen. Brien McMahon (D-Conn.), chair of the Joint Committee on Atomic Energy (JCAE). On September 2, 1950, Marshall's first day in office, he received a memo from McMahon saying that the JCAE believed that a large expansion of the U.S. atomic effort was necessary. Marshall replied that the proposed program "seemed to cover all possibilities."[64] Marshall consulted with the secretaries of the armed forces and then approved the NSC Special Committee report that recommended doubling spending on the already authorized nuclear weapons program to $2.5 billion over the next six years.[65]

In early 1951, McMahon, not satisfied with the progress of the nuclear weapons program, pressured the administration for more details. The JCS objected for reasons of security, and Marshall, with the president's backing, refused the senator's request. Marshall's response revealed his tact in dealing with the senator:

Dear Senator McMahon: I refer to your memorandum, 12 February 1951, in which request is made for certain information concerning our atomic weapons, our ability to deliver them, the selection of targets, our atomic missile development, and other details. Most careful consideration has been given to a series of possible answers to the questions presented by you and, after consultation by the President with me and the Joint Chiefs of Staff, it has been decided that there is no practicable way in which this type of information can be made available without serious risk to our national security. No question as to the integrity of anyone concerned in this matter has arisen. The risk to our national security arises from the fact that answers to the questions propounded cannot be complete in themselves; that is they can serve only to develop further fields for examination. Thus, the ultimate result could only be a complete briefing of our most secret war plans including all the information upon which they are based. Those mentioned above are unanimously of the opinion that this type of information must be held secret by the President, in his capacity as Commander in Chief, and his immediate subordinates.

I believe that when you consider this matter from this point of view you will understand our reticence and agree with the conclusions reached.[66]

In May 1951, Marshall received a request from McMahon to expand the AEC's nuclear weapons production facilities, and Marshall and Lovett met the senator for lunch at the Pentagon on July 5. McMahon expressed his opinion that the nation needed "literally thousands and thousands" of atomic bombs to counter the growing Soviet nuclear stockpile. In response, Marshall and Lovett conceded that some increase in lightweight, tactical nuclear weapons might be useful. It is likely that they were thinking of positioning these weapons in Western Europe to shield North Atlantic Treaty Organization (NATO) partners during the buildup of conventional forces.

McMahon was unrelenting in his push for expanding the nuclear stockpile. On August 21, Marshall received a lengthy letter from McMahon, which contained a call for much greater emphasis on research, development, and use of tactical nuclear weapons. On September 4, Marshall assured McMahon that he had given the letter careful reading and had requested supplemental information on the subject including the views of the Joint Chiefs of Staff. At a lunch with McMahon and others on September 6, Marshall assured "him that U.S. military planners including Eisenhower and the Joint Chiefs were closely studying the potentialities of future improved weapons in defending Western Europe."[67]

By this time, some in the Truman administration were questioning the need for further expansion of the nuclear weapons program. Fredrick Lawton, director of the Bureau of the Budget, asked if "ultimate war aims place a limit upon the extent of the use of atomic bombs."[68] McMahon prevailed, however, and set the U.S. nuclear arsenal on a trajectory to reach a peak of 76,000 warheads in 1976.[69] On September 12, 1951, Marshall quietly handed the leadership of the Defense Department to Undersecretary of Defense Robert Lovett, who continued to carry out the policies that Marshall had put forward for the Korean War and for the future of nuclear weapons. The smooth transition from Marshall to Lovett was yet another example of Marshall's foresight and leadership.

NOTES

1. Larry I. Bland and Sharon Ritenour Stevens, eds., *The Papers of George Catlett Marshall*, vol. 5: *"The Finest Soldier": January 1, 1945–January 7, 1947* (Baltimore: Johns Hopkins University Press, 2003), 311–13.

2. George C. Marshal, *Army and Navy Journal*, November 6, 1945, George C. Marshall Papers, Pentagon Office, Categorical, Speeches and Writings, George C. Marshall Library (hereafter cited as GCML).

3. George C. Marshall, "Our Weapons," *Yank*, October 6, 1945, 6.

4. Bland and Stevens, *"The Finest Soldier,"* 341.

5. Godfrey Hodgson, *America in Our Time: From World War II to Nixon—What Happened and Why* (New York: Doubleday, 1976), 22.

6. John C. Sparrow, *History of Personnel Demobilization in the United States Army* (Washington, D.C.: Department of the Army, Office of the Chief of Military History, 1951), 380.

7. Groves's memorandum to chief of staff, August 24, 1945, microfilm roll 1, M1109, Manhattan Engineering District, GCML.

8. Sean L. Malloy, "'A Very Pleasant Way to Die': Radiation Effects and the Decision to Use the Atomic Bomb against Japan," *Diplomatic History* 36, no. 3 (June 2012): 542.

9. JCS 1477, August 18, 1945, JCS 1477/1, October 30, 1945; CCS 471.6 (8–15–45) sec. 2, cited in James F. Schnabel and Robert J. Watson, *History of the Joint Chiefs of Staff*, vol. 1: *The Joint Chiefs of Staff and National Policy, 1945–1947* (Washington, D.C.: Office of the Chairman of the Joint Chiefs of Staff, Office of Joint History, 1996), 127.

10. Schnabel and Watson, *History of the Joint Chiefs*, 1:130.

11. Ibid.

12. Ibid.

13. Special Message to the Congress on Atomic Energy, 156, Public Papers of Harry S. Truman, Harry S. Truman Library (hereafter cited as HSTL).

14. Ibid.

15. Schnabel and Watson, *History of the Joint Chiefs*, 1:118.

16. Ibid., 1:120.

17. Ibid.

18. Ibid.

19. Katherine Tupper Marshall, *Together: Annals of an Army Wife* (New York: Tupper and Love, 1946), 272–73.

20. Bland and Stevens, *"The Finest Soldier,"* 365.

21. Baruch to Marshall, May 14, 1946, George C. Marshall Papers, GCML.

22. Bland and Stevens, *"The Finest Soldier,"* 660–61.

23. Mark A. Stoler, *George C. Marshall: Soldier-Statesman of the American Century* (Boston: Twayne, 1989), 154.

24. Leonard Mosley, *Marshall: Hero for Our Times* (New York: Hearst, 1982), 190–91.

25. Robert H. Ferrell, ed., *Off the Record: The Private Papers of Harry S. Truman* (New York: Harper and Row, 1980), 109.

26. Dean Acheson, *Present at the Creation: My Years at the State Department* (New York: W. W. Norton, 1969), 140–41.

27. U.S. Department of State, Office of the Historian, "The Acheson-Lilienthal and Baruch Plans, 1946," https://2001-2009.state.gov/r/pa/ho/time/cwr/88100.htm (accessed October 17, 2019).

28. Richard G. Hewlett and Oscar E. Anderson, *A History of the United States Atomic Energy Commission*, vol. 1: *The New World, 1939–1946* (University Park: Pennsylvania State University Press, 1962), 576–78.

29. Ibid., 618–19.

30. Richard G. Hewlett and Francis Duncan, *A History of the United States Atomic Energy Commission*, vol. 2: *Atomic Shield, 1947–1952* (University Park: Pennsylvania State University Press, 1969), 266.

31. Eric F. Goldman, *The Crucial Decade: America, 1945–1955* (New York: Alfred A. Knopf, 1956), 69.

32. David E. Lilienthal, *The Journals of David E. Lilienthal*, vol. 2: *The Atomic Energy Years, 1945–1950* (New York: Harper and Row, 1964), 196–97.

33. Ibid., 197.

34. Lilienthal to Bereton, April 25, 1947, cited in Hewlett and Duncan, *Atomic Shield*, 271.

35. Minutes, Meeting of the Secretaries of State, War, and Navy, September 8, 1947, AEC, cited in Hewlett and Duncan, *Atomic Shield*, 271–72.

36. *Department of State Bulletin*, September 28, 1947.

37. Larry I. Bland, Mark A. Stoler, Sharon Ritenour Stevens, and Daniel D. Holt, eds., *The Papers of George Catlett Marshall*, vol. 6: *"The Whole World Hangs in the Balance": January 8, 1947–September 30, 1949* (Baltimore: Johns Hopkins University Press, 2013), 557.

38. "Minutes of the Combined Policy Committee," January 7, 1948, in Department of State, Office of the Historian, *Foreign Relations of the United States, 1948*, vol. 1, pt. 2: *General; The United Nations* (Washington, D.C.: Government Printing Office, 1976), 679–86.

39. Acheson, *Present at the Creation*, 141.

40. Bland et al., *"Whole World Hangs in the Balance,"* 410.

41. Walter Millis, ed., *The Forrestal Diaries* (New York: Viking, 1951), 432.

42. Marshall to Soviet Ambassador, Washington, D.C., July 6, 1948, in Department of State, Office of the Historian, *Foreign Relations of the United States, 1948*, vol. 2: *Germany and Austria* (Washington, D.C.: Government Printing Office, 1973), 919–21.

43. James V. Forrestal Diaries, July 5, 1948, 2362–2363, Princeton University Library.

44. Forrestal and Millis, 458, cited in Gregg Herken, *The Winning Weapon: The Atomic Bomb and the Cold War, 1945–1950* (Princeton, N.J.: Princeton University Press, 1981), 262–63.

45. Memorandum of Press and Radio News Conference, July 21, 1948, Office of the Special Assistant of State, Verbatim Reports of the Conference, RG 59, National Archives and Records Administration (hereafter cited as NARA).

46. Bland et al., *"Whole World Hangs in the Balance,"* 584–85.

47. Ibid., 597.

48. Avi Shlaim, *The United States and the Berlin Blockade, 1948–1949: A Study in Crisis Decision-Making* (Berkeley: University of California Press, 1983), 572–73.

49. Bland et al., *"Whole World Hangs in the Balance,"* 557.

50. Ibid., 569.

51. Ibid., 572.

52. Harry S. Truman, "Statement in Response to First Soviet Nuclear Test," September 23, 1949, https://digitalarchive.wilsoncenter.org/document/134436.pdf?v=5ff 33129481c51af49c602a780127ec7.

53. "Spiritual Revival Needed for Peace, Marshall Asserts," *New York Times*, May 31, 1950.

54. Forrest C. Pogue, *George C. Marshall*, vol. 4: *Statesman, 1945–1959* (New York: Viking, 1987), 422.

55. Ibid.

56. "A Report to the National Security Council—NSC 68," April 12, 1950, Harry S. Truman Papers, President's Secretary's Files, HSTL.

57. Department of State, Office of the Historian, *Foreign Relations of the United States, 1950*, vol. 7: *Korea* (Washington, D.C.: Government Printing Office, 1976), 159–60.

58. Ibid., 1260.

59. Memorandum, Army Chief of Staff to Joint Strategic Survey Committee, December 3, 1950, box 1, folder 2, "Recently Declassified Documents," NARA; JCS History, vol. 3, pt. 1, 372, cited in Herken, *Winning Weapon*, 332.

60. Matthew Moten, *Presidents and Their Generals: An American History of Command in War* (Cambridge, Mass.: Belknap Press of Harvard University Press, 2014), 254–55; Omar N. Bradley and Clay Blair, *A General's Life: The Autobiography by General of the Army Omar N. Bradley* (New York: Simon & Schuster, 1983), 634–35.

61. Mark A. Stoler and Daniel D. Holt, eds., *The Papers of George Catlett Marshall*, vol. 7: *"The Man of the Age": October 1, 1949–October 16, 1959* (Baltimore: Johns Hopkins University Press, 2016), 395.

62. Ibid.

63. Hewlett and Duncan, *Atomic Shield*, 538–39.

64. ChJCAF to SecDef, September 21, 1950, in Department of State, Office of the Historian, *Foreign Relations of the United States, 1950: National Security Affairs; Foreign Economic Policy* (Washington, D.C.: Government Printing Office, 1977), 1:576–77.

65. Memo for SecDef for ExecSecNSC, September 29, 1950, cited in Alfred Goldberg, ed., *History of the Secretary of Defense*, vol. 2: Doris M. Condit, ed., *The Test of War 1950–1953* (Washington, D.C.: Historical Office of the Secretary of Defense, 1988), 645nn59–60; Memo Asst to DCS/OpsAE HQ SAF for SecAF, September 27, 1950, without initialed agreement of Finletter; Memo for SecDef, September 29, 1950; Memo CNO for SecNavy, September 27, 1950, with signed agreement of Mathews; Memo SecDef for ExecSecNSC, September 29, 1950; Memo SecArmy for SecDef, September 29, 1950—all in CD400.174, RG 330, NARA.

66. Memo Asst to DCS/OpsAE HQ SAF for SecAF, September 27, 1950, without initialed agreement of Finletter, CD400.174, RG 330, NARA; Memo SecDef for ExecSecNSC, September 29, 1950, cited in Condit, *Test of War*, 645nn59, 60; Memo SecArmy for SecDef, September 29, 1950, CD400.174, RG 330, NARA.

67. Stoler and Holt, *"Man of the Age,"* 617–18.

68. Condit, *Test of War*, 470.

69. Steven I. Schwartz, ed., *Atomic Audit: The Cost and Consequences of the U.S. Nuclear Weapons since 1940* (Washington, D.C.: Brookings Institution, 1998), 33.

6

THE PATIENT IS SINKING

Marshall and the European Recovery Program

In April 1947, George C. Marshall cut a frustrated figure onboard the C-54 U.S. Army plane home from the six-week-long Conference of Foreign Ministers (CFM) in Moscow. After a grueling but fast-paced flight with stopovers in Germany, Iceland, and Canada, the secretary of state's delegation finally touched down at National Airport, where President Harry S. Truman greeted them. As Marshall shook Truman's hand on the tarmac, he explained that in Moscow he and his associates "attempted to do our best in the best interest of the United States and of the world, so that the people of the world can have the peace of mind and the comforts of life to which they are entitled." The statement echoed that of the British foreign secretary Ernest Bevin, who upon his departure from Moscow in a similarly hopeful tone claimed that "next time" the CFM met they would reach an agreement on the political principles in Germany.[1] Such pronouncements of hope regarding the postwar world were mere performances for the press corps. The talks in Moscow had not gone well. Marshall had been in the job for less than four months, but he already was arriving at the conclusion that international agreement over Europe's recovery from the recent war was improbable. Three days after his return, on April 28, Marshall delivered a thirty-minute radio address during which he explained his concerns regarding European conditions directly to the American people. Singling out Soviet premier Joseph Stalin, Marshall explained that the "unwillingness of the Soviet authorities to cooperate in establishing a balanced economy for Germany as agreed upon at Potsdam has been the most serious check on the development of a self-supporting Germany, and a Germany capable of providing coal and other necessities for the neighboring states." Marshall further revealed that the recovery of European society had been slower than expected. The consequences were dire. Starvation and desolation were everywhere. "The patient is sinking while the doctors deliberate," Marshall iterated, adding, "Action cannot await compromise through exhaustion. New issues arise daily. Whatever action is possible to meet these pressing problems must be taken without delay."[2] Within a year of Marshall's frustrating homecoming, the United States would launch the European Recovery Program (ERP), the most extraordinary foreign aid program ever undertaken. In size, scope, vision, and consequences, the plan that colloquially would bear Marshall's name made the United States the leader of the Free World. Its impact continues to reverberate through European politics, cultures, and societies. Above all, it established the institutional foundations for the European Union, and it conceived the modern perception of the West.[3]

In collective memory, the Marshall Plan stands on a pedestal. Americans as well as Europeans remember it as the economic development program that rescued Western Europe from poverty, starvation, and communism. This traditional narrative makes the end of World War II in 1945 the axis upon which U.S. foreign policy and modern international history turns. The temptation to divide history into manageable eras is understandable, but such periodization also impacts historical assessments. Focusing too narrowly on the Marshall Plan as a Cold War policy severs the connections between the ideals that inspired American postwar planning policies during World War II and the exceptionalist ideology that drove policy in the aftermath of the war. Of course, the ERP was an economic program and a counter to Soviet policies in Eastern Europe, but it was more than that. At heart, the Marshall Plan was ideological. When understood as part of rather than apart from U.S. postwar planning between 1939 and 1945, the plan aligns with an American vision that specifically aimed to redesign the international political and economic order. This ideological

Secretary of State George C. Marshall seated in his office. February 2, 1947. Courtesy George C. Marshall Library, Lexington, Va.

vision began to circulate in the inner sanctums of U.S. foreign policymaking circles, in the halls of American universities, and among members of a rapidly expanding foreign policy press corps the moment that war broke out. In part, this reflected a need for atonement after Versailles. As George Marshall pointed out shortly after becoming secretary of state, many were of the belief that "the negative course of action followed by the United States" after 1919, including the nation's decision to stand outside the League of Nations, had allowed if not enabled the rise of fascism, "the recent war and its endless tragedies."[4] Following this line of thought, hopeful intellectuals like Clarence Streit and Emery Reeves demanded the pursuit of world federalism or the democratization of global politics as the antidote to future global wars.[5] Such hopeful views influenced postwar planning in the State Department, the White House, and later the Department of the Treasury, as well as by members of the national print media. Henry Luce, the publishing entrepreneur and editor of *Time* and *Life* magazines, is the most frequently cited advocate of a new world order made in the United States' image; however, Luce was far from alone.[6] Almost all these advocates agreed with Harold Moulton, president of the Brookings Institution, that the events of the past three decades meant there was "no such thing as an unobjectionable way to prevent war" but also that peace would "have its price" and that the "United States *must* adopt a policy."[7]

This ideological policy that the Marshall Plan became a prime example of did not emerge in 1945 or at the dawn of the Cold War but, rather, during World War II. Nor was it a shift from isolationism to internationalism because the United States was never isolationist in any meaningful sense. It was the activation of a policy to provide humanity a path to modernity—a vision as old as the Republic.[8] The most powerful advocacy of this emerged in a little and long since forgotten work by the former Republican presidential candidate Wendell Willkie. Published in 1943, his book *One World* made a piercing case for a world inspired and influenced by American ideals.[9] Part Enlightenment part Progressivism, Willkie's vision imagined American guidance and leadership in a world that for the sake of peace and prosperity ought to target the democratization of the international system, champion human rights, liberalize trade, end imperialism, and stamp out political radicalism on the right and the left.

Critics of U.S. foreign policy denounced such ideas as simple economic imperialism—a charge they would also level at the Marshall Plan—but in reality, there was no alternative to U.S. leadership as the curtain came down on World War II. In 1944, then Sen. Harry Truman (D-Mo.) along with two colleagues introduced a resolution demanding that in light of the United States' disproportionate wealth and principles, the nation "cannot, nor does it wish to, shirk leadership in the post-war economic collaboration. Our own industrial accomplishments have nominated us as the Nation that must assume a position to guide others in the pathway of peaceful production." In their view, the nation had "within its grasp a leadership which will determine the happiness . . . of hundreds of millions of people in the years to come [and] can control a destiny which if unwisely used may bring depression and ruin, hunger and death to great numbers of the world's people."[10]

For Truman, the magnitude of these observations became even clearer when he assumed the presidency after Franklin D. Roosevelt's death in April 1945. Across the European continent, the humanitarian and economic situation was dire. Less than two weeks into office, Truman received firsthand reports describing calamitous conditions in Europe. In separate reports, Assistant Secretary of War John J. McCloy and Judge Samuel Rosenman described Central Europe and Germany as on the brink of "complete economic, social, and political collapse . . . unparalleled in history." Except "in the rural, food-raising areas, a dangerously low level of nutrition generally exists; coal production meets not even minimum requirements; ports have suffered great damage by bombing and demolition. Railroads, canals, and highways have been wholly or partially destroyed."[11] During the war, the United Nations Recovery and Rehabilitation Administration (UNRRA) had fought a hopeless battle to remedy this situation. However, lacking a clear mandate, organized bureaucracy, and sufficient resources, UNRRA had merely been a palliative.[12]

Like his predecessor, Truman envisioned that the United Nations along with the Bretton Woods institutions—the World Bank and the International Monetary Fund—would work to solve such despair. In 1945, however, none of these were operational. The United States had to fill the void, and time was of the essence. The collective lesson that Americans drew from the interwar period was that poverty, chaos, and desolation led citizens to surrender liberties for the protection and promises of demagogues. The corrective to war and radicalism in the mold of Hitler and Mussolini was economic health and public prosperity. Humanity's remedy, many Americans believed, was an international one-world order run through the United Nations to secure equality, happiness, and security.

Those who dismiss such an American ideology argue that Truman never aimed to collaborate with either the United Nations or the Soviet Union.[13] Such views, however, derive their logic largely from what followed after the Cold War became a reality. In 1945, the assumption inside the Truman White House was that having won the war, the Allies, acting in concert, would go on to win the peace as well. This is not to say that there were no disagreements when the victorious powers met in July 1945 in Potsdam to coordinate a solution to the postwar situation in Germany and wider Europe. Yet, these disagreements were hardly more than one might expect when major powers jockey for influence. If anything, the Potsdam Agreement signed by the United States, the Soviet Union, and Great Britain (France did not participate but was later granted an occupation zone in Germany) targeted both German war crimes and the re-creation of the European continent. The agreement created the Berlin-headquartered Four Power Allied Control Council and prepared for a two-step process of denazification and democratization. While Moscow and Paris favored a slow process toward German recovery, the American target was a modern, liberal Germany that could quickly take its place in the international system while shedding the cancerous remnants of radicalism.

Perhaps Washington and Moscow could have reached an agreement on this question if the United States had accepted the creation of a new balance of power in Europe. The changes that Washington envisioned to the global order, however, precluded any such traditional arrangement. American liberal modernization policies rooted in Enlightenment thinking were always likely to clash dramatically with the thinking in the Kremlin. After all, international communism possessed its own, entirely different, path to modernity. This ideological cleft and competing visions for the world likely meant that collaboration would have broken down no matter what, but despite international tensions throughout the fall of 1945, Americans continued to hope for global cooperation. However, as 1946 rolled around, events began to expose the illusion of the one-world vision. The first sign came when the Soviet Union withdrew from participation in the Bretton Woods system. Keeping Moscow in the American-designed global economic order would have forced the Soviets to disclose economic data that would expose the war's destruction of the Soviet economy and consequently weaken the public image of international communism.[14] When added to other smaller crises in Europe and the Middle East, the Soviet withdrawal from the Bretton Woods framework indicated that Stalin was not looking to cooperate with the new international system after all.

Meanwhile, the situation in Germany was particularly grim. After the Potsdam Conference, the Allies divided Germany into four occupation zones under the control of American, British, French, and Soviet forces, respectively. Though run as independent areas to be unified as part of the new Germany at a yet to be decided date, very different socioeconomic realities soon emerged. Neither the Soviets nor the French had much interest in the rehabilitation of Germany. Both sought reparations and both had an interest in keeping Germany down. Their obstructionist approach frustrated the head of the American zone, U.S.

Army Gen. Lucius Clay. He witnessed firsthand the consequences of over-population and the rapidly developing refugee crisis that pushed the German people to starvation. In the British zone, officials cut daily rations to around 1,000 calories, while in the American zone rations hovered between 1,200 and 1,500 calories. There is ample reason to suspect that the levels were even lower in the Soviet zone. Frustrated with the lack of a comprehensive approach to handling this humanitarian crisis as well as with his supposed occupation partners, Clay—foreshadowing arguments made by Marshall in Moscow eight months later—explained to Army Chief of Staff Dwight D. Eisenhower that in the absence of zonal unification to provide food and services, the suffering "of the German people will be a serious charge against democracy [and this] will develop a sympathy which may well defeat our other objectives in Germany."[15] Urged by Clay to amplify the American commitment to German independence and recovery, then Secretary of State James Byrnes delivered a powerful speech in Germany in which he insisted that U.S. policy would not allow "Germany to become the satellite of any power. . . . The American people want to return the government of Germany to the German people. The American people want to help the German people to win their way back to an honorable place among the free and peace-loving nations of the world."[16]

The view that European peace and democracy were inseparable from German recovery prevailed within the State Department after Marshall replaced Byrnes in January 1947. The most urgent test of American commitments would come not in Berlin, however, but 1,100 miles to the southeast in Greece. Above all, the Greek Civil War made the Marshall Plan both possible and necessary. Ever since the defeat of Nazi occupation, communist insurgents operating out of neighboring Albania, Bulgaria, and Yugoslavia had threatened to overthrow the Athens government. Throughout the fall of 1946, Greek attempts to secure UN Security Council backing to halt these incursions lost out to Soviet vetoes, thereby exposing the weakness of the infant organization's powers. Historical ties made Britain the sponsor of Greek security, but the costs of World War II had dramatically diminished London's ability to influence global events. As pressure mounted on the Athens government, a growing chorus of Americans called for a greater U.S. role. Sumner Welles, Franklin D. Roosevelt's former undersecretary of state, insisted that if the United States stood on the sidelines now, it would undermine the nation's global democratic mission and its legitimacy as the architect of the postwar world. Two of the nation's most influential reporters, Joseph and Stewart Alsop, agreed. They vocally criticized Washington's lack of action. "[K]eeping your fingers crossed," they stated, "cannot be described as having a policy in the field of world relations . . . , however, crossed fingers seem to be the only visible American response" to communist policies in Europe. Support for Greece in the United Nations was not enough; the Alsops insisted that the United States needed a program to provide support "on a much larger scale, in all economic and political soft spots."[17] After heated debates in the United Nations and mounting international pressure, Moscow finally refrained from vetoing an American-backed plan for a multinational investigative UN mission.[18] American reporters considered this a return to "big power harmony," concluding that Moscow was not "prepared to do anything that would cast doubt on her new policy of cooperation with the west."[19]

Shortly after Marshall replaced Byrnes, Britain informed his office that London could no longer support the Athens government. Almost simultaneously, the U.S. representative in the UN mission to Greece relayed stories of Soviet obstruction of the investigations. He insisted that if the United States failed to act independently, Greece was "a ripe plum ready to fall into [Soviet] hands in a few weeks."[20] In front of a joint session of Congress on March 12, 1947, President Truman responded with the foreign policy doctrine that would come to bear his name. The Truman Doctrine committed American financial aid for Greece and its equally threatened neighbor Turkey but also provided an unlimited pledge to the democratic way of life around the world.[21]

Most scholars argue that Marshall, a traditionally reserved man, found Truman's rhetoric excessive and flamboyant. This was certainly the argument presented by Charles Bohlen, who accompanied Marshall to Moscow and who later played a prominent part in the State Department's policy planning toward Europe. Nonetheless, when given the chance to comment on the draft of the president's speech, Marshall suggested only a few changes. In any case, he himself was not immune to using bold language.[22] Just three weeks earlier, in a speech at Princeton University, Marshall presented the situation in Europe as equally critical. It will, he insisted, "largely determine our future." Quoting Oliver Wendell Holmes, Marshall maintained, "To act is to affirm the worth of an end, and to affirm the worth of an end is to create an ideal." Americans could not be spectators in the new world. The "Fall of Athens," in the Peloponnesian War, Marshall averred, was a critical lesson for anyone seeking "a clear understanding of the institutions upon which human liberty and individual freedom have depended, and the struggles to gain and maintain them." The "basic international issues" of the day required an understanding of the past just as it was acute to recognize "the position that the United States now occupies in the world," including its "responsibility for world order and security." A few weeks later, in an address to the American Red Cross, the secretary of state added that the United Nations remained "the rock upon which this nation has built its hopes for a stable world order." While Marshall still believed in the global influence of American-designed institutions, the situation in Greece was proving, for now, that the United States might need to go it alone.[23]

The Cold War was not the single catalyst of emerging American aid initiatives, but Marshall's State Department clearly saw the European situation as increasingly threatening to the international order. In many countries, food shortages and calamitous economic conditions led to black markets that seriously undermined governments' abilities to maintain order. Simultaneously, across Western Europe, national communist parties promising radical solutions were making headway in polls and elections. In part, the popularity of communism reflected a genuine appreciation for the Soviet Union's wartime efforts, but evidence from Eastern European archives shows that it was also a result of extensive clandestine backing from Moscow, especially in Scandinavia and Belgium but more importantly in France and Italy. The Italian Communist Party (PCI) boasted a "groundswell of support for Communism" that soon reached 2 million members and saw the PCI claim 19 percent of the vote and several cabinet positions. The situation in Italy got the Truman administration's attention, as did analogously unfolding events in France.[24] U.S. Ambassador Jefferson Caffery warned from Paris that the "financial, economic and food crisis . . . has a most depressing effect on French morale." The French people were "beginning to feel that . . . since democracy in France does not appear to produce results, some form of authoritarian government is needed . . . [either] a dictatorship by the Communist Party or an authoritarian regime under [Charles] de Gaulle." In 1946, Maurice Thorez's Communist Party (PCF) took 28 percent of the votes to become the majority party. Only the refusal by other parties to form a coalition prevented Thorez from taking power. The Communist view, according to the ambassador, was that the

> international situation is favorable to . . . the interests of the Soviet Union [and] while [Moscow] is not prepared for war and its military preparations will not be completed for a number of years . . . the necessity to *gain time* . . . while endeavoring to maintain and consolidate positions already

required [is needed]. The policy and tactics of the French Communist Party must follow *closely in line with this perspective.*

The U.S. ambassador to Moscow, Walter Bedell Smith, considered this assessment of Soviet involvement the "most accurate revealing exposé of present Soviet tactics not only in France but throughout the rest of Europe." Communist parties in Europe were responding to Moscow's pulling of the strings.[25]

These were the economic and political realities that Marshall faced as he departed for Europe in March 1947. He first held talks in Paris and Berlin, where he witnessed the social gloom firsthand.[26] The experience left a deep impression on him, but nothing could have prepared him for the indifference that the Soviets displayed toward Europe's suffering. When paired with Soviet support for European communist parties in Germany, France, Italy, and elsewhere, the agenda became clear. While communist insurgents in Greece actively sought to overthrow the government, Moscow's aim in other Western European countries was to push the countries toward economic collapse, to let people, as Marshall later recalled, live like animals, thereby paving the way for local communist parties.[27]

The CFM encounters with Soviet negotiators confirmed the Soviet unwillingness to abide by the Potsdam Agreement and UN principles. As Marshall explained to French foreign minister Georges Bidault, he had arrived with the belief that the best guarantee for success was an "agreement between the Four Powers on a sound basis." Such a basis, he believed, was one that advanced Europe economically and politically and made the continent democratically functional once again. To Marshall this also meant a "global solution" that would "increase the prestige of the U.N." But as he accurately insisted, "the U.N. is a very young child, without tradition, without experience. . . . We must therefore in the immediate future take intermediary measures. The Four Power treaty is . . . in this respect, essential." The expectation was that until the United Nations was strong enough, the big powers needed to handle the urgent problems of recovery and reconstruction. Addressing his peers on March 14, Marshall criticized the Soviet refusal to collaborate toward a democratic Germany. A unified Germany, Marshall insisted, was critical to European security and freedom. Germans made up 65 million of Europe's 350 million people, and as Marshall made clear, the United States "wants one Germany because it wants a Europe which is not divided against itself."[28] Despite Marshall's repeated and similar arguments throughout the remaining four weeks of the conference, there would be no advances in this regard. Apathetic to Germans' suffering, Moscow refused. Soviet policy was to strengthen the communists in its zone while seeking to undermine German recovery.

As president, Roosevelt had firmly believed that the personal relationship he established with his counterparts in Moscow and London would lead to the establishment of an American-inspired "one world" order. Roosevelt's intentions were good, but Stalin's behavior during meetings with Marshall made it clear that the Soviet leader had conned Roosevelt much the way that he was now trying to deceive Marshall. Like Hitler in the 1930s, Stalin continuously provided hints of cooperation along the way on such issues as Germany and nuclear weapons. The reality was that the Soviet premier was willing to collaborate as long as Moscow needed American aid; however, he would cede none of his own objectives.

These were the conclusions that Marshall reached during the CFM and relayed via radio to the American people on April 28 after his return home. Marshall's address spelled out the dire realities in postwar Europe. Bottlenecks in every sector, particularly in coal and energy production, slowed every aspect of modern life. The result, Marshall warned American listeners, would be "deteriorating economic life in Germany and Europe and inevitable emergence of dictatorship and strife." Americans could brook no delay. The reaction back in the United States was one of overwhelming support. "It must be plain to anybody but a dullard," the *Washington Post* insisted, "that noncooperation is Russian policy." Moscow's purpose was to drive the United States out of Europe and subsequently "let it drift into dissolution." For all its concerns, the paper took some comfort from the leader at the helm of U.S. diplomacy. Marshall's address proved that "he carried into the peace not a war mind but a constructive mind. And he knows what he is doing—which as Aristotle put it, will strengthen the energy of his thought at action."[29] Although only the most astute observers at the time took notice, a critical bureaucratic change was taking place inside the State Department, and it would provide Marshall and the subsequent European Recovery Program with intellectual force and piercing clarity to match the situation. The very day Marshall departed Moscow, the reporter James Reston explained to *New York Times* readers that going forward, the secretary of state would be backed by "a new policy planning staff" likely to be headed by "the ablest student of the Soviet Union in the Government," George Frost Kennan. Bohlen, Marshall's interpreter on the Moscow trip, would support Kennan, and the objective of the Policy Planning Staff's would be "long-range plans" developed by an elite group of "a few highly skilled men, free of all obligation for daily decisions on policy." Reston predicted that their first task would be "to analyze the tactics of the Soviet Union and the other powers at the Moscow Conference." It was from this analysis that the principal Cold War doctrine of communist containment became policy.[30]

In the weeks following Marshall's homecoming, a consensus developed inside and outside of the government that confirmed his assessment of Soviet intentions and confirmed the urgent need for European aid. In the reporter Walter Lippmann's view, Americans could afford no illusions. Neither the World Bank nor the American banking community could meet "the deficit of the western European countries." To loan money was no alternative. The sums needed surpassed what Europeans would ever be able to pay back and would merely place Europeans "on the dole." Instead, the money should be an investment "in peace and prosperity." It may need "a different name," but the "revival" of "lend-lease" was necessary.[31] Responding to a speech that Dean Acheson gave in Mississippi, Lippmann insisted that by 1948 Europe would run out of ways to pay for essential commodities. The inevitable political, economic, and humanitarian consequences, he insisted, made it critical that the administration "address itself to the adult and informed population of the United States, and to assume that the American people would rather hear the truth . . . and that they will do their duty when they are presented with a well prepared plan for discharging their duty."[32]

Lippmann's argument about Lend-Lease was pertinent. Winston Churchill may once have called the Lend-Lease program the "most unsordid act," but it was nothing of the kind. It may have appeared generous because Americans were not looking for repayment in money or goods, but the demand for policy concessions told a different story. Lend-Lease had been the first program designed to force America's allies to sign on to an American-organized world order. The Marshall Plan would do something similar. As early as March, Undersecretary of State for Economic Affairs William Clayton, explained to Marshall that the "United States must take up world leadership and quickly to avert world disaster." Clayton reiterated this position in May after returning from a visit to Europe. He found the situation there to be "steadily deteriorating. . . . Millions of people in the cities are slowly starving." In terms of output, productivity, and standard of living, Europe operated far below prewar levels. He warned of revolutions. Echoing Lippmann's suggestion of full public disclosure, Clayton insisted that "if the American people are taken in to the complete confidence of the Administration and told all the facts and only if a sound and workable plan is presented," they would support the endeavor. Clayton wanted the Europeans to come up with a plan, but he was defiantly clear that the *United States must run this show.*" In his view, no one else could.[33]

It was from this platform at Harvard University that George C. Marshall in June 1947 delivered the most famous speech ever given by a secretary of state. Authored largely by Charles Bohlen, it was the crystallization of Marshall's thoughts as they had built since the Princeton address in February.[34] It is commonly claimed that Marshall proposed the ERP in his Harvard speech, but that assessment is an exaggeration. No one knew what it would cost, how long Europeans would need aid, or how to execute such an aid program. So few had been taken into his confidence that no preparations or research had been possible. In blunt terms, there was no Marshall Plan when the secretary took the podium at Harvard, only a vision.

In content and context, however, Marshall's speech was a tour de force. He spoke of desolation, starvation, political and economic instability, and of the United States:

> It is logical that the United States should do whatever it is able to do to assist in the return of normal economic health in the world, without which there can be no political stability and no assured peace. Our policy is directed not against any country or doctrine but against hunger, poverty, desperation and chaos. Its purpose should be the revival of a working economy in the world so as to permit the emergence of political and social conditions in which free institutions can exist. Such assistance, I am convinced, must not be on a piece meal basis as various crises develop. Any assistance that this Government may render in the future should provide a cure rather than a mere palliative. Any government that is willing to assist in the task of recovery will find full cooperation. . . . Any government which maneuvers to block the recovery of other countries cannot expect help from us.

Marshall pledged American support, but echoing Clayton he insisted that the Europeans collectively had to come to an agreement on how such a program might operate and to clarify and specify their exact needs. Only then would Americans set demands.

Marshall's speech has become legendary, but ironically enough, nothing at the time seemed to justify its reputation. The State Department had not publicized any announcement of a major policy shift, and the presence of the press was negligible. If Americans largely overlooked it, however, Europeans did not. Within days, British and French diplomats met, and they soon extended invitations to other European governments to participate in further talks. Among the invitees to Paris was the Soviet Union. It could be no other way. Marshall had made clear that support would be forthcoming to any nation willing to collaborate on the issue of continent-wide recovery. Behind closed doors, however, Kennan and Bohlen had already explained to Marshall that Moscow's response would mirror its decision to pull out of Bretton Woods. The demands for collaboration with noncommunist Europe, the inevitable insistence that to decipher the precise need for aid Moscow would need to open its books, and the extent to which appearing to need an American handout would undermine Moscow's role as the leader of an alternative modernity model made participation improbable. The prediction proved accurate. Although Stalin sent Foreign Minister Vyacheslav Molotov and eighty advisers to the talks in Paris, the purpose was disruption, not collaboration. When Molotov insisted that each nation determine its needs and work bilaterally with the Americans, Bevin and Bidault shot it down, insisting that all Europe, including Germany, be treated as a single unit. In response, Molotov stormed out of the conference and mandated that the Communist governments in Eastern Europe—almost all of which were subservient to the Soviet Union—refrain from participation. When Poland and Czechoslovakia nonetheless sought participation, Moscow humiliated both nations' leaders and forced them to rescind participation. As the Czechoslovakian foreign minister Jan Masaryk recalled his dressing down in the Kremlin, "I went to Moscow as the Foreign Minister of an independent sovereign state. I returned as a lackey of the Soviet Government."[35]

To the Soviets, Marshall's proposal was either an imperialistic scheme or perhaps a reflection of underlying economic problems in the United States. The Soviet ambassador to Washington, Nikolai Novikov, considered it an indication of Washington's desire to use Western Europe as a "tool of U.S. policy," while the Soviet ambassador to the United Nations, Andrei Vyshinski, considered the ERP an attempt to divide Europe into two camps. Any American benevolent rhetoric was simply "demagogic propaganda serving as a smokescreen."[36] The Soviets were wrong in believing that the Marshall Plan was a sign of weaknesses in the American economy. They were right, however, to assume that the plan entailed an American ultimatum. Either the Soviets participate in the "one world" order on an equal basis with other European powers or become responsible for dividing Europe. Stalin's rejection of participation essentially cemented the division of Europe.[37]

The irony was that Marshall always considered the United States a benevolent nation whose intentions other states frequently misunderstood. While the ERP may have sought to force Europeans into a collaborative system with the Americans, it was hardly imperialism. The so-called Cold War revisionists have long disagreed with Marshall's assessment. Scholars such as William Appleman Williams and Carolyn Eisenberg viewed Moscow's actions as natural. In Eisenberg's view, "the formal steps that led to the partition of Germany [and thus of Europe] were initiated by the United States and Britain in violation of the quadripartite framework established at Yalta and Potsdam."[38] Americans surely wanted influence, but if it was an empire, it was, as one scholar insisted, "an empire by invitation."[39]

In response to Moscow's reaction in Paris, Ambassador Bedell Smith summed up the situation from Moscow like this: "The lines are drawn. Our response is awaited. I do not need to point out to the Dept. the repercussions of a failure to meet the Soviet challenge in terms of control of Europe, but of the impact which such a failure would have in the Middle and Far East and throughout the colonial world."[40] As Marshall had foreseen months before, the solution was to go it alone. Bohlen captured the new reality succinctly by the end of August. The United States now faced, he insisted, a "condition in the world which is at direct variance with the assumptions upon which, during and directly after the war, major United States polices were predicated. Instead of unity among the great powers . . . after the war, there is complete disunity between the Soviet Union and the satellites on one side and the rest of the world on the other." There were, he insisted, "in short, two worlds instead of one." Bohlen did not believe that the United States should give up on its "one world" dream, but Washington could not deal with the world as Americans would like it to be but had to deal with the world as it actually was.[41]

Over the summer and fall, officials of the Truman administration launched an extensive lobbying campaign on behalf of the ERP. Not only did they need to persuade Congress to fund the money, they also needed an entirely new bureaucratic infrastructure to operate the program. In 1947, no government agency possessed the skills or resources to run an operation on this scale.[42] Europeans pitched in impressively too. Soon sixteen European nations created the Committee of European Economic Cooperation (CEEC) to prepare the collective request to Washington. While all European governments worried about some loss of sovereignty, Western governments accepted the reality of the new order. Britain was the principal exception. Likely inspired by imperial haughtiness as well as geographical isolation, Bevin hoped that London could assume an independent position as a go-between for Washington and the Continent. Americans dismissed this out of hand. Although Britain's sense of self-importance would resurface on several occasions in the years that followed, the days of European supremacy were over. As the chair of Britain's Defence Research Policy Committee, Sir Henry Tizard, tersely concluded, "We persist in regarding ourselves a Great Power capable of everything and only temporarily handicapped by economic difficulties. We are not a Great Power and never will be again."[43]

By November, the administration pushed through the first $500 million of emergency funding. Although the entire program ran counter to the persuasion of the Republican Party's old guard, opposition steadily dwindled. The many congressional representatives from both parties who visited Europe during the fall of 1947 found it particularly difficult to stand against the ERP. They returned home shocked by what they saw. Congressman Richard Nixon (R-Calif.) considered it "among the most sobering experiences of my life. . . . We found families huddled in the debris of buildings and in bunkers. There was a critical shortage of food, and thin-faced, half-dressed children approached us not to beg, but to sell their fathers' war medals or to trade them for something to eat."[44] Yet, because opposition to foreign aid found much of its support in the upper echelons of the GOP, historians often have overestimated its actual ability to challenge the Marshall Plan. The reality is that a more progressive and internationally minded wing had emerged. Most of the credit has gone to Senator Arthur Vandenberg (R-Mich.), but in many respects Sen. Henry Cabot Lodge Jr. (R-Mass.) was the most important figure. Between November and February, Lodge, whose grandfather had led the charge against Wilson's League of Nations, became the principal Republican advocate for the Marshall Plan and the Truman Doctrine—just as he later would be for NATO. When the GOP leadership, headed by Sen. Robert Taft (R-Ohio), attempted to undermine the Truman administration's ideological approach by insisting that the plan ought to be "limited to specific countries for specific purposes," Lodge led the fight against his own party.[45] Any final opposition evaporated in February 1948 when, in the midst of congressional ERP hearings, Soviet-backed Communists ousted the semiautonomous government in Czechoslovakia. The event, which led to Foreign Minister Masaryk's death by either suicide or murder, enhanced

Europe's collective fear of the Communist threat and pushed all nations closer to the United States.[46] By mid-March, the Senate and the House overwhelmingly approved the Marshall Plan. On April 3, Harry Truman signed the Economic Cooperation Act of the Foreign Assistance Act into law, thereby formally creating the ERP. Within two weeks, the European foreign ministers added their final approval of the ERP. The agreement admitted Germany to the pool of recipient nations, consequently underlining the determination to find a comprehensive solution for Western Europe.

To run the Marshall Plan, the U.S. government created the nonpartisan Economic Cooperation Administration (ECA) to be headed by American automobile executive Paul Hoffman. In its first year of a projected four-year program, the ECA would deliver $4 billion. In total, it would bring close to $13 billion in aid to Western Europe.[47] The original intent had been for considerable amounts of aid to be in the form of loans, but as it became clear that this would weaken European economies further, the Marshall Plan increasingly began arriving in the form of grants. Operating on both sides of the Atlantic, the ECA navigated political and public debates at home while a staff of six hundred, led by the seasoned diplomat Averell Harriman, ran its European offices. A European counterpart, the Organization of European Economic Cooperation (OEEC), worked to maintain European unity and to guarantee Marshall's demand of a collaborative, liberalized continent. This centralized structure proved vital. The OEEC recommended amounts and types of assistance to countries and forced a level of cooperation on the participating states that helped shape a common Western cause. In light of the levels of hunger and desolation, there was a natural desire among European politicians to seek quick remedies to solve immediate problems, but the ECA largely ensured that the most important programs received preference. In places such as Italy, however, where the threat of national communism remained strong throughout 1948, the government had more leeway to utilize resources for the public's immediate need. Generally, however, the ECA targeted reconstruction projects with long-term significance. Electrical plants, agriculture, energy, housing projects, and infrastructure that could improve living conditions in the long term received more support than luxury goods and short-term food supplies. Hoffman's agency also invited European business owners to receive training in the United States in such areas as industrial and agricultural productivity, public administration, tourism, infrastructure, and communication. The creation of the West, in that sense, received a boost not

Secretary of State Dean Acheson (*left*) and Director of the Economic Cooperation Administration Paul Hoffman (*center*) present Gen. George C. Marshall (*right*) with a book detailing the achievements of the Marshall Plan at the celebration of the second anniversary of the establishment of the ECA, held at the Hotel Statler in Washington, D.C. April 3, 1950. Courtesy George C. Marshall Library, Lexington, Va.

simply from shared liberal ideals but from the establishment of shared business and administrative methods.

Politically and economically, the Marshall Plan achieved remarkable results. In quick succession, communist parties lost influence. They were irrelevant in Western European politics by the end of the decade. Only in the eastern zone in Germany, including the Soviet sector of Berlin, did Moscow retain control. In western Germany, U.S. influence led to the unification of the original French, British, and American zones by 1948. That spring, the Western powers met in London and created a new currency for western Germany while also authorizing German delegates to draft a constitution for an independent political state. As had always been the intention, and in stark contrast to the interwar era, Germany was to be welcomed back into the system of states.

In June 1948, Stalin responded by blockading all access points to West Berlin. This draconian step, made possible by the city's location within the Soviet-controlled zone, isolated 2.2 million residents and deprived them of access to resources, including food, medication, and fuel. Critics of American foreign policy insisted that Stalin merely wanted to reopen negotiations over Germany. Marshall disagreed. While the Potsdam Agreement did call for the occupying powers to collaborate on Germany's future, it did not provide anyone veto power. As Marshall wrote a friend in August, Americans had "wrestled for three years in an effort to bring Russia to some form of agreement with respect to Germany and we could be criticized much more justly for our delay in acting as we did at the London Conference than for the manner of our actions."[48] The situation in Berlin also highlighted the significance of ideology. For example, Lucius Clay acknowledged that while there was "no practicality in maintaining our position in Berlin. . . . We are convinced that our remaining in Berlin is essential to our prestige in Germany and in Europe. Whether for good or bad, it has become a symbol of American intent."[49] Within weeks, the United States and the British launched an airlift that for the next eleven months would supply the quarantined city. The Soviet blockade proved Marshall's concerns from April 1947 correct: Moscow was willing to let Western Europeans starve to achieve its political goals.

After Truman's election victory in 1948, Dean Acheson replaced George Marshall as head of the State Department. By then, the Marshall Plan was running smoothly. It would officially come an end on December 31, 1951. The combined economic and ideological effort had dramatically changed Europe. Aggregate industrial production among recipient countries stood at 41 percent above 1938 levels. Total gross national product rose 25 percent. Steel production and oil-refining volume exceeded 1947 expectations. The American demand for lower trade barriers in Europe as a way of increasing inter-European trade led to the removal of up to 75 percent of import restrictions.[50]

In recent years, several historians have questioned any causation between the Marshall Plan and these impressive numbers. Alan Milward, for example, has claimed that recovery was under way before the arrival of ERP support and that the actual impact of Marshall Plan dollars was negligible.[51] Economically Milward's numbers make sense, but he assumes a world in which all else was equal. The Marshall Plan gave Europeans the political confidence to develop independently of the Soviet Union, and it enabled them to make difficult economic choices about government investment. The testimony from recipients tells the story. Bevin famously called it "a life line to sinking men," an act that "brought hope where there was none," while Franz Blücher, vice chancellor of West Germany, considered it "the first fact by which Germany was reintroduced into the family of nations. . . . Without the Marshall Plan we wouldn't have been able to survive."[52] Richard Bissel, the last administrator of the ECA, perhaps captured the impact most succinctly shortly after the ERP ended. "When future historians look back upon the achievements of the Marshall Plan," he asserted, "I believe they will see in it the charge that blasted the first substantial cracks in the centuries-old walls of European nationalism—walls that once destroyed will clear the way for the building of a unified, prosperous, and, above all, peaceful continent."[53] After three decades of war and economic hardship, optimism returned to the American-sponsored half of Europe. Cooperation and unity became the new norm in a region historically dominated by political, economic, and military conflict.

Perhaps the Marshall Plan's most impressive achievement was how it made Western Europe into the political entity now recognizable as the European Union. Though it took statesmen on both sides of the Atlantic to succeed, it was Washington's insistence on ERP cooperation that made this development possible. Surprisingly, it was in France where the formal initiative originated. In 1919 and again in 1945, fears about German recovery dominated French foreign policy. By 1947, however, such insightful officials as Jean Monnet and Robert Schuman, accepting the end of French power, came to acknowledge that postwar recovery demanded continent-wide collaboration. As Monnet saw it shortly after Marshall's Harvard speech, "To tackle the present situation, to face the dangers that threaten us, and to match the American effort, the countries of Western Europe must turn their national efforts into a truly European effort. This will be possible only through a *federation* of the West."[54] This idea found support in Washington and soon across several European capitals. The years that followed saw the creation not only of the OEEC but also of the Council of Europe with its emphasis on human rights and democracy. By 1950, Schuman along with German chancellor Konrad Adenauer proposed the first formal economic unification of the West. Inspired by the Marshall Plan, a new Europe was born. The timing of what eventually became the European Coal and Steel Community proved fortunate. The outbreak of the Korean War in June 1950, an event that also brought Marshall back into the Truman administration as sec-retary of defense, caused Washington to shift its attention from reconstruction toward security policy. By then the European Recovery Program, well ahead of schedule, was already winding down. Black markets were largely limited, and production and trade were beginning to flourish. In 1949, the German problem had been solved by the creation of the Federal Republic in the west, while the Soviet zone became a German Communist state. The western half of the country that had largely been the cause of the emerging postwar conflict took particularly good advantage of ERP support. Over the next few decades, the German *Wirtschafttswunder* made the German economy the strongest in Europe. Yet, rather than emerging as a new threat to continental security, it became the engine of the integrated European project.

American officials supported this European integration from the start. In May 1947, Clayton suggested European recovery and unity necessitated a federation closely tied to the United States. It was an argument that always found plenty of support in the American media too. Those who opposed these commitments largely lost legitimacy because of the Marshall Plan. Taft, who had been the strongest opponent of a permanent, open-ended American ideological commitment and whose seniority in the party made him a natural candidate for the Republican presidential nomination in 1952, found himself handily defeated by Dwight Eisenhower. Running Eisenhower's presidential campaign, Lodge again led the way for the new Republican Party.[55]

The 1949 formulation of the North Atlantic Treaty illustrated that the American commitment to Europe only strengthened with European integration. While there is no doubt that the Soviet threat expedited the Truman Doctrine, ERP, and NATO, it is a mistake to interpret these developments exclusively through a post–World War II prism. These developments, as well as the later European institutional additions that emerged as the Treaty of Rome, the European Community, and then the European Union, were entirely consistent with the American policies originally developed between 1941 and 1945. Two worlds instead of one perhaps, but the western half very much fit what Franklin D. Roosevelt's people had envisioned. This development, as the historian William Hitchcock accurately assesses, created what observers in common parlance now simply refer to as "the West"—a concept basic in name but one that is today understood to mean something extraordinarily specific: "A community of ideas, economic links, and security," as well as a shared set of values and principles stretching from Western Europe to North America.

In the larger context of the Cold War, perhaps the Marshall Plan's greatest legacy was the manner in which it hermetically sealed off Western Europe from Soviet influence. But if the firm American commitment to Western Europe effectively ended the U.S.-Soviet conflict on the continent, it also indirectly cast a darker shadow over U.S. foreign policy beyond the European continent. The two superpowers, driven as they were by ideological inclinations, inevitably shifted the battleground somewhere else. It was ironic that Washington, which had originally promoted the dismantlement of European empires during the war, now found it necessary to engage in the very areas in Africa, Southeast Asia, and elsewhere, from which its alliance partners withdrew. Even so, the American ambition to engage the developing world was unsurprising. After all, the "one world" vision was at heart a quest to reform the world according to American values. The Marshall Plan only seemed to confirm the prospects of such an endeavor. Even before the ERP was one year old, President Truman proposed to expand the modernization and development model well beyond European borders. His Point Four Program became the first attempt to create an American aid program to uplift the developing world. Although this achieved only modest success, by the 1950s and 1960s, modernization theorists within the nation's major universities, whose influence soon stretched directly to the White House, lobbied for American programs not only to aid the developing world, but to uplift and Westernize it. The intentions were good, but Marshall Plan logic failed miserably in the decolonized world, which lacked a history of Western political and economic thinking. Cultures and religions were at odds with Western methods and ideas, and a genuine and often well-founded suspicion of Western intentions doomed many of these projects. So did the pitiful amounts of money that policy makers by then proved willing to commit to development endeavors. Soon, the emphasis on security overshadowed the American determination to aid, most catastrophically in Vietnam.[56]

One might have expected that the Marshall Plan's inspiration for modernization theories—and by indirect extension, the war in Vietnam—might have scarred its reputation. But nothing of the sort happened. If anything, those failed policies have enhanced the ERP's reputation because it allows Americans to remember the "good" Cold War—the one that existed before Vietnam. There are, of course, worthy reasons for admiration. Not only did the Marshall Plan prove overwhelmingly successful in containing Soviet aspirations, Americans could clearly—and in stark contrast to Vietnam—claim the moral high ground in the battle for Europe. Even so, the well-deserved lionization of the Marshall Plan to the plateau of myth had other consequences. For decades now, Americans and foreigners have called for similar Marshall Plans to solve local, national, regional, and global problems. This belief gained particular steam after the collapse of communism in the 1980s and 1990s, when many advocated for a plan for Eastern Europe akin to the one that had saved Western Europe four decades earlier. From the perspective of the present, with Russia again inserting itself in Western elections and politics, it is hard to argue that Westernizing Eastern Europe would not have been worth a more sustained attempt. In the 1990s, however, none of the urgency of the 1940s appeared, nor did the United States possess public officials with the kind of foresight and acumen of Marshall's day. More importantly, there is perhaps little reason to believe that Eastern Europe, given its historical lack of Western Enlightenment influence and democratic principles, would have fared much better than the developing world did in the 1960s and 1970s.

The twenty-first century has not dimmed the calls for more "Marshall Plans" for Africa, Detroit, or the entire developing world. Its very name, Hitchcock correctly asserts, has attained a "talismanic quality."[57] After all, the Marshall Plan immortalized its namesake to such an extent that few nonspecialists currently recall that, as army chief of staff, Marshall was essential to U.S. military planning in advance of D-Day and the man that Franklin D. Roosevelt valued above all. For a nation that venerates World War II—the Good War—to the extent that Americans do, perhaps there can be no greater compliment to the legacy of Marshall's plan.

NOTES

1. John W. Ball, "Two Moscow Reports Prepared by Marshall after Fast Trip Home," *Washington Post*, April 27, 1947; Drew Middleton, "Western Leaders Express Optimism on Leaving Russia," *New York Times*, April 25, 1947.

2. Moscow Meeting of the Council of Foreign Ministers, March 10–April 24, 1947, address by the Secretary of State, *Department of State Bulletin* (May 11, 1947): 919–24.

3. William I. Hitchcock, "The Marshall Plan and the Creation of the West," in Melvyn P. Leffler and Odd Arne Westad, eds., *The Cambridge History of the Cold War*, vol. 1: *Origins* (Cambridge: Cambridge University Press, 2010), 154–74; Michael Holm, *The Marshall Plan: A New Deal for Europe* (London: Routledge, 2017), xxviii–xxix.

4. George C. Marshall, speech at Princeton University, February 22, 1947, in Larry I. Bland, Mark A. Stoler, Sharon Ritenour Stevens, and Daniel D. Holt, eds., *The Papers of George Catlett Marshall*, vol. 6: *"The Whole World Hangs in the Balance," January 8, 1947–September 30, 1949* (Baltimore: Johns Hopkins University Press, 2013) (hereafter cited as *Papers of George Marshall*, 6), 47–50.

5. Clarence K. Streit, *Union Now: A Proposal for a Federal Union of the Democracies of the North Atlantic* (New York: Harper Brothers, 1939); Emery Reeves, *The Anatomy of Peace* (New York: Harper Brothers, 1939).

6. For an extensive discussion of this emerging global role, see Holm, *Marshall Plan*, 7–23.

7. Harold G. Moulton, foreword to Arthur Chester Millspaugh, *Peace Plans and American Choices: The Pros and Cons of World Order* (Washington, D.C.: Brookings Institution, 1942), v–vi; emphasis in original.

8. On ideology and the early Republic, see Gordon S. Wood, *The Idea of America: Reflections on the Birth of the United States* (New York: Penguin, 2011); Michael Holm, "All Paine: The American Mind and the Creation of the League of Nations and the U.N.," in Sam Edwards and Marcus Morris, eds., *The Legacy of Thomas Paine in the Transatlantic World* (London: Routledge, 2018), 51–67.

9. Wendell L. Willkie, *One World* (New York: Simon & Schuster, 1943).

10. *Congressional Record*, 78th Cong., 2nd sess., Senate, March 7, 1944, 2299–2300.

11. John J. McCloy to the president, April 26, 1945, printed in Holm, *Marshall Plan*, 136–37; report of Samuel I. Rosenman to the president, "Civilian Supplies for the Liberated Areas of Northwest Europe," *Department of State Bulletin*, May 6, 1945, 860–62.

12. William I. Hitchcock, *The Bitter Road to Freedom: The Human Cost of Victory in World War II Europe* (New York: Simon & Schuster, 2009), 215–48.

13. Arnold A. Offner, *Another Such Victory: President Truman and the Cold War, 1945–1953* (Stanford, Calif.: Stanford University Press, 2002); Frank Costigliola, *Roosevelt's Lost Alliances: How Personal Politics Helped Start the Cold War* (Princeton, N.J.: Princeton University Press, 2011).

14. Harold James and Marzenna James, "The Origins of the Cold War: Some New Documents," *Historical Journal* 37, no. 3 (September 1994): 615–22.

15. Jean Edward Smith, *Lucius D. Clay* (New York: Henry Holt, 1980), 352–53, 357–58, 379, 384–89.

16. James Byrnes, "Restatement of U.S. Policy towards Germany, Stuttgart," September 6, 1946, *Department of State Bulletin*, September 15, 1946, 496–501.

17. Joseph Alsop and Stewart Alsop, "Crossed Fingers toward Russia," *Washington Post*, December 15, 1946.

18. Holm, *Marshall Plan*, 36–37.

19. "Big Power Harmony: The Council and the Greek Issue," *Washington Post*, December 21, 1946.

20. Oral History Interview with Mark F. Ethridge, Oral History Collection, Harry S. Truman Library (hereafter cited as HSTL); Mark F. Ethridge to the Secretary of State, February 17, 1947, Department of State, Office of the Historian, *Foreign Relations of the United States, 1947*, vol. 5: *The Near East and Africa* (Washington, D.C.: Government Printing Office, 1972), 820–21 (hereafter cited as *FRUS*, followed by year and volume).

21. Harry S. Truman, Special Message to the Congress on Greece and Turkey: The Truman Doctrine, *Public Papers of the President, Harry S. Truman, 1947* (Washington, D.C.: Government Printing Office, 1964), 176–80.

22. Charles E. Bohlen, *Witness to History, 1929–1969* (New York: W. W. Norton, 1973), 261. For Marshall's suggested changes, see Marshall to Dean G. Acheson, no. 1013, March 7, 1947, in *Papers of George Marshall*, 6:67–68.

23. Marshall, speech at Princeton, 49; Marshall, speech to the American Red Cross, March 2, 1947, in *Papers of George Marshall*, 6:58–59.

24. Robert Gellately, *Stalin's Curse: Battling for Communism in War and Cold War* (New York: Alfred A. Knopf, 2013), 285–88; Kaeten Mistry, *The United States, Italy and the Origins of the Cold War: Waging Political Warfare, 1945–1950* (Cambridge: Cambridge University Press, 2014), 48–58.

25. Jefferson Caffery to the Secretary of State, October 29, 1946, in *FRUS, 1946*, 5:468–470; "The Tactics of the French Communist Party According to a Source Maintaining Close Contacts with Important Communists," November 23, 1946, in *FRUS, 1946*, 5:417–77 (emphasis in original); Smith to the Secretary of State, December 20, 1946, in *FRUS, 1946*, 5:478–79.

26. For Marshall's meetings, see *Papers of George Marshall*, 6:63–66.

27. Marshall's reflections printed in Holm, *Marshall Plan*, 166–68.

28. "Memorandum of Conversation between Monsieur Georges Bidault and General Marshall," March 13, 1947, in *Papers of George Marshall*, 6:73–77; "Statement on Reconstruction of Germany on a Democratic Basis," March 14, 1947, in *Papers of George Marshall*, 6:77–79; "Statement to the Eighteenth Meeting of the Council of Foreign Ministers," March 31, 1947, in *Papers of George Marshall*, 6:86–89.

29. "Marshall's Report," *Washington Post*, April 29, 1947.

30. James Reston, "New Policy Staff Will Aid Marshall Frame His Plans," *New York Times*, April 25, 1947; "Policy with Respect to American Aid to Western Europe: Views of the Policy Planning Staff," in *FRUS, 1947*, 3:223–30; John Lewis Gaddis, *George F. Kennan: An American Life* (New York: Penguin, 2011), 265–70.

31. Walter Lippmann, "Marshall and Dulles," *Washington Post*, May 1, 1947.

32. Walter Lippmann, "On Borrowed Time," *Washington Post*, May 10, 1947.

33. William Clayton, "The European Crisis," printed in Holm, *Marshall Plan*, 143–45.

34. Marshall's Harvard speech, printed in Holm, *Marshall Plan*, 146–48; Bohlen, *Witness to History*, 263–64.

35. Holm, *Marshall Plan*, 56–57; Gellately, *Stalin's Curse*, 308–12.

36. United Nations, "Official Records of the General Assembly, Second Session, Plenary Meetings," September 18, 1947, 81–106; Holm, *Marshall Plan*, 53–54, 60.

37. Kennan, *Memoirs, 1925–1950* (Boston: Little, Brown, 1967), 342; Bohlen, *Witness to History*, 264; "Summary of Discussion on Problems of Relief, Rehabilitation, and Reconstruction of Europe," May 29, 1947, in *FRUS, 1947*, 3:234–36.

38. William Appleman Williams, *The Tragedy of American Diplomacy* (New York: W. W. Norton, 1972), 268–72; Carolyn Eisenberg, "Revisiting the Division of Germany," March 1, 2013, http://www.newleftproject.org/index.php/site/article_comments/revisiting_the_division_of_germany.

39. Geir Lundestad, "Empire by Invitation? The United States and Western Europe, 1945–1952," *Journal of Peace Research* 23, no. 3 (September 1986): 263–77.

40. Smith to the Secretary of State, July 11, 1947, in *FRUS, 1947*, 3:327.

41. Memorandum by the Consular of the Department of State (Bohlen), August 30, 1947, in *FRUS, 1947*, 1:763–65.

42. Michael Wala, "Selling the Marshall Plan at Home: The Committee for the Marshall Plan to Aid European Recovery," *Diplomatic History* 10, no. 3 (July 1986): 247–65.

43. For an excellent assessment of this British sense of self-importance, see Derek Leebaert, *Grand Improvisation: America Confronts the British Superpower, 1945–1957* (New York: Farrar, Straus and Giroux, 2018); and Robert Pearce, *Attlee* (London: Routledge, 1997), 166.

44. Richard M. Nixon, *Leaders: Profiles and Reminiscences of Men Who Have Shaped the Modern World* (New York: Warner, 1982), 136–37.

45. On Vandenberg see Hendrik Meijer, *Arthur Vandenberg: The Man in the Middle of the American Century* (Chicago: University of Chicago Press, 2017), 300–312; Ben Steil, *The Marshall Plan: Dawn of the Cold War* (New York: Simon & Schuster, 2018), 192–97; and Holm, *Marshall Plan*, 46–47, 65–72.

46. Dorothy Thompson, "Jan Masaryk Found One Answer," *Life*, March 22, 1948.

47. Adjusted for inflation, the equivalent amount for 2018 would be approximately $135 billion. The United States' total foreign aid budget in 2018 stood at approximately $50 billion.

48. Marshall to Gen. Charles G. Dawes, August 3, 1948, in *Papers of George Marshall*, 6:515.

49. Jean E. Smith, ed., *The Papers of General Lucius D. Clay: Germany, 1945–1949* (Bloomington: Indiana University Press, 1974), 2:677.

50. For a good analysis of the ERP's economic impact, see John Killick, *The United States and European Reconstruction, 1945–1960* (London: Routledge, 2000).

51. Alan S. Milward, *The Reconstruction of Western Europe, 1945–1951* (London: Methuen, 1984), and his review of the scholarly debate on this issue, "Was the Marshall Plan Necessary?" *Diplomatic History* 13, no. 2 (1989): 231–52.

52. Holm, *Marshall Plan*, xvii.

53. "Achievements of the Marshall Plan," *Department of State Bulletin*, January 14, 1952, 43–45.

54. Jean Monnet, *Memoirs* (New York: Doubleday, 1978), 272–73.

55. Walter Lippmann, "U.S. Reasons for European Union," *Washington Post*, May 17, 1947; Michael Holm, "Also Present at the Creation: Henry Cabot Lodge Jr. and the Coming of the Cold War," *Journal of the Historical Society* 10, no. 2 (June 2010): 203–29.

56. Andrew David and Michael Holm, "The Kennedy Administration and the Battle over Foreign Aid: The Untold Story of the Clay Committee," *Diplomacy and Statecraft* 27, no. 1 (March 2016): 65–92.

57. Hitchcock, "Marshall Plan," 154.

7
AN ALLIANCE BY DEFAULT
Marshall and the North Atlantic Treaty

On June 5, 1947, Secretary of State George C. Marshall accepted an honorary degree at Harvard University. In his acceptance speech, Marshall proposed what would become the European Recovery Program (ERP), colloquially known as the Marshall Plan, which helped propel Western Europe's economic and psychological recovery from the devastation of World War II, shored up the West's defenses against the Communist threat, and bound together a transatlantic alliance that still stands, even some thirty years after the end of the Cold War. In streamlined histories of the Cold War, the Marshall Plan, following closely on President Harry Truman's March 1947 request for aid for Turkey and Greece, eventually known as the Truman Doctrine, was appears but one step toward the North Atlantic alliance, which formed in April 1949. Yet Marshall and his newly appointed chief strategist, George F. Kennan, had a different design in mind: a closely joined economic and political bloc, not a military alliance. Kennan's vision of containment, the American Cold War policy objective followed by

The official flag of the Allied Atlantic Command, North Atlantic Treaty Organization. April 7, 1952. U.S. Navy. Courtesy Harry S. Truman Library, Independence, Mo.

all administrations from Truman's to Ronald Reagan's, was neither global nor militarized. Strobe Talbott, himself a former deputy secretary of state, lauded Marshall for an early application of "soft power."[1] As the Cold War heated up, Marshall adjusted his thinking, recognizing the need for a formal alliance. The North Atlantic Treaty Organization (NATO) was the outgrowth of crisis management in 1948 more than the result of a blueprint in 1947.

Marshall retired from the State Department in January 1949, but he rejoined the Truman administration in September 1950, replacing the spendthrift and overwhelmed defense secretary Louis A. Johnson. Amidst widespread fear that the Korean War signaled an impending Soviet offensive in Europe, Marshall helped transform NATO from a political coalition to a military organization. Jules Moch, France's defense minister, recalled this was "a time when the pessimist thought that a new war with Russia would come in three months, and the optimists said in six months," though he, like Marshall, trusted in atomic deterrence and did not expect a Soviet attack.[2] By the end of 1950, NATO had appointed its first military commander, with Truman coaxing Dwight

D. Eisenhower, the former supreme Allied commander in Europe during World War II, to take the reins at headquarters in Paris. Soon thereafter, American army divisions began to arrive in Germany to bolster the small constabulary force. By 1952, instead of two divisions there were six, and NATO leaders agreed at their summit in Lisbon that the alliance should build toward ninety active-duty and ready-reserve divisions to defend the central front in Germany, France, and the Low Countries. Marshall played his part in these changes from his office at the Pentagon in 1950–51, and he closely observed transatlantic conversations about the rearmament of West Germany. With his health in decline, he retired for good in September 1951.

Marshall thus was active in the formation of NATO in two distinct phases. First, he was a critical figure in the creation of the alliance framework in the context of a containment policy that was defined primarily for Europe and that was not yet militarized. By the time he rejoined the Truman administration, the underpinning philosophy of containment had changed. Following the August 1949 test of an atomic bomb by the Soviets and the Communist victory in the Chinese Civil War in the fall, Truman and his closest advisers determined that it was necessary to build hydrogen bombs. Strategy planners in the State Department proposed a new approach outlined in NSC-68: accelerated nuclear but also conventional rearmament, with a defense budget of up to $50 billion per year instead of Truman's desired $13 billion limit. If not for the outbreak of the Korean War, it seems unlikely that Truman would have adopted NSC-68, but the threat perception heightened in summer 1950 and Marshall's second stint in Truman's cabinet occurred in a period of global and militarized containment.

From the vantage point of the twenty-first century, it is tempting to assume that the transatlantic alliance emerged from an inevitable split after 1945 of Europe into opposing ideological and military camps. As political scientist James McAllister notes, this assumption has afflicted political science theories, but it has also made inroads among historians.[3] Yet the breakdown of the World War II alliance did not occur in one sharp blow—at the Potsdam Conference in July 1945, for example. Instead, it developed over time and took perhaps nearly two years to harden.[4] The United States drifted into the Cold War without a clearly delineated policy, and even though there were signs of consensus around containment of the Soviet Union in 1946, it was only in the spring and summer of 1947 that an American strategy emerged.[5] It did so along two tracks: (1) a politicoeconomic system to draw Europe closer to the United States and deny the Soviet Union access to resources without a long-term commitment of American ground forces, and (2) ad hoc delivery of military aid that morphed into firmer alliances in the coming years. The two tracks were integrated to some extent in July 1949 when the Senate ratified the North Atlantic Treaty. But even then, the long-term presence of American military forces on the European continent was not assured, language in Article 5 about the obligation to come to the aid of an ally under attack had been kept ambiguous to assure Senate approval of the treaty, and only the Korean War codified militarized containment.[6]

In the winter of 1947, President Truman turned to George Marshall as secretary of state. In so doing, he pegged an able administrator and strategic thinker, but not a Cold War hardliner. Truman wanted a more efficient State Department that could help shape U.S. foreign policy. During Franklin D. Roosevelt's presidency, the Joint Chiefs of Staff (JCS) and Henry Morgenthau's Treasury Department had defined the core principles of U.S. European policy.[7] Marshall had been in the eye of the storm. As chief of staff of the army, he had served as the architect of mobilization and of American strategy in World War II. Truman had sent Marshall to China in December 1945, to broker peace between Chiang Kai-shek's Nationalist government and Mao Zedong's Communists, who had been in an uneasy coalition during the war against Japan but had previously fought a bloody civil war. Marshall worked on this futile project for over a year before returning to Washington.[8]

Marshall had thus observed the earliest postwar crises from a different vantage point than most American foreign policy elites. Despite tensions in Iran, Turkey, and Greece, he still held out hope for continuation of some aspects of the World War II alliance. In the meantime, he imparted his high expectations in staff work on a disorganized State Department. Undersecretary Dean Acheson noted the "calmness, orderliness and vigor" with which Marshall "has taken hold of this baffling institution."[9] Robert A. Lovett, who succeeded Acheson in mid-1947, thought the department had many talented members but lacked "rational organization."[10] Soviet Union expert Charles Bohlen concluded Marshall brought "greater clarity in the operation of the State Department than I had seen before or have seen since," thus pointing subtly to the importance of a leader who was prepared to delegate tasks to his handpicked aides—men like Lovett and Kennan—and kept the improved system performing at its best.[11]

As he traveled to the March–April 1947 foreign ministers meeting in Moscow, Marshall explained to French president Vincent Auriol that any regional pact in Western Europe had to be integrated within the framework of the United Nations. Pointing to the Treaty of Dunkirk, signed just two days earlier, which linked France and Great Britain in an effort to contain a reemerging Germany but that also offered the nucleus for an anti-Soviet coalition, Marshall plainly still hoped for cooperation of the powers that had won World War II. At a time when the Soviets were most interested in extracting reparations from Germany and the French feared a revived German state and angled for more of its coal production, the main security goal for Marshall remained the demilitarization of Germany.[12] He hoped to attain a four-power agreement of the victorious allies that would include a peace treaty for Austria. This, however, was secondary to Europe's "economic restoration and development," as Marshall told French prime minister Paul Ramadier, adding, "There can be no real security except on a world-wide basis."[13] Putting economics at the center of security policy, Marshall alleviated a concern of Secretary of the Navy (and soon-to-be Secretary of Defense) James V. Forrestal, who said: "The only areas where I am not sure about [Marshall's] equipment are, first, the economic background and second, awareness of the nature of Communist philosophy."[14]

The Moscow meeting opened Marshall's eyes to the new reality of the Cold War. Bohlen, who attended as his chief adviser, noted Marshall's recognition that Joseph Stalin desired to obstruct European economic recovery as a means to assure Soviet hegemony on the Continent. "All the way back to Washington," Bohlen recalled, "Marshall talked of the importance of finding some initiative to prevent the complete breakdown of Western Europe."[15] One day after his return from Moscow, Marshall asked Kennan, a foreign service officer who was then at the National War College and whom Acheson had first approached in January about a new position at the State Department, to join his staff immediately and begin working on strategy planning.[16] Kennan recalled that Marshall had come to realize that cooperation with the Soviets was "a pipe dream" and that the Kremlin "had a political interest in seeing the economies of the Western European peoples fail under anything other than Communist leadership."[17]

Desiring to shape policy rather than merely implement it, Marshall knew the State Department needed to develop a coherent strategic vision. Forrestal, who lamented "a notable lack of any central planning on American policy," applauded Marshall's move to create an in-house think tank.[18] Marshall asked Kennan, who had emerged as the premier expert on the motivations and designs of the Soviets, to lead the new Policy Planning Staff.[19] To facilitate communication, Marshall gave him the office next to his own. For the next twenty months, they worked closely together in building America's Cold War strategy.[20] Kennan and Marshall agreed that Europe had to be at the center of it. For Kennan, this derived from the study of international relations and Russian history.[21] For Marshall, it had been a lived reality since the summer of 1939, one he had come to accept by late 1940—despite his frustration with Great Britain and his threats to shift the weight of the American war effort to the Pacific theater—and one that did not end with victory in 1945. Marshall also recognized that the United States could not effect the desired political outcome in China and the Far East, while the economic problems facing Europe could be resolved.[22] Marshall remarked on the "striking similarity" of the emerging U.S. Cold War strategy to the Europe-first approach in World War II in a conversation with French prime minister Henri Queuille in November 1948.[23] Marshall remained committed to a multilateral framework within the confines of the United Nations as the sole guarantor of stability and security, and he concluded the United States had to be actively involved in shaping that world system.[24]

Why did Marshall perceive economics as a potential solution to the crises in Europe? Like most U.S. officials, he assessed the immediate threat in the winter of 1947 to be social and political rather than military in nature. After six years of war and a frustrating year and one-half of at best slow recovery, severe winter weather added to the sense of foreboding across the continent. If communist parties won elections in France and Italy or communist-led insurgents toppled the pro-British regime in Greece, then Western Europe as a whole would be destabilized. Most of Eastern Europe was already under the control of the Soviet Union, though Stalin still allowed Czechoslovakia's democratically elected government space to function in which the Communist Party did not have full control. Marshall and his advisers predicted that would not last. In his November 7, 1947, "resume of the world situation," Marshall informed Truman and the cabinet that the Soviets remained bent on "virtual domination over all, or as much as possible, of the European land mass." Thanks to improved stability in Western Europe and American firmness, the Soviet Union had been forced to retrench on the eastern half of the European continent. Notably, Marshall spoke about a political threat and did not raise the specter of an outright attack. Examples were the civil war in Greece, where Marshall feared a renewed push, and the volatile politics of France and Italy, where Stalin could order the local communist parties "to resort to virtual civil war."[25] The assessment was, in fact, testament to the work of Kennan's Policy Planning Staff, which had submitted PPS/13 on November 6 as the basis for Marshall's remarks.[26]

The state of affairs in Germany, where Britain and the United States had joined their occupation zones in an economic union, remained unresolved. As cooperation on the joint governing body for all four occupation zones deteriorated, at first as much due to French reluctance as Soviet intransigence, the German question came to the fore.[27] The situation in 1947 did not call for an anti-Soviet military alliance, but it did require better coordination of American aid to European nations. By year's end, Ernest Bevin, the staunchly anticommunist British foreign secretary who hoped to forge a European military alliance in coalition with the United States and Canada, alerted a still hesitant George Marshall to the need for "some form of union, formal or informal in character . . . backed by the United States."[28] Marshall told Bevin in January 1948 that the United States would help him create a European pact, but he did not support outright American backing. The problem, as Lovett put it to British ambassador Lord Inverchapel, was that "you are in effect asking us to pour concrete before we see the blueprints."[29]

Calls for a military alliance grew louder in 1948. By that spring, officers in Washington could be excused for believing that the Soviets were ratcheting up the pressure. First, the Czechoslovak Communist Party seized power in February. In early March, the son of the country's founder and leader of the centrists, Foreign Minister Jan Masaryk, died under suspicious circumstances. Then in June Stalin ordered all access routes on land and by water to the western sectors of Berlin closed. Even before the Berlin Blockade, the U.S. commander in Germany, Gen. Lucius D. Clay, had alerted Washington to what he considered increasingly aggressive Soviet intentions. Throughout early 1948, American policy makers also eyed with suspicion Soviet overtures regarding a defense pact to Finland and Norway, the latter a rumor seized upon by Bevin as a means to persuade Washington to enter into an alliance.[30] If the coup in Prague had come in response to the desire of the Czechoslovak government to participate in the ERP, the Berlin Blockade was an attempt to prevent currency reform in the three western zones of occupation in Germany and the formation of a western German state. It did not work and, after nearly a year of careful noninterference with the Allied airlift, Stalin called off the blockade.[31]

In the midst of these and other crises, notably in China and Palestine, Marshall feared that the United States lacked the means to meet its challenges. In his words, "The trouble was that we are playing with fire while we have nothing with which to put it out."[32] Marshall hoped, ultimately in vain, that universal military training, which was then under consideration in Congress, would produce enough American military personnel.[33] He rejected suggestions that military aid to European nations could be added to the ERP. Doing so, Marshall concluded, would unduly affect their economic recovery and might turn away neutrals such as Sweden and Switzerland. His prescription was to treat military aid on a bilateral basis.[34]

The West had just then begun to mobilize for the Cold War. On March 17, shortly after the coup in Prague, Britain, France, Belgium, the Netherlands, and Luxembourg formed the Brussels Pact, a defensive alliance also known as the Western Union Defense Organization.[35] Washington backed the group and did not oppose the objective of dual containment of Germany and the Soviet Union.[36] The point for the United States, as Marshall's right-hand man Lovett put it, was to "make clear that we were not willing to become bound to an unequivocal contract to come to their assistance unless and until they manifested a desire to help themselves." Lovett estimated the need for military assistance at over $3 billion.[37] Against Kennan's advice, Marshall had supported the talks that led to the treaty. The initiative had come from Bevin, after another futile meeting of the foreign ministers of the wartime allies in December 1947. In general, the push for a transatlantic military alliance came from European policy makers, even though there were American diplomats who agreed on the need for such an alliance.[38] Marshall and Lovett remained cautious, but in between hospitalizations at Walter Reed Hospital, Marshall worked hard at keeping Washington, London, and Paris in close alignment.[39] Nevertheless, in mid-1948, he still thought in terms that matched Truman's March message to the Brussels Pact nations: the United States sought to be associated—not allied—with Western Europe. This stance included the intent to defend friends against aggressors, but it did not allow for treaty obligations.[40]

Marshall and Kennan parted ways on the alliance question in the second half of 1948. Kennan later decried that he "failed to exert any effective influence" in the emergence of NATO. He thought it "took, from the start, a course adverse in important respects to my own concept of what we ought to be attempting."[41] Kennan insisted that militarization of containment was unnecessary, and he feared that it would play into the hands of the Soviet Union, tie down American soldiers and resources in Europe, and accelerate the arms race. Marshall, on the other hand, began to see the need for greater U.S. involvement in Germany and Western Europe in the early months of the Berlin Blockade.[42]

In the summer and fall of 1948, talks between Marshall, Bevin, and their French colleague Robert Schuman turned to a firmer American commitment. Marshall supported the emerging North Atlantic pact, just as he had applauded the Senate resolution put forward by Arthur Vandenberg (R-Mich.) in June that permitted U.S. officials to enter into talks about a Western alliance.[43] Vandenberg and Marshall had developed a close relationship at the Rio de Janeiro conference in 1947 that yielded the Inter-American Treaty of Reciprocal Assistance, which included a mutual defense commitment that soon served as a model for NATO's Article 5.[44] The Vandenberg Resolution was a joint venture: the Senate Foreign Relations Committee chair had negotiated its text with Robert Lovett.[45] Even so, the resolution still pointed at the United States as an associated power and did not suggest that the Senate would easily ratify a formal alliance treaty. Marshall, Lovett, and Vandenberg did not foresee the need for formal U.S. participation in NATO.[46] Freed to negotiate, Marshall noted that Western Europe needed to build up military forces behind the shield provided by the American monopoly on atomic weapons.[47] Bohlen suggested NATO would provide Western Europeans with "that sense of security . . . they felt so essential if recovery was to go forward."[48] Marshall took pride in its creation and told his official biographer, Forrest Pogue, in a 1956 interview, "I started NATO, actually, from the first jump. I got every living soul, one after the other, in talk to me personally on the thing and to get them stirred up to do this business."[49]

A seemingly increased risk of war brought on by the Berlin Blockade had accelerated the shift in Marshall's thinking. In hindsight, the Berlin Airlift may have looked like a triumph of improvisation, but in the first months it seemed that war could erupt soon, and Marshall was concerned about the commitment and preparedness of Britain and France. At the State Department, European Affairs Officer John Hickerson and his assistant Theodore Achilles combated Kennan's and Bohlen's doubts about NATO as well as the opposition of the JCS, who feared that too much assistance for Europe would mean less money for their own armed forces.[50] The emergence of an informal transatlantic bureaucratic network mirrored how officials in the United States and Western Europe had worked together during World War II, and a similar dynamic drew the United States closer to the war in French Indochina.[51] Until mid-1948, Marshall had spent much of his time working on the ERP, building relations with Latin America, and monitoring the civil wars in Greece and China as well as the deepening crisis in Palestine. Thereafter, more of his energy went toward diplomatic and military questions of a transatlantic alliance.

In mid-September, just as defense officials and State Department planners considered how likely it was that U.S. forces would use atomic bombs in the defense of Western Europe—Truman suggested that they would be allowed to do so—British and French officials expressed discomfort with American aggressiveness over Berlin.[52] Subsequently, Marshall pushed hard for U.S. military assistance to France and its Brussels Pact partners. At an October 10 meeting with Forrestal and the chiefs of the armed services, he connected arms shipments of "ground equipment" to the confidence of Europeans in the United States. The psychological effect, Marshall stressed, would be "electrifying." Better yet to send a larger contingent of American troops, but Marshall realized that the U.S. armed forces had insufficient personnel strength for such a deployment.[53] According to Forrestal, Marshall assumed that Congress would provide the funding for a full-blown military assistance program.[54] Marshall had long considered military assistance a viable tool of foreign policy. As army chief of staff in 1945, he had been in favor of a comprehensive military aid policy to replace the Lend-Lease approach of World War II. In 1946, on his mission to China, he had attempted to use military assistance as leverage. In 1947 and 1948, Marshall had pushed for a standardized military aid program for Latin America and Western Europe. Yet Marshall continued to consider military assistance in political and psychological terms, and even as late as November 1948, he tied it more closely to American credibility than to building up armies that could defend Western Europe.[55]

Concerning Marshall's strategic vision, historian Michael J. Hogan concluded he anticipated the New Look defense policy and associated nuclear deterrence strategy that would come to define the Dwight D. Eisenhower administration in the 1950s.[56] Marshall hoped that U.S. atomic weapons would deter the Soviets from launching an attack. Western resolve had finally put the Soviets on the defensive in Berlin. Now Washington had to help fund the buildup of Brussels Pact armies with a greater sense of urgency.[57] These armed forces, for which a unified command under British field marshal Bernard Law Montgomery had just been created, should be closely integrated, and, given the Soviets' numerical advantage, it was critical not to duplicate strengths within the alliance. For Marshall, this meant French and other continental European ground forces should carry the brunt of deterrence or warfighting on land, while Britain and the United States were to provide sea and airpower as well as military aid.[58]

During his final visit to Paris as secretary of state, coming at the end of a long tour of European capitals and just weeks before undergoing the overdue procedure to have a kidney removed, Marshall told Queuille that France should not waste limited resources on building air and sea forces. Marshall bluntly "mentioned our dearth of manpower in the American ground forces and said that in the case of an emergency it would be a year or perhaps even a year and a half before such American troops could be sent to France in substantial numbers."[59] Woefully inadequate numbers of ground forces notwithstanding, Marshall declared himself "much surprised" when he heard from Gen. Emile Antoine Béthouart, the French high commissioner in Austria, about the need to consider West German rearmament.[60] It seems Marshall did not fully grasp the appeal of national sovereignty. This foreshadowed an issue that has bedeviled the alliance since its inception: integration, as Marshall would have liked it, was never a realistic proposition.

Marshall officially retired in January 1949. His successor, Acheson, effectively in charge at the State Department from late November 1948, completed the North Atlantic Treaty negotiations and helped oversee the creation of the Mutual Defense Assistance Program. Two weeks after the treaty had been signed, Marshall touted its necessity in a speech in North Carolina: "The Atlantic Pact will, I think, bring the day much nearer when we can breathe the air of peace and security once again. But the path will be rugged, the issue will require inflexible determination, and we must make up our minds to it."[61] With the treaty awaiting Senate ratification, Marshall lent his voice to the effort to persuade doubters. In his address to the Foreign Policy Association in New York, Marshall called the treaty "one of the most determined steps the United States has ever taken in its history," and he painted it as a necessary measure to protect freedom, security, and "the general welfare of civilization." It fit well within Marshall's fundamental principles: patience and firmness toward the Soviet Union.[62] Marshall had stressed the theme of shared Western values before; he considered the United States part of European "governmental procedures and an advanced civilization."[63] Marshall summed up the shifting weight from economics to military means in his remarks at the Marshall Plan Anniversary Dinner on June 5, with President Truman in attendance: "A feeling of security is essential to Europe and to the world. Improved economy helps tremendously to that end, but in the light of conditions as they exist today, that alone is not enough. The Atlantic Pact is significant of the future steps that are necessary to a restored Europe."[64]

Reading the most thorough account of NATO's genesis, Lawrence Kaplan's *NATO 1948*, one might get the impression that Marshall, who was reserved to the point of appearing distant, did not actively pursue a formal alliance with Western Europe. Acheson appears as the driving force. Drawing that conclusion would overlook Marshall's method—letting his carefully selected staff work out the particulars—and especially the critical role Robert Lovett played in 1948.

Lovett, too, struck his European negotiating partners as reserved, at times even cagey about whether the United States was prepared to make a formal commitment to come to their defense. After the 1948 elections, however, when Truman had won and the Democrats reclaimed the majority in the Senate, it became apparent that Lovett, and by implication Marshall, moved more quickly toward alliance and a military assistance program.[65] In that respect, Marshall's 1956 assessment of having been the instigator of NATO does not seem overly far-fetched.

In the summer of 1949, Marshall remained active in advocating for a military assistance program. President Truman had encouraged Congress to allocate funding on July 25, only hours after senators had voted to ratify the North Atlantic Treaty. On July 29, Marshall spoke with Republican foreign policy expert John Foster Dulles, who stressed that a spending bill could gain congressional approval if it requested military aid for Western Europe, Turkey, Greece, Korea, and the Philippines. The wording of the current proposal, Dulles noted, could allow for U.S. aid to South America, Germany, and Japan, which would raise the hackles of the opposition. Marshall sought to dispel Dulles's concerns by pointing out that the law would be integrated within the existing treaty relationships, and he also tried to persuade a doubtful Dulles that it made sense to arm even a small number of combat divisions that could not by themselves defend Western Europe. It was better to do that, Marshall noted, than to let these forces deteriorate. After all, he concluded, "a beginning had to be made and the earlier the moment of the beginning the better it would be for all of us."[66] Three days later, Marshall appeared before the House Committee on Foreign Affairs and noted that the Mutual Defense Assistance Act, which asked for $155 million in U.S. appropriations to be enhanced by some $700 million that would be spent by other NATO members, was long overdue.[67]

Less than two weeks after the United States entered the Korean War, Truman traveled to Marshall's home in Leesburg, Virginia, to raise the possibility of Marshall becoming secretary of defense.[68] The effects of the war on NATO were dramatic: in Kaplan's words, it converted the alliance from treaty to organization.[69] Much had been left unresolved by the North Atlantic Treaty. Did Article 5 firmly commit the United States to the defense of Western Europe? In the debate that preceded Senate ratification, protreaty witnesses stressed that it did not commit the United States to go to war without a vote in the Senate. Was it possible to share the burden of the common defense? In 1949 and 1950 it made sense for the United States to provide the lion's share of resources, but how long could that be maintained? Could sufficiently strong armed forces be built to deter a Soviet attack? Would that require a West German army?[70] In their meeting with Marshall on July 1, Acheson, Bohlen, and Kennan learned that the general remained convinced that Europe was the "area of greatest strategic importance."[71] By then Truman recognized that Louis Johnson, who had antagonized Acheson, was not the right defense secretary to conduct a war, oversee the expansion of the armed forces, and help guide discussions with European allies. To make the still unsettled Defense Department work, Truman turned once more to Marshall, who had the experience and gravitas for the job.

Marshall needed Congress to waive the rule that no officer who had retired within the last decade could serve as defense secretary. If that part proved uncontroversial, the confirmation hearing before the Senate Armed Services Committee brought vitriol, especially from those who held Marshall responsible for insufficient U.S. support for Chiang Kai-shek. The question of European policy did not centrally come into focus: Marshall evaded answering William Knowland's (R-Calif.) questions on West German rearmament and Spain's entry into NATO on the grounds that he had not received detailed information since his retirement from the State Department. Some of the hearing was bruising, most notably when committee chairman Millard Tydings (D-Md.) read questions posed by William Jenner (R-Ind.), who was not a member of the committee, about Marshall's character, his role in the defeat of the Nationalists in the Chinese Civil War, and his relationship to Dean Acheson. Marshall garnered a positive vote, albeit one that did not match his unanimous confirmation in 1947.[72] He intended to serve for six months to see U.S. armed forces through the gravest crisis, but he ultimately stayed for one year before handing off the reins to his trusted undersecretary, Robert Lovett, who managed much of the department's day-to-day operations under Marshall.[73] NATO now had the full support of the administration; Johnson, uneasy with foreign alliances and concerned that providing military assistance meant spending less on U.S. armed forces, had done so only grudgingly.[74]

Back at work in Washington in late September, Marshall forged a close alignment with Acheson, Kennan's successor Paul Nitze, and the JCS on maintaining the primary strategic emphasis on Europe and NATO. Acheson thought the new arrangement "unique in the history of the Republic."[75] Yet much of their time and energy was taken up by events in Korea, where Gen. Douglas MacArthur's amphibious landing at Inchon and the breakout of the U.S. Eighth Army from the perimeter around Pusan turned the tide of the war and necessitated serious considerations of U.S. and UN war aims. Marshall also was immediately drawn into the American effort to rearm West Germany, spearheaded by Acheson at the NATO foreign ministers meeting in New York.[76] Marshall's task was to persuade the defense ministers of France (Jules Moch, who was opposed to German rearmament) and Britain (Emanuel Shinwell, whose government backed rearming Germany in principle but wondered about ways to do so). Moch expressed grave concerns about West German divisions and later noted the skepticism of the French government: "We thought it was not necessary, that we had enough troops and that the rearmament of Germany was a kind of scandal."[77] At their mid-October meeting, he told Marshall: "Germany would, as always, side with the strongest force [and] German units could not be relied upon to defend the West."[78]

Marshall responded cautiously: perhaps it was unnecessary to begin German rearmament with entire divisions, but they were "the most efficient unit from a purely military standpoint . . . [and] sooner or later the organization would come to the division unit."[79] He nonetheless got the necessary concessions to move the project ahead, at least partly because he had helped Acheson divorce the questions of German rearmament, NATO command under an American general or admiral, and buildup of European armed forces, which the Defense Department had previously insisted were an inseparable package.[80] It helped that other European leaders, most vocally Italian foreign minister Count Carlo Sforza, advocated for German rearmament. The relationship between the United States and West Germany was getting closer too. High Commissioner for Germany John J. McCloy, a former assistant secretary of war who was well acquainted with Marshall, briefed Chancellor Konrad Adenauer on what had transpired at the New York meetings. The goal, McCloy told a favorably inclined Adenauer, was to build one European army rather than a group of national armies, except for those forces needed in French Indochina and other colonial settings.[81]

Marshall's portfolio included chairing NATO's Defense Committee, which had to determine how West German armed forces were to be integrated into the alliance.[82] Marshall ranked among those officials in Washington who wondered whether the Soviets did not intend to draw the United States into a wider war in Asia before striking themselves against Germany and Western Europe. Consequently, Marshall's argument to keep the Korean War limited to the peninsula rested at least in part on the fear that the United States might otherwise not be able to come to the aid of her NATO partners.[83] Steering France and Britain toward a joint position on German rearmament, and even defining a clear U.S.

stance, proved difficult even as Marshall presided over the discussions with NATO allies in the fall of 1950.[84]

Marshall retained three fundamental concerns about the defense of Western Europe. First, he still did not believe it was practicable to deploy U.S. forces to every potential trouble spot. It was cheaper to send assistance to France than to deploy additional U.S. divisions in Europe. The French army was planning to add five combat divisions in 1951 to its five already stationed at home and in Germany and to reach twenty divisions in 1953, despite the strain put on budget, personnel, and logistics by the war in Indochina.[85] Second, he thought that so long as Congress was unwilling to underwrite universal military training, there would not be enough American ground forces. Third, it was therefore critical to find ways to enhance Western Europe's armies, both by building up the French and rearming the Germans. In an October 9 conversation with Acheson, Secretary of the Treasury John Snyder, and ECA officer Richard Bissell, Marshall floated the idea of replicating the program then practiced in Korea, where local draftees augmented American units: "perhaps as an initial step, we might contemplate incorporating German platoons in American divisions." Doing so would help reduce cost and bring U.S. units to full strength.[86] With alarming reports arriving from his commanders in Germany who deemed Western Europe indefensible without West German forces, Marshall understood the urgency of the situation, but like almost everyone else in the military and civilian hierarchy, he saw no clear path forward that would not antagonize France, where the public was opposed to German rearmament.[87] Moch estimated that a vote in parliament would see a ten-to-one majority against such a step.[88]

The Joint Chiefs of Staff were the most forceful advocates of a West German army that might allow NATO to defend territory east of the Rhine and Ijssel Rivers. The JCS hoped for ten to fifteen German divisions, though they suggested that attaching German battalions to U.S. divisions could serve as a stopgap solution. Marshall was disappointed by their deliberations, which offered no clues on how to sell such a policy to the French. The end of German occupation of France was just over half a decade in the past, and fears of German militarism still ran deep. Yet while Marshall quibbled with the Joint Chiefs of Staff on the path to a German army, he agreed with their conclusion that NATO needed a commanding general and that Dwight Eisenhower was the best choice.[89]

In the meantime, the French parliament had voted to reject a West German national army, German divisions for a NATO force, or the formation of a German general staff. When the NATO defense ministers met in Washington at the end of October 1950, the French proposal, named after Prime Minister René Pleven, was on the table. This cleared the path for Eisenhower as supreme commander and suggested a multinational force built on a cadre of French officers. Yet that did not meet the approval of most other Western European governments, and hardly anyone thought it militarily sound. Marshall was no exception, and he impressed on the assembled politicians the need to build a credible deterrent force: "that gap in military strength we must now close as quickly as possible."[90] Marshall knew that doing so required German arms, and he hoped that moving the issue from the realm of politics to military consideration would help resolve the stalemate. In Acheson's thorough reporting to David Bruce, the U.S. ambassador in Paris, Marshall was the attempted peacemaker and Moch the immovable obstacle.[91]

Politics aside, German rearmament and European military integration had taken on a life of its own against the backdrop of the Korean War. Henry Byroade, an army officer who was working as the State Department's German affairs expert, noted that it would have been ideal to effect European political and economic integration before turning to military matters, but "we didn't think we had time for all that. So what we were really trying to do was to start out with the military first, which is very, very difficult. If you already had the political and economic, the military would have flowed along much easier."[92] The crucial decisions had been made in advance of the December foreign ministers meeting at Brussels. This included the militarization of American strategy, a step Marshall now also found necessary: from 1950 to 1953 U.S. military aid to Europe would come to total $12 billion, nearly as much as Marshall Plan aid from 1948 to 1951. Already in 1951 U.S. defense spending rose to some $43 billion.[93]

Marshall understood why the French hesitated to accept a German army roughly on par with their own, but like JCS Chairman Omar Bradley and Shinwell, he thought the European army plan was infeasible. Moreover, the turn of events in Korea, where China had joined the war and U.S. and UN forces were being pushed back all the way to the south of Seoul, had soured the mood. At a press conference on November 30, Truman even seemed to suggest there were active considerations to use atomic bombs in Korea, and he implied that General MacArthur had the authority to do so.[94] Acheson and Marshall, meanwhile, had defined U.S. strategy as one of containing the war in Korea while "we must liquidate the French objection to the development of a European Army," as the secretary of state put it at a late-November NSC meeting.[95] Truman, Marshall, and Acheson reinforced the need to consider the defense of Europe as the foremost challenge in the Anglo-American discussions of early December.[96] France, too, was under great pressure in Indochina, where the possibility of Chinese intervention could no longer be discounted.[97] In this context, the NATO partners agreed to a compromise proposed by the U.S. representative to the North Atlantic Council, Charles Spofford: build Pleven's proposed European Defense Community but allow for German national regiments to serve under NATO command.[98] This attempt at appeasing the French while gaining German personnel was bound to require further adjustments, and it took years to accomplish. In the short run, it provided the necessary cover to commence NATO's conversion from political statement to military alliance.

NATO's force buildup, still largely on the shoulders of American soldiers and taxpayers, added to the demands of the war in Korea. In 1952, the United States spent over half of the federal budget on defense and war fighting. Despite his own and Lovett's efforts to keep military spending at least somewhat restrained, Marshall oversaw a massive increase of the armed forces: the army, whose ground forces were "in a woeful state of deficiency," was set to double in size by July 1951 to 1.26 million officers and men.[99] Marshall managed to rein in the armed services to a point: their initial request of $95 billion for 1952 was reduced to just over $60 billion.[100] Overall, the U.S. armed forces doubled in size within one year—between March 1950 and March 1951—to over 2.9 million officers and men on active duty on its way to 3.6 million in 1953.[101] By 1952, 400,000 of them served in Europe.[102]

This riled up opposition in the Senate. Republicans like Robert Taft (R-Ohio) but also such conservative Democrats as Walter George (D-Ga.) and left-leaning Democrats like Paul Douglas (D-Ill.) doubted the wisdom of committing American troops for undefined duration and putting them in harm's way on the European continent. Hearings in the winter of 1951 featured Eisenhower, who reported that Europeans were determined to build up their defenses with American assistance but that U.S. leadership was needed in the meantime. Acheson thought Marshall, who stated the administration's conviction that four new army divisions had to be sent to Europe, "drove his counterattack with devastating effect."[103] Still, despite the defeat of a Senate resolution aimed at halting the deployment to Europe, the debate showed that the shape of NATO was not a foregone conclusion. Internationalism and U.S. commitment to Europe were not in doubt; returning hundreds of thousands of American soldiers to Europe, however, was not preordained.[104]

When René Pleven met with Truman, Marshall, and Acheson at the end of January 1951, talks started with the Indochina War but soon turned to the defense of Europe. Pleven, who professed commitment to the political, economic, and military integration of West Germany in a Western European bloc, relayed concern about the military buildup. Could the United States defend Western Europe before NATO armies were ready? Would not the Soviets attack before it was too late? While Truman bluntly pointed at nuclear weapons development, Acheson and Marshall stressed the need to build up NATO's conventional forces. Marshall saw it as the only alternative to accepting Soviet predominance, and he feared the French commitment in Indochina might get in the way of presenting sufficient strength in Europe, a point conceded by Gen. Alphonse Juin, the inspector general of the French military. Marshall was more circumspect on atomic deterrence claiming that "for the moment time is on our side" yet conceding "that this may not be the case in one and one-and-a-half to two years from now." Pleven offered reassurance: his government still aimed to build the nine-hundred-thousand-man army by 1953 that was required for NATO's defense plans. When Juin raised questions about U.S. capabilities to reinforce NATO in the first three months of a war, Marshall responded that airpower could be brought in immediately but that shipping limitations would curtail the numbers of troops the United States could send. One potential solution, noted by Omar Bradley, was that heavy equipment and weaponry for such divisions could be stored in France so as to reserve the sealift capacity for the soldiers themselves.[105]

By mid-February 1951, Marshall could tell senators that defensive capabilities in the NATO area were taking form. He stressed that this development had made the United States itself more secure. The primary goal was not war fighting but deterrence; yet should another world war erupt, the United States and its allies were building toward a likely victory. "Fundamental to all our efforts," he noted, "is the immediate start towards the creation in Western Europe of strong and integrated forces—land, sea, and air—in such a proportion to one another as appears reasonable and practicable." He assured senators that "United States forces will constitute only a minor portion of these integrated forces—the major portion being furnished by Western European nations. This is particularly true in the matter of ground forces." Marshall confirmed that four U.S. Army divisions were to join the two that were already in Europe, fewer than critics of the commitment to NATO had feared. This was not in itself sufficient, Marshall concluded, but it offered a solid core for NATO's expanding armed forces and a morale boost for Western Europeans. He did not have to state that six divisions constituted the largest U.S. overseas deployment in peacetime and that the main American contributions were to come in sealift and airpower as well as in munitions production. This was the burden-sharing approach Marshall had in mind, and he could reassure senators that General Eisenhower's command position meant an American would ensure that the European partners lived up to their promises.[106]

It was now Eisenhower's task "to whip into shape a team of twelve sovereign states, in a period short of all-out war, and secure their acceptance of certain roles and their wholehearted support in carrying out their assigned missions," Marshall told students and faculty at Columbia University, adding that "Eisenhower can do that job" and had the full confidence of the European partners, but that his was still "a responsibility for the leader without historic precedent." Marshall expressed the hope that six American combat divisions filled a double role: they boosted morale and "would help make free Europe hard to conquer," thus giving "an imprudent aggressor something to think about before he dare set out on a hostile venture." He acknowledged such a move might entice the Soviets to attack before NATO had attained its defensive posture, but he thought there was "always a risk in positive action but the risk becomes far greater if we hesitate to act with courage, intimidated to the point that we become paralyzed and do nothing." After all, Marshall concluded, "our antagonist needs no excuse, that government will strike whenever it chooses. It has no tempering public opinion to consider. It has few standards of integrity, or honor to observe."[107]

As the strategic situation in Korea slowly turned back in America's favor in the spring of 1951, Marshall emphasized this was not the time to let down one's guard. He told *U.S. News and World Report* in March that "the best we can hope for, as I see it, is a prolonged tension rather than an all-out war." This would at least allow the United States and its allies—in Europe and elsewhere—to "build up our strength and our resources, get organized in Western Europe, which General Eisenhower, Supreme Commander in Europe, is trying to do," and hope for a speedy end to the Korean War. Americans could, as the interviewers summed up Marshall's thoughts, face "inconvenience now or war later."[108]

NATO had a long way left to go. Eisenhower had just told Marshall that NATO was still "more an idea or concept than it is a real organization." He missed the clarity of purpose that had characterized the Allied effort in World War II and bemoaned the complexity brought by the number of allies and the constant interference of political issues in what should be military affairs.[109] Eisenhower did not specify it, but the unresolved path to West German rearmament, a brief flirtation by the French with a Soviet offer to push for a demilitarized Germany, a debate in Britain over whether an American admiral was acceptable for NATO's Atlantic Command, and the gap between force requirements and force levels were at the forefront. Regarding the latter, Eisenhower's command estimated by 1954 a need for ninety-seven combat divisions one month into a war, but only seventy-four were committed, including thirty-one active divisions in peacetime instead of the required forty-six. The Military Committee assumed lower requirements and greater commitments, but even then NATO forces were likely to be short three divisions in peacetime and ten after a month of fighting.[110]

Two days after the Senate approved the deployment of an infantry division in April, Marshall authorized Bradley to inform the allies that two more infantry divisions and an armored division were to follow later in 1951 and the air force was set to deploy three more fighter bomber wings, a light bomber wing, and a tactical reconnaissance wing to add to NATO's firepower.[111] If Marshall hoped this would reassure Western Europeans, he was to be disappointed. Belgium's prime minister, Joseph Pholien, asked the question many other political and military leaders had in mind: were six U.S. combat divisions adequate? Marshall hedged in his response. He had, he told Pholien, revealed that four divisions were to be sent because doubters in Congress had to be mollified and this was the maximum the United States could send in 1951. When pressed on future additional deployments, Marshall offered that this would be determined later. The crucial issue to him was not the number of divisions, but the precedent that the president had the power to send them.[112]

Marshall underscored the urgency of German rearmament throughout the summer of 1951. In a July policy discussion with Acheson, Bradley, and Lovett, he made clear there was time to wait until the question of a European integrated army had been resolved. Lovett noted that this matter was also a domestic political problem: positive steps toward West German rearmament were needed to signal to Congress that America's allies were resolved to build up their strength. Failing that, Congress could opt to reduce military aid. Acheson had in mind negotiations built on the offer of full sovereignty for West Germany, approving a clearly defined plan for arming and training German soldiers, and an agreement in principle on the "European Defense Force." Truman approved the resulting policy paper as NSC-115 in early August. Washington had clearly staked out its position: Germany was to be admitted as a NATO member, but the United States, Britain, and France were to retain the right to station troops in Germany; Berlin remained in their responsibility; and any future peace settlement, territorial adjustments, or unification could not be negotiated without their consent.[113]

As for Congress, Marshall told Eisenhower that the members of the House Armed Services Committee who had just returned from a visit of several NATO countries were impressed with the progress they had observed. Even so, on July 21 he asked Eisenhower to send his deputy, Gen. Alfred M. Gruenther, to Washington to quell opposition in the hearings on the Mutual Defense Assistance Program.[114] Marshall himself urged senators to approve a $6.2 billion military aid bill for 1952, roughly 10 percent of what the United States spent on its own armed forces. To soften the blow, Marshall noted that economic aid had "largely achieved its major objectives" and that the Truman administration was asking for only $2.3 billion in nonmilitary foreign aid. NATO allies were already doing their share: "They are providing for their own forces all the facilities, pay, individual equipment, administrative and housekeeping supplies, and as much of the major arms and equipment as they can produce in time to meet scheduled demands." Marshall added, "They are contributing the land, the bases, and certain logistic facilities that we require in their territories. They have increased their training program, their length of military service, and their defense budgets." Burden sharing in NATO was never merely an issue of directly measurable expenditures and force levels. With respect to the latter, NATO partners had promised enough troops so that the United States would have to provide just 15 percent of all land, sea, and air forces.[115]

In a November 1956 interview with Forrest Pogue, Marshall recalled the need to tread lightly from 1950 to 1951. The United States and its allies simply did not have the strength built up to confront the Soviet Union more forcefully outside of the Korean War, and diplomacy had to be conducted from a weaker position than would be the case by the mid-1950s. Marshall carefully distinguished this from the path to World War II: "We tried not to appease, but just to go easy."[116] Another difficulty appeared in the close linkage of politics and military affairs. In April 1951, when President Truman dismissed MacArthur, Marshall supported the principle of civilian control of the military over his inclination to give a free hand to the commander on the ground. It had been a hard decision that must have taken up much of his time and energy. For the moment, it further intensified the extreme partisanship in Washington that had helped to push foreign policy on a more militarized and aggressive course.[117]

By the time Marshall retired, for the third time, in September 1951, he could look at NATO with some confidence. The Fourth Infantry Division and Second Armored Division had arrived in Germany, and two National Guard infantry divisions were on their way. The alliance had a clear command structure, with Eisenhower in Paris and the Military Committee and Standing Group to consider defense plans and force requirements. Yet how to attain West German rearmament and build sufficient forces for the defense of Western Europe remained an open question until late 1954, though few doubted its necessity. The transitions to come—from Marshall to his alter ego Lovett at the Pentagon, less than a year later the handover of SHAPE from Eisenhower to Matthew B. Ridgway, and in early 1953 Eisenhower's inauguration as Truman's successor—did not fundamentally alter the foundation and structures in place, even though Eisenhower would impose a more immediately nuclear-deterrence-focused strategy on the alliance. Marshall himself expressed the greatest shift in his June 1951 testimony for the Mutual Security Act: as Western Europe's economies had strengthened, the threat shifted from a political and economic to a military one. Under his guidance, U.S. policy had helped bring along NATO to maintain public confidence and keep Western Europe stable and prosperous. The cost may have been great, but Marshall believed in peace through strength and found the price the U.S. government paid much preferable to the war that he was sure would erupt if Congress did not authorize troop deployments and military assistance packages.[118]

Marshall was deeply affected by his experiences in the military, and he believed in the effectiveness of well-managed bureaucracies. Moreover, he had observed the importance of government intervention in the economy in the 1930s.[119] The New Deal had stalled and it was the mass mobilization for World War II—and the government contracts that came with it—that finally defeated the Great Depression.[120] This was a case of warfare and welfare states coming into balance, and it presented Marshall a paradigm: economic prosperity and sociopolitical stability were just as essential to a thriving state and society as security based on military means. In 1947, he assumed that the economic recovery of Western Europe would present a sufficient deterrent to the Soviet Union. In the course of 1948, he came to realize the need for military assistance and an American commitment to the emerging alliance in Europe. As secretary of defense, he helped transform the transatlantic alliance from what amounted to little more than a statement of principles to an organization that could dissuade the Soviets from attacking Western interests in Europe. His work for European economic recovery made Marshall a Nobel laureate: he was awarded the Peace Prize in 1953. In his Nobel lecture, Marshall noted the tragic history of the first half of the twentieth century and drew from the enduring lessons of the Pax Romana. His theme was less about the immediate need for strong defenses than about the long-term necessity of the West standing together, and he emphasized education and democracy as antidotes to tyranny and poverty. Military strength, economic prosperity, and Western civilization were to be the foundation of renewed peace for the world.[121]

NOTES

1. Strobe Talbott, "Brookings in War and Peace," in *The Marshall Plan and the Shaping of American Strategy*, ed. Bruce Jones (Washington, D.C.: Brookings Institution, 2017), 1–18, esp. 13–14.

2. Interview with Jules Moch, April 29, 1970, by Richard D. McKinzie and Theodore A. Wilson, 22–25, Harry S. Truman Library (hereafter cited as HSTL), https://www.trumanlibrary.org/oralhist/mochj.htm#transcript. The quotation is on 22–23.

3. James McAllister, *No Exit: America and the German Problem, 1943–1954* (Ithaca, N.Y.: Cornell University Press, 2002), 5–20. For inevitability see Melvyn P. Leffler, *A Preponderance of Power: National Security, the Truman Administration, and the Cold War* (Stanford, Calif.: Stanford University Press, 1992).

4. Michael Neiberg, *Potsdam: The End of World War II and the Remaking of Europe* (New York: Basic, 2015).

5. Wilson Miscamble, *From Roosevelt to Truman: Potsdam, Hiroshima, and the Cold War* (Cambridge: Cambridge University Press, 2007).

6. William I. Stueck, *The Korean War: An International History* (Princeton, N.J.: Princeton University Press, 1995). For an insider's recollection on making Article 5 palatable to senators, see Oral History Interview with Theodore Achilles, by Richard D. McKinzie, November 13, 1972, 38–40, HSTL, https://www.trumanlibrary.org/oralhist/achilles.htm#transcript.

7. Mark A. Stoler, *Allies and Adversaries: The Joint Chiefs of Staff, the Grand Alliance, and U.S. Strategy in World War II* (Chapel Hill: University of North Carolina Press, 2000); Benn Steil, *The Marshall Plan: Dawn of the Cold War* (New York: Simon & Schuster, 2018).

8. Daniel Kurtz-Phelan, *The China Mission: George Marshall's Unfinished War, 1945–1947* (New York: W. W. Norton, 2018).

9. Acheson to Henry L. Stimson, January 25, 1947, in *Among Friends: Personal Letters of Dean Acheson*, ed. David S. McLellan and David C. Acheson (New York: Dodd, Mead, 1980), 64–65.

10. James Forrestal, notes on Lunch with Admiral Sherman and Under Secretary Lovett, in Walter Millis, ed., *The Forrestal Diaries* (New York: Viking, 1951), 279.

11. Charles E. Bohlen, *Witness to History, 1929–1969* (New York: W. W. Norton, 1973), 259, 268–71.

12. Minutes of a Conversation between the Secretary of State and the President of France (Auriol), March 6, 1947, in Department of State, Office of the Historian, *Foreign Relations of the United States, 1947*, vol. 2: *Council of Foreign Ministers; Germany and Austria* (Washington, D.C.: Government Printing Office, 1972), 190–95; Leffler, *Preponderance of Power*, 152–54.

13. Editors' note on Conversation between the President of the Council of Ministers (Ramadier) and Marshall, March 6, 1947, in Larry I. Bland, Mark A. Stoler, Sharon Ritenour Stevens, and Daniel D. Holt, eds., *The Papers of George Catlett Marshall*, vol. 6: *"The Whole World Hangs in the Balance": January 8, 1947–September 30, 1949* (Baltimore: Johns Hopkins University Press, 2013) (hereafter cited as *Papers of George Marshall*, 6), 63–64.

14. Forrestal to Paul Smith, March 10, 1947, in Millis, *Forrestal Diaries*, 254.

15. Bohlen, *Witness to History*, 263.

16. John Lewis Gaddis, *George F. Kennan: An American Life* (New York: Penguin, 2011), 253, 264–65.

17. George F. Kennan, *Memoirs, 1925–1950* (Boston: Little, Brown, 1967), 325.

18. Forrestal, notes on Cabinet Luncheon, April 28, 1947, in Millis, *Forrestal Diaries*, 266–68. The quotation is on 267.

19. Mark A. Stoler, *George C. Marshall: Soldier-Statesman of the American Century* (Boston: Twayne, 1989).

20. Kennan, *Memoirs*, 345.

21. Gaddis, *George F. Kennan*.

22. Mark A. Stoler, "George C. Marshall and the 'Europe-First' Strategy, 1939–1951: A Study in Diplomatic as well as Military History," Marshall Lecture at the American Historical Association Annual Meeting, New York, January 4, 2015, https://marshallfoundation.org/marshall/wp-content/uploads/sites/22/2014/04/EDStoler.pdf.

23. Editors' note, Meetings with the Prime Minister of France and with the Foreign Ministers of France and Great Britain, November 18–19, 1948, Paris, in *Papers of George Marshall*, 6:624–26. Marshall is quoted on 624.

24. Speech at Princeton University, February 22, 1947, in *Papers of George Marshall*, 6:47–50.

25. Memorandum for the President, November 7, 1947, in *Papers of George Marshall*, 6:238–44. The quotations are on 239.

26. Report by the Policy Planning Staff PPS/13, November 6, 1947, in Department of State, Office of the Historian, *Foreign Relations of the United States, 1947*, vol. 1: *General; The United Nations* (Washington, D.C.: Government Printing Office, 1973), 771–77.

27. Marc Trachtenberg, *A Constructed Peace: The Making of the European Settlement, 1945–1963* (Princeton, N.J.: Princeton University Press, 1999), 3–93.

28. Quoted in Chester J. Pach Jr., *Arming the Free World: The Origins of the United States Military Assistance Program, 1945–1950* (Chapel Hill: University of North

Carolina Press, 1991), 144; State Department officer Theodore Achilles recounts the episode: Achilles interviewed by McKinzie, November 13, 1972, 9–14, https://www.trumanlibrary.org.

29. Quoted in Pach, *Arming the Free World*, 146; Marshall to Bevin, January 20, 1948, and Lovett to Inverchapel, February 2, 1948, in *FRUS, 1948*, 3:8–9, 17–18.

30. Geir Lundestad, *The United States and Western Europe since 1945: From "Empire" by Invitation to Transatlantic Drift* (Oxford: Oxford University Press, 2003), 8.

31. Daniel F. Harrington, *Berlin on the Brink: The Blockade, the Airlift, and the Early Cold War* (Lexington: University Press of Kentucky, 2012).

32. Forrestal, notes on Meeting—National Security Council, February 12, 1948, in Millis, *Forrestal Diaries*, 370–73. Marshall is quoted on 373.

33. Statement to the Senate Armed Services Committee, March 17, 1948, in *Papers of George Marshall*, 6:407–9; editors' note, in ibid., 409–10.

34. Statement to the House Committee on Foreign Affairs, March 3, 1948, in *Papers of George Marshall*, 6:391–95; editors' note, in ibid., 395–96.

35. Lawrence S. Kaplan, *NATO 1948: The Birth of the Transatlantic Alliance* (Lanham, Md.: Rowman & Littlefield, 2007).

36. Only Germany is mentioned by name. See https://www.nato.int/cps/en/natohq/official_texts_17072.htm?selectedLocale=en.

37. Forrestal, notes on Cabinet meeting, April 23, 1948, in Millis, *Forrestal Diaries*, 424–25. His conversation with Lovett, from which the quote is drawn, is on 425.

38. Lundestad, *United States and Western Europe*, 48; Kenneth Weisbrode, *The Atlantic Century: Four Generations of Extraordinary Diplomats Who Forged America's Vital Alliance with Europe* (Cambridge, Mass.: Da Capo, 2009), 83–127.

39. Marshall to Kenneth Royall, August 23, 1948, in *Papers of George Marshall*, 6:526–27; Gaddis, *George F. Kennan*, 303–7.

40. This position also found expression in NSC 1/7, March 30, 1948, and NSC 1/9, April 13, 1948; Kaplan, *NATO 1948*, 88–99.

41. Kennan, *Memoirs*, 397.

42. McAllister, *No Exit*, 156–63.

43. Lawrence J. Haas, *Harry and Arthur: Truman, Vandenberg, and the Partnership That Created the Free World* (Washington, D.C.: Potomac, 2016).

44. Arthur H. Vandenberg Jr., ed., *The Private Papers of Senator Vandenberg* (Boston: Houghton Mifflin, 1952), 365–72.

45. Ibid., 404–7.

46. Kaplan, *NATO 1948*, 92–98.

47. Meetings with Foreign Ministers, October 4–6, 1948, in *Papers of George Marshall*, 6:567–73, esp. 568–69.

48. Quoted in Hal Brands, *What Good Is Grand Strategy? Power and Purpose in American Statecraft from Harry S. Truman to George W. Bush* (Ithaca, N.Y.: Cornell University Press, 2014), 35.

49. Larry I. Bland, ed., *George C. Marshall: Interviews and Reminiscences for Forrest C. Pogue* (Lexington, Va.: George C. Marshall Foundation, 1991), 561.

50. Kaplan, *NATO 1948*, 84–92. JCS opposition softened at the end of summer 1948, but serious doubts remained. Ibid., 140–42.

51. Kaplan, *NATO 1948*, 119–22; Stoler, *Allies and Adversaries*; Mark Atwood Lawrence, *Assuming the Burden: Europe and the American Commitment to War in Vietnam* (Berkeley: University of California Press, 2005); Weisbrode, *Atlantic Century*, 99–104, for the network around Jean Monnet.

52. Millis, *Forrestal Diaries*, 486–91.

53. Memorandum of Meeting with the Secretary of Defense and Service Chiefs, October 10, 1948, in *Papers of George Marshall*, 6:581–88.

54. Millis, *Forrestal Diaries*, 500–502.

55. Pach, *Arming the Free World*, esp. 49–61, 81–86, 130–59, and 202–4.

56. Michael J. Hogan, *A Cross of Iron: Harry S. Truman and the Origins of the National Security State, 1945–1954* (Cambridge: Cambridge University Press, 1998), 164–65.

57. Conversations with Bevin, Schuman, and Paul-Henri Spaak on October 4–6, 1948, in *Papers of George Marshall*, 6:567–73.

58. Meetings with the Prime Minister of France and with the Foreign Ministers of France and Great Britain, November 18–19, 1948, in *Papers of George Marshall*, 6:624–26. Marshall reiterated his position in House and Senate testimony on the Mutual Defense Assistance Program on June 7, 1950; editors' note, in Mark A. Stoler and Daniel D. Holt, eds., *The Papers of George Catlett Marshall*, vol. 7: *"The Man of the Age": October 1, 1949–October 16, 1959* (Baltimore: Johns Hopkins University Press, 2016) (hereafter cited as *Papers of George Marshall*, 7), 99–101.

59. Meetings, November 18–19, 1948, Paris, in *Papers of George Marshall*, 6:624–26. The quotation is on 624.

60. Memorandum of Conversation with General Béthouart, November 5, 1948, in *Papers of George Marshall*, 6:609–10.

61. Remarks at a Savings Bond Dinner Hosted by Governor Kerr Scott, April 19, 1949, in *Papers of George Marshall*, 6:694–96. The quotation is on 695.

62. *Papers of George Marshall*, 6:699–705. The quotations are on 701. On his concern about public opinion, see Marshall to Carlisle H. Humelsine, April 10, 1949, in ibid., 685–87.

63. Marshall's address to the Chicago Council on Foreign Relations and the Chicago Chamber of Commerce: Speech on the Situation in Europe, November 18, 1947, in *Papers of George Marshall*, 6:259–66. The quotation is on 260.

64. *Papers of George Marshall*, 6:713–17. The quotation is on 716.

65. Kaplan, *NATO 1948*, 165–223.

66. Marshall to Acheson, July 29, 1949, in *Papers of George Marshall*, 6:740–41. The quotation is on 741.

67. Editors' note, Testimony on the Mutual Defense Assistance Act of 1949, August 1, 1949, in *Papers of George Marshall*, 6:741–43.

68. *Papers of George Marshall*, 7:xxiv, 130.

69. Lawrence S. Kaplan, *NATO and the United States: The Enduring Alliance* (Boston: Twayne, 1988), 33.

70. Lawrence S. Kaplan, *The United States and NATO: The Formative Years* (Lexington: University Press of Kentucky, 1984), 121–44.

71. Kennan, July 1, 1950, in Frank Costigliola, ed., *The Kennan Diaries* (New York: W. W. Norton, 2014), 257–59.

72. The vote was 57–11. U.S. Senate, Committee on Armed Services, *Hearing on the Nomination of General of the Army George C. Marshall as the Secretary of Defense, September 19, 1950* (Washington, D.C.: Government Printing Office, 1950). Marshall's responses to Knowland are on 3–5, and Jenner's questions are on 20–25.

73. Forrest C. Pogue, *George C. Marshall*, vol. 4: *Statesman, 1945–1959* (New York: Viking, 1987), 427.

74. Jeffrey A. Larsen and Robert M. Shelala II, *Rearming at the Dawn of the Cold War: Louis Johnson, George Marshall, and Robert Lovett, 1949–1952* (Washington, D.C.: Office of the Secretary of Defense, Historical Office, 2012). Johnson had dismissed the Brussels Pact as an outdated balance-of-power alliance. See Kaplan, *NATO and the United States*, 35.

75. Dean Acheson, *Present at the Creation: My Years in the State Department* (New York: W. W. Norton, 1969), 441.

76. Sheldon A. Goldberg, *From Disarmament to Rearmament: The Reversal of U.S. Policy toward West Germany, 1946–1955* (Athens: Ohio University Press, 2017).

77. Moch interview, 1970, 26, https://www.trumanlibrary.org.

78. R. E. Beebe, Memorandum of Conversation, October 16, 1950, in *Papers of George Marshall*, 7:199–203. Moch's quotation is on 199.

79. Lucius Battle, Memorandum of Conversation, New York, September 23, 1950, in Department of State, Office of the Historian, *Foreign Relations of the United States, 1950*, vol. 3: *Western Europe* (Washington, D.C.: Government Printing Office, 1977), 1391–94. Marshall's quotation is on 1393.

80. Dean Acheson, *The Struggle for a Free Europe* (New York: W. W. Norton, 1971), 136–39.

81. Gespräch Adenauers mit McCloy, September 24, 1950, in *Akten zur Auswärtigen Politik der Bundesrepublik Deutschland, 1949/50: September 1949 bis Dezember 1950*, ed. Hans-Peter Schwarz (Munich: R. Oldenbourg, 1997), 352–60.

82. Doris M. Condit, *History of the Office of the Secretary of Defense*, vol. 2: *The Test of War, 1950–1953* (Washington, D.C.: Office of the Secretary of Defense, Historical Office, 1988), 322–23.

83. Jessup, Memorandum on NSC meeting, November 28, 1950, in Department of State, Office of the Historian, *Foreign Relations of the United States, 1950*, vol. 7: *Korea* (Washington, D.C.: Government Printing Office, 1976), 1243.

84. Lord [Hastings] Ismay, *NATO: The First Five Years, 1949–1954* (Utrecht: Bosch, 1954), 34.

85. Col. R. E. Beebe, Memorandum of Conversation, October 10, 1950, in *Papers of George Marshall*, 7:187–88; Maj. Gen. L. L. Lemnitzer, Memorandum of Conversation, October 13, 1950, in ibid., 194–99.

86. Paul Nitze, Memorandum of Conversation, October 9, 1950, in *FRUS, 1950*, 3:364–66. Marshall's quotation is on 366. See also Marshall's statement to the American

Legion Convention, October 5, 1950, and the transcript of his remarks to the Conference of Mayors, October 6, 1950, in *Papers of George Marshall*, 7:177–78, 179–82.

87. Paper Prepared by McCloy, Handy, and Taylor, August 29, 1950, in Department of State, Office of the Historian, *Foreign Relations of the United States, 1950*, vol. 4: *Central and Eastern Europe; The Soviet Union* (Washington, D.C.: Government Printing Office, 1980), 867–87; Marshall to Lay, October 18, 1950, in ibid., 893–94.

88. Beebe, Memorandum of Conversation, October 16, 1950, in *Papers of George Marshall*, 7:201.

89. Marshall, Memorandum for the President, October 20, 1950, in *Papers of George Marshall*, 7:206; Condit, *Test of War*, 323–25.

90. Editors' note on the NATO Defense Ministers Meeting, October 28–31, 1950, in *Papers of George Marshall*, 7:218–20. Marshall's quotation is on 219.

91. Acheson to Bruce, October 29, 1950; October 30, 1950; October 31, 1950; and November 3, 1950—all in *FRUS, 1950*, 3:415–31.

92. Oral history interview with Henry Byroade by Niel M. Johnson, September 21, 1988, 89, HSTL, https://www.trumanlibrary.org/oralhist/byroade.htm#oh2.

93. Robert L. Beisner, *Dean Acheson: A Life in the Cold War* (Oxford: Oxford University Press, 2006), 376–79.

94. Harry S. Truman, "The President's News Conference," November 30, 1950, in Gerhard Peters and John T. Woolley, *The American Presidency Project*, http://www.presidency.ucsb.edu/ws/?pid=13673.

95. Phillip Jessup, Memorandum of Conversation, November 28, 1950, in *FRUS, 1950*, 7:1242–49. Acheson's quotation is on 1247.

96. Especially prominent in the December 6 discussions were Minutes of Truman-Attlee Conversations, Third Meeting, December 6, 1950, in *FRUS, 1950*, 3:1739–46; and Fourth Meeting, December 6, 1950, in ibid., 1746–58.

97. A. C. Murdaugh, Memorandum of Conversation, January 5, 1951, in *Papers of George Marshall*, 7:320–22.

98. Condit, *Test of War*, 325–32.

99. Editors' note on Marshall's Senate Testimony, December 8 and 11, 1950, in *Papers of George Marshall*, 7:291–93. Marshall's quotation is on 292.

100. Hogan, *Cross of Iron*, 308–23. See 323 for the 1952 defense budget.

101. Marshall to Truman, March 20, 1951, in *Papers of George Marshall*, 7:440–41.

102. Ismay, *NATO*, 40.

103. Acheson, *Present at the Creation*, 495.

104. On the debate in 1951, see Phil Williams, *The Senate and U.S. Troops in Europe* (London: Palgrave Macmillan, 1985), 43–107.

105. Minutes of the Second Meeting between Truman and Pleven, January 30, 1951, in Department of State, Office of the Historian, *Foreign Relations of the United States, 1951*, vol. 4, pt. 1: *Europe: Political and Economic Developments* (Washington, D.C.: Government Printing Office, 1985), 315–27. The quotation is on 320.

106. Statement before the Senate Foreign Relations and Armed Services Committees, February 15, 1951, in *Papers of George Marshall*, 7:380–84. The quotations are on 382.

107. Remarks at Columbia University, March 5, 1951, in *Papers of George Marshall*, 7:419–22. The quotations are on 420.

108. Marshall's interview for the April 13, 1951, issue of *U.S. News and World Report*, March 26, 1951, in *Papers of George Marshall*, 7:441–55. The quotations are on 442–43.

109. Eisenhower to Marshall, March 12, 1951, summarized and quoted in the notes from Marshall to Eisenhower, March 21, 1951, in *Papers of George Marshall*, 7:455–56.

110. Walter S. Poole, *History of the Office of the Joint Chiefs of Staff*, vol. 4: *The Joint Chiefs of Staff and National Policy, 1950–1952* (Washington, D.C.: Office of the Chairman of the Joint Chiefs of Staff, Office of Joint History, 1998), 120–36.

111. Marshall to U.S. Representative, Standing Group, April 6, 1951, in *Papers of George Marshall*, 7:472–74.

112. Editors' note on meeting with Pholien, Washington, April 9, 1951, in *Papers of George Marshall*, 7:477–78.

113. Editorial note, Acheson and Lovett to Truman, in Department of State, Office of the Historian, *Foreign Relations of the United States, 1951*, vol. 3, pt. 1: *European Security and the German Question* (Washington, D.C.: Government Printing Office, 1981), 847–49, 849–52.

114. Editors' note on Conversations on a European Defense Force, July 16, 1951; Marshall to Eisenhower, July 16, 1951; Marshall to Eisenhower, July 21, 1951—all in *Papers of George Marshall*, 7:583–85, 585–86, 591–92.

115. Statement to the Senate Foreign Relations and Armed Services Committees on the Mutual Security Program, July 27, 1951, in *Papers of George Marshall*, 7:597–99.

116. Bland, *George C. Marshall*, 328.

117. H. W. Brands, *The General versus the President: MacArthur and Truman at the Brink of Nuclear War* (New York: Doubleday, 2016).

118. Statement before the House Foreign Affairs Committee on the Mutual Security Program, June 29, 1951, in *Papers of George Marshall*, 7:569–75.

119. Nicolaus Mills, *Winning the Peace: The Marshall Plan and America's Coming of Age as a Superpower* (Hoboken, N.J.: John Wiley and Sons, 2008), ix–x, 35–48.

120. James T. Sparrow, *Warfare State: World War II Americans and the Age of Big Government* (Oxford: Oxford University Press, 2011).

121. Marshall to the Nobel Committee, January 31, 1953; Nobel Prize Lecture, December 11, 1953—both in *Papers of George Marshall*, 7:747–48, 810–16.

RETURN TO THE PENTAGON

Marshall and the Korean War

On July 24, 1950, George Catlett Marshall dashed off a note to his goddaughter and confidante, Rose Page Wilson. "I have been trembling on the edge of being called again into public service in this crisis," wrote the general, "but I hope I get by unmolested, but when the President motors down and sits under our oaks and tells me of his difficulties, he has me at a disadvantage."[1]

Twenty days earlier, on Independence Day, President Harry Truman had indeed motored to Marshall's home in Leesburg, Virginia, to discuss the crisis in Korea, which had begun when the Korean People's Army (KPA) of Communist North Korea violated the thirty-eighth parallel and invaded South Korea on June 25. Truman and his advisers incorrectly assumed that the Soviet Union had instigated the attack.[2] South Korea, officially the Republic of Korea (ROK), was led by President Syngman Rhee; though corrupt, it was at least partially democratic and recognized by the United Nations.[3] "I felt certain that if South Korea was allowed to fall communist leaders would be emboldened to override nations closer to our own shores," Truman wrote in his memoirs, predicting such an outcome would have led to both "a third world war" and the discrediting of the United Nations. If he was also spurred by the intense public criticism he had received after China had become a Communist country in 1949, it went unmentioned in his memoirs.[4] Truman had authorized naval and air support of the ROK on June 25. After a June 27 UN Security Council resolution authorizing military action, he also ordered ground support on June 30.[5] Truman discussed these events with Marshall on July 4 and, according to a White House memorandum, "was very much heartened by General Marshall's warm endorsement of the President's recent actions."[6]

Whether directly or obliquely, Truman apparently raised the possibility of Marshall becoming the secretary of defense that day under the oaks of Leesburg, which explains the general's comment to Rose that he was "trembling on the edge of being called again into public service" but hoped to escape "unmolested."[7] His reluctance was understandable. He was now sixty-nine years old, and Truman had already called him out of retirement once. He had retired from the army in 1945, only to be asked the next day by Truman to be his special presidential envoy to China. That morphed into a momentous stint as the secretary of state, which ended with his second retirement in January 1949. Even this second retirement had come with an asterisk, because Marshall had agreed to serve as the president of the American Red Cross. By April 28, 1950, he had traveled an estimated 35,000 miles on Red Cross business. Still, he had found time during the winter of 1949–50 to spend with his wife, Katherine, at their winter home in Pinehurst, North Carolina. When not traveling for the Red Cross, he had enjoyed many hours of horse riding, hunting, and fishing. The president was suggesting that he trade these happy moments for the weight of running the Pentagon during a time of undeclared war.[8]

Truman had lost confidence in the current secretary of defense, Louis A. Johnson. A "brusque" and "bullying" man, according to military historian Allan Millett, Johnson did not get along well with other members of the cabinet. Moreover, he had now been discredited by his support for small defense budgets prior to the Korean War.[9] In contrast to the president's lack of trust in Johnson, Truman had almost limitless confidence in General Marshall.[10] In his already distinguished public career, Marshall had demonstrated remarkable skill in working with all branches of the armed forces, as well as with the State Department, Congress, and American allies. At a time when the United States once again found itself needing to wage coalition warfare and build up its armed forces, he was a much better choice for defense secretary than the abrasive Johnson.[11]

On September 6, Truman asked Marshall directly if he would head the Pentagon. The general agreed, though he expressed concern that his appointment might bring criticism of Truman from those who held Marshall responsible for the collapse of Chiang Kai-shek's Nationalist government in China in 1949. Far from dissuading Truman, however, the president saw this concern as further evidence of the general's greatness of character. Marshall told Truman he was only willing to serve for six months, or perhaps a year. He wanted Robert A. Lovett, a trusted protégé who had once served as his undersecretary of state, to be the deputy secretary of defense. With Marshall's reluctant willingness confirmed, Truman forced a weeping Johnson to sign his letter of resignation on September 12, effective September 19.[12]

Before Marshall could be confirmed, however, both houses of Congress had to approve a special one-time exception to the 1947 National Security Act, which denied eligibility for the office of defense secretary to any former commissioned officers of the armed forces who had been retired for fewer than ten years. During the hearings concerning this matter, Sen. William Jenner (R-Ind.) savaged Marshall as "a front man for traitors" and a "living lie." Another Republican senator, however, Leverett Saltonstall from Massachusetts, offered a heartfelt defense of the general, arguing that "if ever there was a life spent in the interest of our country, a life that is not a lie, it is the life of George C. Marshall." In spite of Jenner's invective, both houses approved the exception. The Senate then voted 57–11 to approve Marshall's nomination as secretary of defense, and he was sworn in on September 21.[13]

In addition to Lovett, Marshall had already forged relationships with several people with whom he would be working. His relationship with the president dated back to when he was the army chief of staff and Truman was a senator. He had gained Truman's respect by cooperating in the senator's investigation of wasteful spending within the War Department. The current secretary of state, Acheson, had preceded Lovett as the undersecretary of state during Marshall's tenure in the State Department. Gen. Omar Bradley, chairman of the Joint Chiefs of Staff (JCS), had served with Marshall on the faculty of the Infantry School at Fort Benning in the early 1930s, when Marshall was the assistant commandant, and had gone on to command the Twelfth Army Group in Europe during World War II. Another member of the JCS was the army chief of staff, Gen. J. Lawton "Lightning Joe" Collins, who had likewise served on the Benning faculty with

EXTENSION OF THE DRAFT ACT

"Extension of the Draft Act." Cartoon by James T. Berryman in the *Washington Evening Star* depicting Chief Justice Fred M. Vinson (*right*) swearing in George C. Marshall (*center*) as secretary of defense in front of President Harry S. Truman (*left*). Circa 1950. Courtesy Harry S. Truman Library, Independence, Mo.

Marshall before commanding the VII Corps in Europe. A third JCS member was the air force chief of staff, Gen. Hoyt Vandenberg, who had worked with Marshall in the War Department at the beginning of World War II.[14]

One man who could not in any meaningful way be considered a Marshall protégé, however, was Gen. Douglas MacArthur, the newly appointed commander-in-chief of UN forces in Korea. MacArthur—a Medal of Honor recipient, the loser and subsequent liberator of the Philippine Islands during World War II, and the democratizer of Japan—had already enjoyed one of the most storied careers in American military history. His recent appointment as UN commander was in addition to his roles as head of the Far East Command and supreme commander for the Allied Powers in Japan.[15]

Marshall and MacArthur were both born in 1880, and both were now five-star generals. Each had made a name for himself during World War I, though Marshall's had been as a staff officer—he had planned the Meuse-Argonne offensive—while MacArthur's had been as a decorated combat commander. MacArthur received permanent promotion to brigadier general in 1920, but Marshall not until 1936. During MacArthur's tenure as army chief of staff from 1930 to 1935, he irritated Colonel Marshall by ordering his transfer from Fort Moultrie, South Carolina, to the Illinois National Guard in Chicago. Marshall protested, but to no avail. Promotions eventually caught up with Marshall, and he too became chief of staff from 1939 to 1945, a tenure coinciding with World War II. During the war, MacArthur became the commander of the Southwest Pacific Theater at Marshall's insistence. This was only one of many gestures of support that Marshall made toward MacArthur throughout the war, including recommending him for the Medal of Honor.[16] Nevertheless, the two men differed significantly over grand strategy. Whereas Marshall generally favored the Europe-first strategy, MacArthur was always oriented toward the Pacific.[17]

Not only did Marshall return to the Pentagon with several already formed relationships, he also brought with him a set of beliefs. He ardently believed in the importance of civilian control of the military. Just as in World War II, he still believed that Europe was more vital to American security than Asia. Having spent time in China himself, he believed that the Chinese Communists were heavily influenced by the Soviets, of whom he had acquired a late but hard-earned distrust.[18] Forrest Pogue, Marshall's official biographer, also noted his "long opposition" to U.S. troops becoming involved in a ground war in Asia.[19] Unfortunately, it was too late to prevent this; American troops were very much at war in Asia when Marshall was sworn in as secretary of defense on September 21.

The invasion of South Korea came at a time of smaller defense budgets and reduced troop strength for the United States. As of June 30, nine of the army's ten divisions were understrength, as were both marine divisions.[20] Moreover, the Joint Chiefs of Staff could not commit all U.S. troops to Korea because they had to consider the possibility that the KPA's invasion of South Korea was merely the first prong of a larger global offensive by the Soviets or their allies; while American forces were occupied in Korea, other communist armies might strike at Formosa (Taiwan), Japan, or Berlin.[21] By September, those U.S. troops who had been sent, as well as their ROK allies, had all been pushed into a defensive perimeter ringing the port of Pusan on the peninsula's southeast coast. MacArthur proposed a daring scheme to reverse the fortunes of war, however. He would sail the X Corps around the tip of Korea to land at Inchon, while the Eighth Army broke out of the Pusan perimeter. Inchon presented daunting challenges with its tricky tides, and the JCS vainly suggested that MacArthur seek a safer landing site. He refused. The Inchon landings proceeded on September 15, and they succeeded spectacularly. Bradley groused that it was the "luckiest military operation in history." Lucky or not, MacArthur had been vindicated, while the JCS "seemed like a bunch of nervous Nellies to have doubted."[22] They would be hesitant to question MacArthur again.[23]

When Marshall became the defense secretary, the Inchon landing had just occurred. He now supported the momentous decision to allow MacArthur to conduct military operations north of the thirty-eighth parallel. On September 27, the Joint Chiefs of Staff transmitted a directive to that effect. Marshall, Acheson, and Truman all approved. It stated:

> Your military objective is the destruction of the North Korean armed forces. In attaining this objective you are authorized to conduct military operations, including amphibious and airborne landings or ground operations north of the 38° parallel in Korea, provided that at the time of such operation there has been no entry into North Korea by major Soviet or Chinese Communist forces, no announcement of intended entry, nor a threat to counter our operations militarily in North Korea.

MacArthur was explicitly forbidden from allowing any of his forces to enter or attack either China or the Soviet Union. To diminish the danger of intervention by either of these Communist countries, MacArthur was instructed that "as a matter of policy, no non-Korean ground forces will be used in the northeast provinces bordering the Soviet Union or in the area along the Manchurian border."[24]

Marshall heard a rumor that Gen. Walton Walker, commander of the Eighth Army, would pause at the thirty-eighth parallel to regroup. The defense secretary feared that such an operational pause might prove uncomfortable to America's friends in the United Nations, since it might force them formally to approve operations north of the parallel. He suspected that they would prefer being presented with a fait accompli. He wrote to MacArthur on September 29, 1950, laying out these fears. "We want you to feel unhampered tactically and strategically to proceed north of [the] 38th parallel," he stressed, probably not realizing what a wide loophole he had just opened.[25] South Korean troops, compelled by

President Rhee, began crossing the parallel as early as the next day, though it would be another week before U.S. troops ventured across. MacArthur made a mistake, however, in ordering a second amphibious landing at Wonsan, which unnecessarily complicated his logistics and delayed the UN advance into North Korea. Most of the KPA force escaped.[26]

The Chinese foreign minister, Zhou Enlai, warned on October 3 that China would intervene militarily if UN forces other than South Koreans crossed the thirty-eighth parallel. The warning went largely unheeded in Washington, but Mao Zedong on October 8 ordered Chinese troops into North Korea.[27] Meanwhile, MacArthur's September 27 orders had not contemplated a scenario in which the Chinese invaded North Korea after his forces had crossed into North Korea themselves. The Joint Chiefs remedied this by drafting an addendum, approved by Marshall, Acheson, and Truman, and transmitted to MacArthur on October 9. In such a scenario, the UN commander should continue military engagement as long as there was "a reasonable chance of success." "In any case," the JCS told MacArthur, "you will obtain authorization from Washington prior to taking any military action against objectives in Chinese territory."[28] Even though Zhou issued another warning on October 10, MacArthur dismissed the threat of Chinese intervention during the Wake Island conference with Truman and his advisers on October 15. In private, MacArthur told Truman that "the victory was won in Korea" and assured him "the Chinese Communists would not attack." During the larger meeting, the UN commander said he expected formal resistance would end in Korea by Thanksgiving and hoped to send the Eighth Army back to Japan by Christmas. He thought there was "very little" chance that either the Chinese or the Soviets would intervene in North Korea. Should Chinese troops try "to get down to Pyongyang there would be the greatest slaughter" because of the UN advantage in airpower.[29]

After taking Pyongyang and Wonsan, MacArthur drove his men northward toward the Yalu River. Even though the September 27 directive stipulated that "no non-Korean ground forces" were to be employed near the Manchurian border, the UN commander gave permission to Walker and the X Corps commander, Gen. Edward M. Almond, to use American troops near the border on October 24. The JCS asked MacArthur why he had disregarded their policy against the use of non-Korean troops near the border. MacArthur replied, in part, that his September 27 instructions had been superseded by Marshall's September 29 admonition to "feel unhampered tactically and strategically to proceed north of [the] 38th parallel." This was a dubious interpretation of

Marshall's words; the defense secretary had meant to prod the UN commander to send his forces across the parallel as quickly as possible, not give him operational carte blanche for the rest of the war. The Joint Chiefs of Staff chose not to pursue the incident any further, but MacArthur had damaged his credibility in their eyes. Chairman Bradley thought that MacArthur's order to use American troops in northernmost Korea was "not technically insubordinate" but "very close." Collins said the JCS recognized that MacArthur had "violated a policy in this case without consulting us" and feared he might do so again in an even "more serious" matter.[30]

In spite of MacArthur's assurances that the Chinese were unlikely to attack, they did in late October, inflicting severe casualties upon the ROK II Corps and U.S. First Cavalry Division.[31] When the Joint Chiefs asked for an update, MacArthur replied on November 4 that the situation was still murky but that he doubted the Chinese were actually interceding with their "full potential military forces." He thought it illogical for them to do so, argued the evidence did not yet suggest they were, and urged the JCS not to leap to "hasty conclusions." The Joint Chiefs of Staff found MacArthur's assessment "utterly reassuring."[32]

That reassurance soon vanished, however, when they learned that MacArthur had subsequently ordered his air forces to bomb the bridges over the Yalu River. He gave these orders without first clearing them with the JCS, but Lovett, the deputy defense secretary, caught wind of them through back channels. On the morning of November 6, he consulted with Acheson and Dean Rusk, the assistant secretary of state for East Asian and Pacific affairs. The three men worried that stray bombs might explode in Manchuria and fretted about the international complications that might ensue from such an accident. The British would likely be angered, since the United States had promised not to attack Manchuria without consulting them. It might complicate the U.S. attempt to persuade the UN Security Council to condemn the Chinese incursion. Worse yet, because of the Sino-Soviet Treaty, it might even draw the Soviet Union into the war. Lovett telephoned Marshall, who agreed that the proposed attacks were ill-advised unless UN troops were in danger, an important caveat. Acheson called Truman, who was in Missouri preparing to vote in his hometown of Independence the next day. Truman's views were similar to Marshall's. The president was willing to bomb the bridges if UN troops were in imminent peril but agreed with Acheson that MacArthur should furnish proof that this was actually the case before the mission proceeded.[33]

The Joint Chiefs of Staff quickly cabled MacArthur instructions to suspend all air strikes within five miles of the Manchurian border and requested an explanation why he thought it necessary to bomb the bridges. Because of the fourteen-hour time difference, the telegram arrived in Tokyo in the early hours of November 7, just in time to scrub the mission.[34] MacArthur responded to the JCS message with a fiery one of his own, in which he lodged the "gravest protest that I can make." Chinese troops and equipment were now "pouring" across the Yalu bridges "in large force," necessitating the destruction of those structures. "Every hour that this is postponed will be paid for dearly in American and other United Nations blood," he darkly prophesied. Heaping more rebuke upon the JCS, he scolded, "I cannot overemphasize the disastrous effect, both physical and psychological, that will result from the restrictions which you are imposing." He demanded that the matter be taken directly to Truman for executive decision; otherwise, he refused to accept responsibility for the military "calamity" that was likely to occur.[35]

It was still November 6 in Washington when MacArthur's immoderate message arrived. The bleak situation it described was in stark contrast to the reassuring tones of his November 4 cable. When Truman learned of MacArthur's diatribe, he authorized the attacks, which was in keeping with his earlier willingness to do so if UN lives were at stake. The JCS wrote MacArthur, noting with much understatement that the situation had "considerably changed" since his assessment just two days earlier and authorizing him to attack the Korean side of the bridges. His planes were prohibited from violating Manchurian airspace, however. The Joint Chiefs reminded the general of the grave consequences that might follow if American bombs accidentally fell on Manchuria. Such an error might bring general war with China, or worse yet the Soviets, in which case the operation would end up costing, rather than saving, UN lives.[36]

Ultimately, the attacks on the bridges were only partly successful and did little to keep Chinese troops out of North Korea.[37] Bradley thought that he and the rest of the JCS committed "the worst possible error" by failing to reprimand MacArthur for not consulting them before ordering the bridge attacks. Marshall biographer Ed Cray broadened this criticism to include the defense secretary. Among Marshall and the four service chiefs, he argued, only Marshall had sufficient stature to restrain MacArthur on such occasions as this. Yet Bradley's memoir defended Marshall, arguing that the defense secretary was reluctant to interfere with MacArthur because it was not his place to intrude into JCS oversight of a commander in the field. Pogue concurred, noting that Marshall would not have tolerated similar intrusion by Secretary of War Henry Stimson during World War II.[38]

MacArthur sent two cables to the JCS on November 7. In one, he surprisingly suggested that subsequent intelligence had confirmed his initial assessment of November 4 that Chinese forces were *not* engaged in full-scale intervention, though they still might compel his own troops to retreat. Thus, in the course of three days, the UN commander had argued that the Chinese were unlikely to intervene fully, that they were about to wipe out his entire command, and that they were unlikely to intervene fully though he still might have to retreat. It was little wonder that Acheson thought him "mercurial," though in fairness to MacArthur, Chinese forces on November 6 had unexpectedly begun to disengage and pull back.[39] In MacArthur's second message, he complained about the restrictions against operating in Manchurian airspace, arguing that this constraint gave enemy planes a safe haven. His concerns actually found a sympathetic audience among the JCS and Marshall. They favored allowing UN fighter planes to engage in "hot pursuit" of enemy warplanes a short distance into Manchuria, but Truman refused because of negative reaction from America's UN allies.[40]

On November 7, Marshall sent a message of his own to MacArthur, in response to the UN commander's heated cable the day before. Though the defense secretary adopted a conciliatory tone, he showed his support for the Joint Chiefs of Staff. In response to MacArthur's implication that the JCS had been acting without consulting the president, Marshall informed him that, to the contrary, Truman had been receiving "almost hourly" updates on the situation in Korea. He reminded the general that more was at stake than merely the tactical situation in northern Korea because of the "delicate situation" posed by Washington's efforts to persuade the UN Security Council to condemn China. Though he assured the general that the administration was "intensely desirous of supporting you," he cautioned that the present conflict in Korea "could so easily lead to a world disaster."[41]

The controversies surrounding MacArthur's use of U.S. troops near the Yalu River and his orders to bomb the bridges were both early signs that he was less concerned about the dangers of risking general war with China and the Soviets than were many of Truman's advisers, including Marshall. This difference of opinion only deepened. On November 8, the JCS asked MacArthur if, in light of Chinese intervention in Korea, he thought it time to reexamine his assigned mission of destroying North Korean military forces. MacArthur forcefully replied the next day that it would be "fatal" to settle for any mission that stopped short of destroying "all resisting armed forces in Korea" and assisting it to become "a united and free nation." It was "immoral" to leave "any portion" of North Korea in Chinese hands. He planned to resume offensive operations soon. "I recommend with all the earnestness that I possess," he implored, "that there be no weakening at this crucial moment and that we press on to complete victory which I believe can be achieved if our determination and indomitable will do not desert us."[42]

The Joint Chiefs of Staff believed differently, which is clear from a November 9 memorandum. While they stopped short of formally suggesting modification of the UN commander's current mission, they considered three military options. The first—the MacArthur option—was to drive the Chinese out of North Korea, but this might require more troops, of which the United States had few available at the moment. The second was to find and hold a defensible line somewhere south of the Manchurian border. This option was "apparently feasible" and perhaps temporarily "expedient" while Chinese intentions were yet unclear, though the JCS were loath to get quagmired in Korea. The third option was voluntarily to evacuate the Korean Peninsula and leave it in Communist hands, but this option would "so lower the worldwide prestige of the United States that it would be totally unacceptable." The real significance of the document, however, lies in its preference for a political solution to the Korean War—if possible through the United Nations—rather than a military one. Marshall endorsed the memorandum, so this reflected his thinking as well. That the JCS expressed this preference *before* the second, more devastating, Chinese offensive of late November is all the more telling. "From the military standpoint," they argued, "the continued commitment of U.S. forces in Korea is at the expense of the more useful strategic deployment of those forces elsewhere." This sentence effectively summarized the view that not only the Joint Chiefs of Staff but also Marshall and Truman took regarding the Korean War. It was a view with which MacArthur disagreed so intensely, so often, and so publicly that it eventually cost him his job.[43]

The UN commander launched his offensive on November 24, but the Chinese began their second offensive the next day, hitting MacArthur's troops hard. "We face an entirely new war," MacArthur admitted to the JCS on November 28, informing them that he would now shift to the defensive.[44] The Chinese offensive wrought angst and uncertainty in Washington. At a National Security Council meeting on November 28, there was general consensus that the United States should avoid total war with China, a view shared by Marshall. He did not want to get "sewed up in Korea" and thought the United States should extricate itself while simultaneously retaining national honor, though he was unsure how to do this.[45] Secretary Acheson wanted MacArthur to "find a line that we can hold," but MacArthur soon dashed hopes of holding any defensive line across North Korea, arguing he did not have enough troops to do so. He suggested reinforcing his command with Nationalist Chinese troops from Formosa, a proposal the JCS met with skepticism because it might "disrupt" the UN alliance.[46]

On December 2, Marshall was still fretting about the "great dilemma of determining how we could save our troops and protect our national honor at the same time," though acknowledging that the United States could not conscientiously merely abandon South Korea. At a Pentagon war council on December 3, there was discussion of the possibility of a UN cease-fire, but Acheson worried that the Chinese would demand too great a price in exchange, perhaps admission to the United Nations or U.S. abandonment of Formosa. That same day, the JCS wrote MacArthur acknowledging that "the preservation of your forces is now the primary consideration," and authorizing him to consolidate his troops into coastal beachheads.[47] These were trying times; in fact, Bradley found them more trying than even the Battle of the Bulge had been. "We have lived with danger for some years," Marshall told the staff of the American Red Cross on December 4. "Now that danger has become acute. The events of the next few weeks—or even days—may determine the course of our civilization for long years to come."[48]

Finally, Truman and his advisers received some good news on December 8. General Collins had just returned from a trip to Japan and Korea at Marshall's urging. Having seen the situation firsthand, the army chief of staff was confident that the Eighth Army would make an orderly retreat to Pusan. While acknowledging that the First Marine Division was in a "serious" fight near the Changjin (Chosin) Reservoir, he was optimistic that the X Corps would be able to evacuate the Hamhung–Hungnam area by sea and disembark at Pusan, as well. Reassembled UN troops should then be able to hold out in Pusan "indefinitely." In short, Collins did not think the UN forces were actually "in a critical condition" or that they were in imminent danger of being expelled from the peninsula.[49]

As the administration groped for a way to meet Marshall's twin hopes of extrication from Korea yet with honor intact, it became clear that, in order to avoid negotiating with the Chinese from a position of weakness, UN forces were first going to have to inflict significant casualties upon the enemy. This was the position that Marshall took.[50] On December 29, the Joint Chiefs of Staff informed MacArthur that "successful resistance to Chinese–North Korean aggression at some position in Korea and a deflation of the military and political prestige of the Chinese Communists would be of great importance to our national interests." He was now to "defend in successive positions"—that is, conduct an orderly, fighting withdrawal from one defensive line to another—and inflict "such damage to hostile forces" as he could while incurring a minimum of losses himself.[51]

To MacArthur, this message indicated that Washington had lost the "will to win." If only he was permitted to use his "full military might, without artificial restrictions," he believed that he could both "save Korea" and so damage the military and industrial capabilities of Communist China that it would be rendered harmless for "generations to come." To that end, he wrote back to the JCS on December 30 suggesting a blockade of China, destruction of Chinese factories by airpower as well as naval gunfire, and employment of Nationalist Chinese troops not only as reinforcements in Korea but also on "diversionary" missions against the mainland of China itself. Addressing the concern that broadening the war would result in full-scale war with China, he replied that China was already fully engaged. He could not say whether the Soviets would become involved, but this did not seem to trouble him.[52]

After serious consideration by the Joint Chiefs of Staff, they sent a negative reply on January 9. There could be no blockade of China without the agreement of the United Nations, particularly the British. The JCS rejected bombing targets in China, unless the Chinese attacked U.S. interests outside of Korea first. They rejected sending Nationalist Chinese troops to Korea. Although they made a tantalizing suggestion that such troops likely had "greater usefulness elsewhere," they did not authorize their use against China. Instead, the JCS reaffirmed their earlier instructions to MacArthur to fight defensively from one position to the next, maximizing enemy casualties while minimizing his own. They would continue to consider MacArthur's proposals, but in the end, never agreed to any of them.[53]

A major turning point in the war occurred on December 23, when General Walker died in a jeep accident. At MacArthur's urging, the Pentagon promptly replaced him with Gen. Matthew B. Ridgway, who had served under Marshall in Tientsin, China, during the 1920s. He had also graduated with Collins in the West Point class of 1917, then briefly served under him during the Normandy invasion, during which Ridgway parachuted into France as the commander of the Eighty-Second Airborne Division. Later, he rose to command the XVIII Airborne Corps, and more recently, was serving as Collins's deputy chief of staff for operations and administration in the Pentagon.[54]

Meanwhile, the Chinese army was losing much of its potency. About one-third of its combat troops had already become casualties, either because of combat or the extremely cold conditions. The further southward it pushed, the more its supply problems worsened. Some of the initial advantages enjoyed by the Chinese, such as high morale and the element of surprise, had disappeared. UN forces, meanwhile, still enjoyed superiority in airpower, armor, artillery, and communications.[55] In addition to these advantages, they now had Ridgway, one of the outstanding American combat commanders of the twentieth century. On December 31, Chinese forces launched their third offensive, which pushed Ridgway's Eighth Army below the thirty-eighth parallel, forcing him once again to evacuate Seoul. MacArthur predicted on January 10 that his current troop limitations and operational restraints would make the "military position of the command in Korea untenable," but events soon proved him mistaken. Ridgway's forces began to strike back in late January and started regaining lost ground.[56]

The question arose whether they should be permitted once again to conduct operations north of the thirty-eighth parallel. On February 23, Acheson recommended against "a general advance north of the general vicinity of the 38th parallel." Before submitting this recommendation to Truman, he ran it by Marshall first. The defense secretary consulted the Joint Chiefs of Staff, as well as the secretaries of the army, navy, and air force, and received conflicting advice. While the three service secretaries agreed with Acheson, the JCS disagreed, and Marshall sided with them. In a letter to Acheson asking him not to submit the recommendation to Truman, Marshall argued that UN forces needed "freedom of action and freedom of maneuver." Acheson relented, leaving Ridgway free to operate north of the parallel as opportunities presented. In the meantime, the Eighth Army commander launched on March 7 Operation RIPPER, which liberated Seoul and pushed enemy troops back across the parallel.[57]

While the Eighth Army was battling the Chinese People's Liberation Army, Marshall was engaged in the "great debate" over the size and role of the U.S. armed forces. Congress and the Truman administration had drastically decreased defense spending after World War II, from $83.0 billion in fiscal year 1945, to $9.1 billion in fiscal year 1948, and $13.7 billion in fiscal year 1950.[58] The armed forces shrank from 12.1 million personnel in 1945 to 1.5 million in mid-

1950. Nine of the army's ten divisions and both marine divisions were under-strength.[59] Truman disingenuously blamed Congress, the news media, and the American people for these reductions in defense spending, but Millett argues that the president had been their "principal architect."[60] Now one of Marshall's responsibilities was to help rebuild his country's armed forces one final time. "I was getting rather hardened to coming in when everything had gone to pot and there was nothing you could get your hands on," he later observed, "and darned if I didn't find the same thing when I came into the Korean War. There wasn't anything."[61]

The proponents of expansion had received a boost back in April 1950, when the National Security Council advanced the first draft of NSC-68, a white paper calling for the buildup of U.S. national defenses to serve as a deterrent to Soviet aggression. Debate ensued within the administration over adopting NSC-68, but the onset of the Korean War—and the limited options imposed on the Pentagon because of the reductions to the armed forces—gave momentum to advocates of a larger military.[62]

The initial defense budget for fiscal year 1951, which ran from July 1, 1950, to June 30, 1951, was just $13.3 billion. That budget was not signed until September 6, 1950, more than two months into the fiscal year and more than two months since the North Korean invasion in June. Secretary Johnson already had requested additional defense funding from Congress in July, and Congress passed a supplemental budget bill on September 23, which included $11.7 billion more for defense.[63] Even with the defense budget now grown to $25 billion, the Joint Chiefs of Staff argued that roughly $20 billion more was still needed in the current fiscal year in order to pursue the robust military structure envisioned by NSC-68. Consequently, the Pentagon requested on December 1 a little more than $16.8 billion of additional spending.[64]

That December, Marshall played a central role in making the administration's case for more defense funds, though the recent Chinese offensive made members of Congress receptive to the request. In fact, at times Marshall found himself explaining why he was not asking for *more* than the $16.8 billion. During a hearing before a House subcommittee on December 1, he explained that unless the country was actually in a general war, "this is about as fast as you can efficiently digest these sums of money."[65] In testimony before the Senate Appropriations Committee on December 9, Marshall again stressed that it was "better not to try to rush things beyond the immediate capability of expansion."[66] On December 13, Truman, Marshall, Acheson, and others met with eighteen congressional leaders from both parties to advocate additional funding. Marshall explained to lawmakers that while the United States should have sufficient strength to defend in Korea, it needed additional troops to maintain the security of Japan and Western Europe.[67]

In the end, Congress granted all but $49 million of the amount requested by the Department of Defense. With this $16.8 billion, plus an additional $6.4 billion in May, the defense budget for fiscal year 1951 ended up being $48.2 billion, while actual outlays during the fiscal year were $23.6 billion.[68] From June 30, 1950, to the same date in 1951, armed forces personnel more than doubled, from 1.5 million to 3.2 million. The army grew to fifteen full-strength divisions, plus three more below strength. The marines now had two full-strength divisions, plus a regimental combat team. The air force now maintained seventy-two combat wings, up from forty-two during the prior year. The navy's ship-force level had risen from 634 vessels to 980; it now operated twenty-six aircraft carriers instead of fifteen and eighty-three submarines instead of seventy-two.[69]

A larger military became the norm during the Cold War. Defense spending reached $46.1 billion in fiscal year 1952 and never fell below $42 billion again. According to Cray, Marshall had "shaped United States military policy for another generation."[70] Two caveats should be added, however. First, Marshall had by no means accomplished this singlehandedly; NSC-68 existed even before his return to Truman's cabinet in September 1950. Second, the military policy that emerged was not precisely the one Marshall would have chosen, since it did not include universal military training, which he regarded as an essential component.[71] Nevertheless, Marshall played a prominent role in increasing the size of the U.S. military during the Cold War.

Marshall also found himself in the middle of the sad drama surrounding Truman's decision to relieve MacArthur in April 1951. The UN commander vehemently differed with Truman, as well as with Marshall and the Joint Chiefs of Staff, over the wisdom of expanding the war into Manchuria, and, more broadly, the importance of the Far East to American security. That MacArthur held dissenting views was not necessarily a problem. That he would not quit sharing his views publicly was a big problem indeed.

He had only been UN commander for a couple of months when he wrote a public letter to the Veterans of Foreign Wars that implied criticism of Truman for not properly understanding the importance of Formosa. Truman learned of the letter in advance and ordered MacArthur to withdraw it, which he did, though it still appeared in the September 1 edition of *U.S. News and World Report*. The president was so frustrated that he considered replacing MacArthur with Bradley as the UN commander.[72] After UN fortunes rose with Inchon and fell with the Chinese foray into North Korea, MacArthur made a series of injudicious remarks, which appeared in the *New York Times* in early December. In an interview conducted by *U.S. News and World Report*, but appearing first in print in the *Times* on December 2, MacArthur complained that the rules of engagement forced upon him were an "enormous handicap, without precedent in military history." In the same edition of the *Times*, he complained to Hugh Ballie, the president of United Press, about the Europe-first orientation favored by Truman, Marshall, and the JCS. It was "fallacious" to believe that the expenditure of military effort in Asia detracted from the security of Europe, he opined. "If the fight is not waged with courage and invincible determination to meet the challenge here, it will indeed be fought, and possibly lost, on the battlefields of Europe."[73]

These indiscretions raised the ire of the president, who wrote a letter to Acheson and Marshall on December 5 stating that "military commanders and diplomatic representatives" serving abroad "should be ordered to exercise extreme caution in public statements, to clear all but routine statements with their departments," and to avoid communicating directly with the media regarding either foreign policy or military policy. The Joint Chiefs of Staff forwarded the letter to MacArthur for his "guidance and appropriate action."[74]

Nevertheless, MacArthur soon committed additional indiscretions. By mid-March, UN forces had sufficiently bloodied the Chinese army that the Truman administration was ready to negotiate. Before Truman could issue a communiqué offering to do so, MacArthur beat him to the punch with a pronouncement of his own on March 24. The UN commander's communiqué created a firestorm in Washington for its bellicosity and its implied criticism of Truman. After mockingly recounting the military and industrial limitations of the Chinese, MacArthur declared:

Even under the inhibitions which now restrict activity of the United Nations forces and the corresponding military advantages which accrue to Red China, it has been shown its complete inability to accomplish by force of arms the conquest of Korea.

The enemy therefore must by now be painfully aware that a decision of the United Nations to depart from its tolerant effort to contain the war to the area of Korea through expansion of our military operations to his coastal areas and inferior bases would doom Red China to the risk of imminent military collapse.

So inflammatory was MacArthur's message that the president did not even bother to send his own offer of negotiation. Moreover, Truman understandably regarded this as a violation of his December policy. The president, according to his memoirs, now silently resolved to relieve the UN commander.[75]

MacArthur had actually already committed another indiscretion, though it would still take a few days to play out. Congressman Joseph Martin, the Republican minority leader, had written to him on March 8, soliciting his views on the Korean situation, particularly the use of Nationalist Chinese troops. MacArthur replied on March 20, four days before his controversial communiqué to China. He not only endorsed the use of the Nationalist Chinese but also laid bare his fundamental disagreement with Truman and Marshall over grand strategy:

> It seems strangely difficult for some to realize that here in Asia is where the Communist conspirators have elected to make their play for global conquest, and that we have joined the issue thus raised on the battlefield; that here we fight Europe's war with arms while the diplomats there still fight it with words; that if we lose the war to communism in Asia the fall of Europe is inevitable, win it and Europe most probably would avoid war and yet preserve freedom. As you pointed out, we must win. There is no substitute for victory.

Martin formally read MacArthur's letter in Congress on April 5, which set in motion the final train of events culminating in MacArthur's relief.[76]

From April 6 to April 9, Marshall took part in a series of meetings regarding MacArthur's fate. The defense secretary's first impulse was caution. During a Friday morning meeting on April 6, which included Truman, presidential assistant Averell Harriman, Acheson, and Bradley, Marshall was fearful that relieving MacArthur might make Congress unwilling to pass the increased military appropriation the Department of Defense was seeking.[77] Later—probably during a meeting with Bradley, Acheson, and Harriman in the defense secretary's office that same afternoon—Marshall suggested summoning MacArthur to Washington for consultation before making a final decision about his relief. Acheson, all too aware of the UN commander's "histrionic abilities" with the public and influence on the armed forces, was horrified at the possible spectacle of MacArthur's return to the nation's capital, arrayed "in the full panoply of his commands," ready to defend his reputation and position. Acheson persuaded Marshall to drop the idea.[78]

Marshall was still reluctant to recommend MacArthur's relief on Saturday, April 7. Bradley believed there were other reasons for his reticence besides his fear regarding defense appropriations. Marshall and Bradley were both concerned that it might be difficult to prove a formal charge of insubordination against the UN commander. The JCS chairman also suspected Marshall dreaded the "savage right-wing political assault" that he knew would come his way if he supported MacArthur's dismissal, and believed Marshall did not want to give credence to rumors that he held a long-standing grudge against MacArthur. After meeting with Truman on Saturday morning, Bradley and Marshall considered, then abandoned, a last-minute plot to save MacArthur's job by writing him a stern letter to "shut up."[79]

On Sunday, April 8, the Joint Chiefs of Staff convened and, according to Collins, decided to "concur in the relief of General MacArthur by the President." Collins and the other chiefs of staff were "a sad and sober group of men" as they trooped to Marshall's office at 4:05 P.M. to share their decision. Marshall "made no comment of his own," according to Bradley, but instructed him to inform Truman the next morning. At the climactic meeting on Monday, April 9, Bradley summarized the views of the JCS for Truman. Though Bradley did not have voting rights on the JCS as chairman, his memoirs note that "it was clear to Truman that I concurred with the JCS views, as did Marshall." Truman and Acheson both remembered Marshall stating his concurrence directly. Though initially reluctant to support MacArthur's relief, the secretary of defense had finally swung around. With the concurrence of Harriman and Acheson, who were also present, Truman finally informed his advisers that he had already decided to relieve MacArthur several days earlier. The news went public on Wednesday, April 11, at the awkward hour of one in the morning, Washington time.[80] Truman assured the public that it was with "deep regret" that he had reached his decision. "I was sorry to have to reach a parting of the way with the big man in Asia," he wrote to Gen. Dwight Eisenhower the next day, "but he asked for it and I had to give it to him."[81] MacArthur returned to the United States to a hero's welcome, intensified by public opposition to Truman. In spite of the headaches MacArthur had caused, Marshall treated him courteously, coordinating the general's famous appearance before a special joint session of

Congress on April 19 and attending a ceremony in his honor at the Washington Monument on that same date.[82]

The dismissal of MacArthur prompted a Senate investigation, in which the defense secretary was required to testify for seven days. Marshall drew a careful contrast between MacArthur's views and those of the administration. He assured senators that while he, Truman, and the Joint Chiefs of Staff intended to stop Communist "aggression" in Korea, they also "persistently sought to confine the conflict to Korea and to prevent its spreading into a third world war." MacArthur, by contrast, "would have us, on our own initiative, carry the conflict beyond Korea against the mainland of Communist China, both from the sea and from the air." This would have risked not just a wider war with China, but war with the Soviets and America's abandonment by its allies. Marshall had not been troubled that MacArthur disagreed with the administration. "What is new," he explained, "and what has brought about the necessity for General MacArthur's removal, is the wholly unprecedented situation of a local theater commander publicly expressing his displeasure at and his disagreement with the foreign and military policy of the United States."[83] It later fell to Bradley to utter the most memorable line from the MacArthur hearings. Addressing MacArthur's proposal to widen the war against China, the JCS chairman observed, "This strategy would involve us in the wrong war, at the wrong place, at the wrong time, and with the wrong enemy."[84]

MacArthur's relief necessitated a shuffling of the UN command structure. At the same April 9 meeting, Marshall and Bradley recommended that Ridgway assume MacArthur's various command positions, and that Gen. James Van Fleet take Ridgway's place as commander of the Eighth Army. Van Fleet had been one of Collins's trusted subordinates as the commander of the Eighth Infantry Regiment, Fourth Division, VII Corps, during the Normandy invasion. Van Fleet had not initially been a favorite of Marshall's, however. Army lore has it that Marshall, as army chief of staff, had been reluctant to promote him because he confused him for another officer with a similar last name who had a drinking problem. Millett suggested that the real reason for Marshall's reticence had been Van Fleet's mediocrity as a staff officer. He was anything but mediocre as a combat commander, however, and was commanding III Corps by the end of the war. Marshall, in fact, later admitted that he was "probably the most aggressive and hard driving corps commander developed by [the] U.S. during the war." More recently, Van Fleet had directed the military mission to Greece, in support of the Truman Doctrine.[85]

Secretary of Defense George C. Marshall (*center*), Gen. Matthew B. Ridgway (*back left*), and Lt. Gen. James A. Van Fleet (*back right*), commanding general of the Eighth Army, prepare to depart by jeep for X Corps headquarters in Hongchon, Korea. June 8, 1951. Courtesy George C. Marshall Library, Lexington, Va.

UN soldiers continued to pummel Chinese and North Korean troops in the months after Ridgway was bumped up to UN commander and Van Fleet was assigned to command the Eighth Army. Exercising the latitude that Marshall preserved for them, UN forces pushed generally north of the thirty-eighth parallel, occupying lines more defensible than the parallel itself.[86] In June, Marshall traveled to Japan to confer with Ridgway. The UN commander accompanied him to Korea, where they flew through dangerously foul weather so Marshall could view the front. Back in Japan, Marshall admitted to Ridgway that even he had not realized conditions were so bad. According to Col. James T. Quirk, who was also present, Marshall contemplated advising Truman to warn the Chinese that if they did not agree to end the war in Korea, "we are going to give them a taste of the atom."[87]

No atomic attacks proved necessary to produce peace, though it did require two agonizing years of negotiations between the Communists and the United Nations. Meanwhile, soldiers continued to suffer death or injury: 45 percent of American casualties in Korea occurred *after* the truce talks began.[88] Finally, the delegates—though none from South Korea—signed an armistice on July 27, 1953, recognizing a permanent division between North and South Korea near the thirty-eighth parallel.

Marshall had long since retired by then. True to his word, he stepped down as defense secretary on September 12, 1951, just a few days short of one full year. During his year running the Pentagon, he had taken part in several important decisions.[89] The decision to allow MacArthur to conduct operations north of the thirty-eighth parallel in September 1950 was deeply consequential, because it led to Chinese intervention. Yet there was no realistic opportunity to destroy the Korean People's Army without doing so. If UN forces had merely chased the KPA across the parallel before leaving Korea, the Republic of Korea would scarcely have been any safer than it had been in June 1950, before the North Korean invasion.

The decision to deny MacArthur's request to expand the war into Manchuria was especially significant. While it made it much harder—though probably not militarily impossible—to defeat the Chinese in Korea, it also quite possibly avoided a potential World War III.[90] MacArthur, however, with his penchant for grandiosity, was temperamentally unsuited to fight the sort of limited war that his superiors in Washington requested of him.

Marshall's successful effort in preserving Ridgway's freedom of action north of the parallel in the spring of 1951 was also important, for at least three reasons.

It prevented the parallel from becoming an artificial barrier behind which Communist forces could regroup, thus empowering UN forces to engage and attrit them north of the parallel; it allowed UN forces to recapture some ground north of the parallel, which ultimately became South Korean territory; and it enabled them to occupy lines that were more easily defensible than the strictly east–west latitude line had been.[91]

Marshall's contributions as defense secretary to enlarging the military enhanced his already firmly established reputation as a builder of armies. In mid-1950, the United States simply did not possess armed forces large enough to project power in Asia and Europe simultaneously, as the doctrine of containment required. Beginning with fiscal year 1951, however, larger defense budgets and force structures became the norm. Even so, the United States would learn soon enough the limits of its military power in the jungles of Vietnam.

Though Marshall had been reluctant to recommend MacArthur's relief from command, he was finally persuaded to do so. In the final months of his long public-service career, Marshall thus reaffirmed the principle of civilian control over the military, one of his bedrock beliefs. It is regrettable that the MacArthur-Truman controversy ended the way it did, and it is tempting to wonder if Marshall might have been able to save MacArthur from himself if he had intervened forcefully earlier. But to have done so would have violated another of his beliefs, that the responsibility to oversee a theater commander was properly vested in the Joint Chiefs of Staff, not the secretary of defense.

Finally, Marshall's tenure as defense secretary proved again his remarkable sense of duty. It not only cost him a year of his life but also subjected him to intense stress and withering criticism from the hard-right wing of the Republican Party.[92] In accepting Marshall's resignation in September 1951, Truman acknowledged that "one time after another" he had "responded to the call to public service" and had done so in exemplary fashion. "You have earned your retirement many fold," the president closed, "and I wish you many good years at Leesburg."[93]

NOTES

1. Marshall to Rose Page Wilson, July 24, 1950; Marshall to F. Trubee Davison, April 28, 1950—both in Mark A. Stoler and Daniel D. Holt, eds., *The Papers of George Catlett Marshall*, vol. 7: *"The Man of the Age": October 1, 1949–October 16, 1959* (Baltimore: Johns Hopkins University Press, 2016) (hereafter cited as *Papers of George Marshall*, 7), 146. The author would like to thank the following for assistance in locating sources used in this chapter: David Clark of the Harry S. Truman Library, Emillia Cline of Harding University's Brackett Library, and Bill Sabin of Arkansas State University's Dean

B. Ellis Library. He would also like to thank his wife, Natalie, not only for proofreading and making valuable suggestions, but most of all, for her love and support even while she became a research widow during the last several weeks of 2018.

2. For the pervasive view that the Soviets had instigated the KPA invasion, see Dean Acheson, *Present at the Creation: My Years in the State Department* (New York: W. W. Norton, 1969), 405; Omar N. Bradley and Clay Blair, *A General's Life: An Autobiography* (New York: Simon & Schuster, 1983), 563–64; J. Lawton Collins, *War in Peacetime: The History and Lessons of Korea* (Boston: Houghton Mifflin, 1969), 78; and James F. Schnabel, *Policy and Direction: The First Year*, United States Army in the Korean War (Washington, D.C.: Center of Military History, 1992), 75, https://history.army.mil/html /books/020/20-1/CMH_Pub_20-1.pdf. Max Hastings argues that such an assumption was not illogical given Soviet behavior in Eastern Europe after World War II; see *The Korean War* (New York: Simon & Schuster, 1987), 339. In reality, Joseph Stalin reluctantly had acquiesced to North Korean dictator Kim Il-sung's desire to conquer South Korea based upon the false assumption that Truman would not respond militarily; see Allan R. Millett, *The War for Korea, 1950–1951: They Came from the North* (Lawrence: University Press of Kansas, 2010), 12, 46–49; and Hastings, *Korean War*, 51.

3. Allan R. Millett, *The War for Korea, 1945–1950: A House Burning* (Lawrence: University Press of Kansas, 2005), 148–58, 190, 255–56.

4. Harry S. Truman, *Memoirs*, vol. 2: *Years of Trial and Hope* (Garden City, N.Y.: Doubleday, 1956), 333. For the criticism of Truman and its effect upon policy, see Hastings, *Korean War*, 48–49.

5. Schnabel, *Policy and Direction*, 70; UN Security Council resolution, July 7, 1950, Department of State, Office of the Historian, *Foreign Relations of the United States, 1950*, vol. 7: *Korea* (Washington, D.C.: Government Printing Office, 1976), 211 (hereafter cited as *FRUS*, followed by year and volume).

6. Memorandum for File, July 8, 1950, Korea: July 1950, box 71, Subject File, George M. Elsey Papers, Harry S. Truman Library.

7. For Truman's inquiry, see *Papers of George Marshall*, 7:130n4. For Marshall's comment, see Marshall to Wilson, July 24, 1950, in ibid., 146.

8. Mark A. Stoler, *George C. Marshall: Soldier-Statesman of the American Century* (Boston: Twayne, 1989), 145; Marshall to F. Trubee Davison, April 28, 1950, in *Papers of George Marshall*, 7:86.

9. Millett, *They Came from the North*, 57–58, 144; Forrest C. Pogue, *George C. Marshall*, vol. 4: *Statesman, 1945–1959* (New York: Viking, 1987), 420–22.

10. Bradley and Blair, *General's Life*, 542; Millett, *They Came from the North*, 145.

11. Pogue, *Statesman*, 436–38; Stoler, *George C. Marshall*, 181.

12. Pogue, *Statesman*, 422; Millett, *They Came from the North*, 239.

13. Pogue includes a useful discussion of these events, including the Jenner and Saltonstall quotations, in *Statesman*, 424–28. He does not separate the Senate debate over the amendment from the debate over Marshall's confirmation, however; cf. *Papers of George Marshall*, 7:157–58n1, 160–63.

14. Stoler, in *George C. Marshall*, mentions Marshall's relationship with Truman (138), Acheson (156, 184), and Bradley, Collins, and Vandenberg (184). Pogue discusses Bradley, Collins, and Vandenberg in *Statesman*, 438–40.

15. For a list of MacArthur's commands, see *Papers of George Marshall*, 7:125.

16. For general biographical information on Marshall and MacArthur, see *Webster's American Military Biographies* (Springfield, Mass.: G. & C. Merriam, 1978), 253–54, 273. For MacArthur's transfer of Marshall, see Debi Unger and Irwin Unger with Stanley Hirshson, *George Marshall: A Biography* (New York: Harper, 2014), 66–68. For various gestures of support made by Marshall, see Stoler, *George C. Marshall*, 118–19; Unger and Unger, *George Marshall*, 246, 252, 354; and Pogue, *Statesman*, 22.

17. For more on Marshall's strategic thought during World War II, see Stoler's chapter on this subject in *George C. Marshall*, 89–108; for MacArthur's, see ibid., 118–19.

18. Stoler, *George C. Marshall*, x; Millett, *House Burning*, 93; Truman, *Years of Trial and Hope*, 399; Pogue, *Statesman*, 152, 520.

19. Pogue, *Statesman*, 62.

20. Walter S. Poole, *History of the Office of the Joint Chiefs of Staff*, vol. 4: *The Joint Chiefs of Staff and National Policy, 1950–1952* (Washington, D.C.: Office of Joint History, 1998), 20, http://www.jcs.mil/Portals/36/Documents/History/Policy/Policy_V004.pdf.

21. Collins, *War in Peacetime*, 78–81; Bradley and Blair, *General's Life*, 534, 557–58; Schnabel, *Policy and Direction*, 79; Matthew B. Ridgway, *The Korean War* (1967; repr., New York: Da Capo, 1986), 35.

22. Collins, *War in Peacetime*, 85, 123–26; Bradley and Blair, *General's Life*, 556–57.

23. Collins, *War in Peacetime*, 141–42; Ridgway, *Korean War*, 42, 61. Hastings quotes Maj. Gen. Charles Bolté: "We were all rather scared of him. When you considered what he had been." Hastings, *Korean War*, 194.

24. The first eleven paragraphs of the September 27 JCS directive are reprinted in *FRUS, 1950*, 7:781–82, while the final paragraph is on 785. For the approval process, see Marshall to Truman, September 27, 1950, in *Papers of George Marshall*, 7:168 (and 168–69nn2–3).

25. Marshall to MacArthur, September 29, 1950, in *Papers of George Marshall*, 7:171 (and n1).

26. Roy E. Appleman, *South to the Naktong, North to the Yalu: June–November 1950*, United States Army in the Korean War (Washington, D.C.: Center of Military History, 1961), 615, 623, https://history.army.mil/html/books/020/20-2/CMH_Pub_20-2.pdf; Bradley and Blair, *General's Life*, 567–68, 578; Ridgway, *Korean War*, 41–44; Millett, *They Came from the North*, 281–82; Hastings, *Korean War*, 125–26.

27. Julius Holmes to Acheson, October 3, 1950, in *FRUS, 1950*, 7:839. For Washington's dismissal of the threat, see Bradley and Blair, *General's Life*, 569–70; Truman, *Years of Trial and Hope*, 361–62. For Mao's orders, see Millett, *They Came from the North*, 294.

28. JCS to MacArthur, October 9, 1950, in *FRUS, 1950*, 7:915. For the approval process, see Lovett to Truman, October 7, 1950, in ibid., 911–12 (and n1). Zhou's October 10 warning, quoted in editorial note, in *FRUS, 1950*, 7:913–14.

29. Truman, *Years of Trial and Hope*, 365; Wake Island conference memorandum, in *FRUS, 1950*, 7:948–60.

30. James F. Schnabel and Robert J. Watson, *History of the Joint Chiefs of Staff*, vol. 3: *Joint Chiefs of Staff and National Policy*, pt. 1: *1950–1951, The Korean War* (Washington, D.C.: Office of Joint History, 1998), 118–19, http://www.jcs.mil/Portals/36/Documents /History/Policy/Policy_V003_P001.pdf. Bradley and Collins both discuss this, though they misdate Marshall's "unhampered" message as September 30. Bradley and Blair, *General's Life*, 578–79; Collins, *War in Peacetime*, 181. Collins's quotation is from Schnabel and Watson, *Joint Chiefs of Staff and National Policy*, pt. 1, 119.

31. Appleman notes that the Chinese had "disastrously" crippled the ROK II Corps by November 1 and that the U.S. Eighth Cavalry Regiment, First Cavalry Division, suffered about six hundred casualties at Unsan in early November. Appleman, *South to the Naktong*, 675, 708.

32. MacArthur to JCS, November 4, 1950, reprinted in Truman, *Years of Trial and Hope*, 373; Bradley and Blair, *General's Life*, 583.

33. Millett, *They Came from the North*, 308–9; Memorandum of conference between Acheson, Lovett, and Rusk, in *FRUS, 1950*, 7:1055–57; Truman, *Years of Trial and Hope*, 373–75; Acheson, *Present at the Creation*, 463–64; *Papers of George Marshall*, 7:226–28.

34. JCS to MacArthur, November 6, 1950, in *FRUS, 1950*, 7:1057–58; Millett, *They Came from the North*, 308–9.

35. MacArthur to JCS, November 7, 1950, reprinted in Truman, *Years of Trial and Hope*, 375.

36. Bradley and Blair, *General's Life*, 585–87; Truman, *Years of Trial and Hope*, 375–76; JCS to MacArthur, November 6, 1950, in *FRUS, 1950*, 7:1075–76.

37. Schnabel and Watson, *Joint Chiefs of Staff and National Policy*, pt. 1, 129.

38. Bradley and Blair, *General's Life*, 587; Ed Cray, *General of the Army: George C. Marshall, Soldier and Statesman* (New York: Simon & Schuster, 1991), 700; for Pogue's observation, drawn from a letter he wrote to Blair, dated August 19, 1982 (after Bradley's death), see *General's Life*, 587, as well as 720, chap. 58, n14. Bradley's memoir is problematic because he died before his collaborator, historian Clay Blair, wrote the section on the Cold War period. Blair chose to finish the project while still writing in Bradley's voice, drawing upon interviews, Bradley's correspondence, and other sources. Bradley and Blair, *General's Life*, 10–11.

39. MacArthur to JCS, November 7, 1950, in *FRUS, 1950*, 7:1076–77; Acheson, *Present at the Creation*, 465; Hastings, *Korean War*, 137–38.

40. Schnabel, *Policy and Direction*, 247–50; Bradley and Blair, *General's Life*, 594.

41. Marshall to MacArthur, November 7, 1950, in *Papers of George Marshall*, 7:228.

42. JCS to MacArthur, November 8, 1950, in *FRUS, 1950*, 7:1097–98; MacArthur to JCS, November 9, 1950, in ibid., 1107–10.

43. JCS Memorandum, November 9, 1950, in *FRUS, 1950*, 7:1117–21; for Marshall's concurrence, see Marshall to Acheson, November 10, 1950, in ibid., 1126.

44. Schnabel and Watson, *Joint Chiefs of Staff and National Policy*, pt. 1, 147–49; MacArthur to JCS, November 28, 1950, in *FRUS, 1950*, 7:1237–38.

45. Notes on NSC meeting, November 28, 1950, in *FRUS, 1950*, 7:1242–49; Truman, *Years of Trial and Hope*, 386; Acheson, *Present at the Creation*, 469. Marshall also expressed opposition to a general war with China in a December 7 meeting between Truman and British prime minister Clement Attlee; see *FRUS, 1950*, 7:1455.

46. Acheson's remark was made during the November 28 NSC meeting (cited above), in *FRUS, 1950*, 7:1246. MacArthur rejected holding a line in separate cables to the JCS dated November 30 and December 3, 1950, in ibid., 1259–60, 1320–22. Regarding MacArthur's proposal to use Nationalist Chinese troops, see JCS to MacArthur, November 29, 1950, in ibid., 1253–54 (and n1).

47. Memorandum by Lucius D. Battle of meeting held on December 2, 1950, dated the next day, in *FRUS, 1950*, 7:1310–12; Memorandum of meeting held on December 3, 1950, in ibid., 1323–34; JCS, quoted in Schnabel and Watson, *Joint Chiefs of Staff and National Policy*, pt. 1, 162.

48. Bradley and Blair, *General's Life*, 581; Marshall, Remarks to American Red Cross staff, December 4, 1950, in *Papers of George Marshall*, 7:283–84.

49. Marshall encouraged Collins to go to the Far East during a war council on December 1, 1950; see *FRUS, 1950*, 7:1278. Collins reported during a December 8 meeting between Truman and Attlee; see *FRUS, 1950*, 7:1468–72.

50. Marshall advocated this view during the MacArthur hearings; see *Papers of George Marshall*, 7:507. According to Millett, Marshall and Bradley both favored this position by early December; Millett, *They Came from the North*, 359. See also Hastings, *Korean War*, 185.

51. JCS to MacArthur, December 29, 1950, in *FRUS, 1950*, 7:1625–26.

52. Douglas MacArthur, *Reminiscences* (New York: McGraw-Hill, 1964), 378; MacArthur to JCS, December 30, 1950, in *FRUS, 1950*, 7:1630–33.

53. JCS to MacArthur, January 9, 1951, in *FRUS, 1951*, vol. 7, pt. 1, 41–43; Schnabel, *Policy and Direction*, 317–22, 328–30.

54. Collins, *War in Peacetime*, 236; Pogue, *Statesman*, 472–73; *Webster's American Military Biographies*, 350.

55. Millett, *They Came from the North*, 356.

56. Schnabel, *Policy and Direction*, 308–9, 333–34; MacArthur to Army Department, January 10, 1951, in *FRUS, 1951*, vol. 7, pt. 1, 55–56.

57. Acheson to Marshall, February 23, 1951, in *FRUS, 1951*, vol. 7, pt. 1, 189–94; Marshall to Acheson, March 1, 1951, in ibid., 202–6, 203n2; Schnabel, *Policy and Direction*, 351–54.

58. Cray, *General of the Army*, 706; Office of Management and Budget (OMB), *Historical Tables* (Washington, D.C., 2018), 122–23, table 6.1, https://www.whitehouse.gov /wp-content/uploads/2018/02/hist-fy2019.pdf (accessed October 8, 2019).

59. According to 1997 data from the Department of Defense, personnel levels were 12,055,884 in 1945 and 1,459,462 in 1950. *Selected Manpower Statistics: Fiscal Year 1997* (Washington, D.C.: Directorate for Information Operations and Reports, 1997), 51, table 2-11, https://apps.dtic.mil/dtic/tr/fulltext/u2/a347153.pdf. According to Walter Poole, the personnel level as of June 30, 1950, was 1,453,544; statistics regarding army and marine divisions are also from Poole; see *Joint Chiefs of Staff and National Policy*, 4:20.

60. Truman, *Years of Trial and Hope*, 325, 345, 414; Millett, *They Came from the North*, 111–12 (see also 54–57, 77).

61. Quoted in Stoler, *George C. Marshall*, 183. Stoler observes that this was the third time Marshall had to build up U.S. forces (183). The first had been during World War I, when, as aide to the flu-stricken Gen. J. Franklin Bell, he had been "virtually in charge of the mobilization effort in the Eastern Department" in 1917 (35). The second was during World War II.

62. For the text of NSC-68, see *FRUS, 1950*, 1:234–92. Millett discusses NSC-68 and defense spending in *They Came from the North*, 65–66, 145–46, 366–68.

63. Doris Condit, *History of the Office of the Secretary of Defense*, vol. 2: *The Test of War, 1950–1953* (Washington, D.C.: Office of the Secretary of Defense, Historical Office, 1988), 223–27, https://permanent.access.gpo.gov/gpo58448/OSDSeries_Vo12 .pdf; Poole, *Joint Chiefs of Staff and National Policy*, 4:24.

64. Condit, *Test of War*, 233–37.

65. U.S. Congress, House, *Second Supplemental Appropriation Bill for 1951: Hearings before Subcommittees of the Committee on Appropriations*, 81st Cong., 2nd sess., December 1, 1950, 18, https://hdl.handle.net/2027/umn.31951d03496123b (accessed October 8, 2019).

66. Quoted in *Papers of George Marshall*, 7:291–92.

67. Truman, *Memoirs*, 2:420–22; Millett, *They Came from the North*, 366–67.

68. Condit, *Test of War*, 240; OMB, *Historical Tables*, 123, table 6.1.

69. See Poole, *Joint Chiefs of Staff and National Policy*, 4:20, 46; Condit, *Test of War*, 238, table 3. Air force strength is from Condit. Ship force levels are from Naval History and Heritage Command, "US Ship Force Levels," https://www.history.navy .mil/research/histories/ship-histories/us-ship-force-levels.html.

70. OMB, *Historical Tables*, 123–30, table 6.1; Cray, *General of the Army*, 706.

71. Marshall, Statement before the Preparedness Subcommittee of the Senate Armed Services Committee, in *Papers of George Marshall*, 7:326–28.

72. MacArthur, "Formosa Must Be Defended," *U.S. News and World Report*, September 1, 1950, 32–34; Bradley and Blair, *General's Life*, 550–51; Truman, *Years of Trial and Hope*, 354–56.

73. "Texts of Comments by MacArthur on Korean War," *New York Times*, December 2, 1950, late city ed.; Joseph Fromm, "MacArthur's Own Story: An Interview with the U.N. Commander in Chief," *U.S. News and World Report*, December 8, 1950, 16–17.

74. Truman's letter, dated December 5, 1951, and JCS cover comment are reprinted in Collins, *War in Peacetime*, 280.

75. MacArthur's March 24, 1951, communiqué is embedded within Acheson's telegram of same date, in *FRUS, 1951*, vol. 7, pt. 1, 265–66; see also Truman, *Years of Trial and Hope*, 439–45.

76. Martin's letter to MacArthur, dated March 8, 1951, and MacArthur's reply, dated March 20, 1951, are reprinted in U.S. Congress, Senate, Committees on Armed Services and Foreign Relations, *Military Situation in the Far East*, 82nd Cong., 1st sess., 1951, pt.

5, 3543–44, https://hdl.handle.net/2027/mdp.39015005249118 (accessed October 8, 2019); see also *Papers of George Marshall*, 7:478.

77. Truman, *Years of Trial and Hope*, 447–48; Bradley and Blair, *General's Life*, 631–32; Acheson, *Present at the Creation*, 521; Pogue, *Statesman*, 481.

78. Acheson, *Present at the Creation*, 521–22; cf. Bradley and Blair, *General's Life*, 632; *Papers of George Marshall*, 7:479. Acheson mistakenly remembered that the Friday afternoon meeting occurred in his office, rather than Marshall's. He also could not remember whether Marshall made his suggestion Friday afternoon or Saturday morning, but according to Bradley and Blair, it was Friday afternoon. It seems improbable that Marshall would have raised the point in Truman's presence Saturday morning.

79. Bradley and Blair, *General's Life*, 633.

80. Collins, *War in Peacetime*, 283; Bradley and Blair, *General's Life*, 634–36; Truman, *Years of Trial and Hope*, 448; Acheson, *Present at the Creation*, 522.

81. Truman's statement regarding MacArthur, dated April 11, 1951, and Truman's letter to Eisenhower of April 12 are both in box 116, folder Truman, Harry S. (1), Eisenhower Pre-Presidential Papers, Principal File, Eisenhower Library.

82. Marshall to MacArthur, April 16, 1951, in *Papers of George Marshall*, 7:487–88 (and nn1–2); Pogue, *Statesman*, 484.

83. Marshall, Statement before the Senate Committee on Armed Services and the Committee on Foreign Relations, May 7, 1951, in *Papers of George Marshall*, 7:501–5. For a synopsis of Marshall's seven-day testimony, see ibid., 505–16.

84. Bradley and Blair, *General's Life*, 640. The authors make it clear that Bradley was criticizing MacArthur's proposal for a wider war against China, not the initial decision to support South Korea.

85. Bradley and Blair, *General's Life*, 635; Collins, *War in Peacetime*, 294–95; Millett, *They Came from the North*, 428; *Webster's American Military Biographies*, 450–51; Marshall, quoted in Pogue, *Statesman*, 398.

86. Ridgway, *Korean War*, 190.

87. Quoted in Pogue, *Statesman*, 487–88.

88. Hastings, *Korean War*, 329.

89. See Stoler's insightful assessment of Marshall's tenure as secretary of defense; Stoler, *George C. Marshall*, 190–92.

90. After inflicting heavy casualties upon the Chinese in the spring of 1951, it appeared that UN troops had the opportunity to launch a potentially devastating attack, which they did not take. See Millett, *They Came from the North*, 443, 448; and Hastings, *Korean War*, 229, 281.

91. The Joint Chiefs had warned against allowing the territory north of the thirty-eighth parallel to become a safe haven in which enemy troops could concentrate; see attachment to Marshall's letter to Acheson, March 1, 1951, in *FRUS, 1951*, vol. 7, pt. 1, 202–6.

92. Besides Jenner, Joseph McCarthy (R-Wisc.) severely criticized Marshall on the Senate floor on June 14, 1951. Cray, *General of the Army*, 721–23.

93. Truman, quoted in *Papers of George Marshall*, 7:629–30.

9

THE FREEDOM TO SERVE

Marshall and Racial Integration of the U.S. Military

The Korean War marked a pivotal time in U.S. history. It was the first "hot war" of the greater Cold War that pitted Western capitalism against Soviet communism and the first time that U.S. policy makers attempted to prosecute a war of limited aims after having fought the most destructive war in the twentieth century. On the faraway Korean Peninsula, racial integration became an important issue with respect to fielding an effective force and furthering the goals of a U.S. government determined to present itself—in opposition to the Soviet Union's style of communism—as a bastion of equality and freedom. With severely depleted forces and equipment after Department of Defense downsizing in the aftermath of World War II, U.S. forces scrounged together troops from home and overseas units to organize a response to the North Korean attack on its southern neighbor. In the first phase of the conflict, U.S. forces were augmented with South Korean troops, yet African American units in the army remained segregated. Such organization was cause for concern for many reasons, U.S. President Harry S. Truman having ordered racial integration as official policy two years prior being chief among them. Moreover, the rigorous fighting during this period led to mounting casualties, which in turn resulted in a further-depleted force. In this tense climate, company and regimental commanders began integrating units to fill those that were left understrength. It was Gen. Matthew B. Ridgway as a member of the higher echelon, however, who facilitated the process of racial integration in the U.S. Army, ending the major roadblock to equality in the armed forces that African Americans had been struggling to transcend since the American Civil War.

Who was Matthew Ridgway? What qualities did he possess that led him to climb the promotion ladder to become the commander-in-chief of the Far East Command and be in a position to effect change on racial policy in the U.S. Army? Neither of these questions can be answered without a similar analysis of George C. Marshall, who was Ridgway's mentor and friend but also the U.S. policy maker responsible for setting more military and diplomatic policy than any other American leader in the twentieth century. Throughout a forty-three-year army career, culminating in his position as the fifteenth army chief of staff and subsequent posts as the fiftieth secretary of state and third secretary of defense, Marshall was involved directly and indirectly with the racial policies of the army for half a century. All policies regarding racial integration from 1939 until the army had officially integrated flowed through him. Serving under Marshall in multiple capacities since the mid-1920s, Ridgway cemented a lasting relationship with him that offered Ridgway later opportunities to rise through the ranks, chances to learn the inner workings of politics in the War Department and Washington, D.C., and experiences to realize the injustice and inefficiency of maintaining a racially segregated army.

Racial integration was the culmination of a long and arduous process that had been argued over since the American Civil War. African American civil rights leaders correctly had surmised that in the history of civil-military relations in the United States, nothing spelled out loyalty to the nation more than the ideal of the citizen-soldier. Understanding this, they adopted the strategy of using the military as the route to equality. Initially, that approach meant securing legislation that provided for a permanent role for African Americans in the U.S. Army. Historically, they had only been allowed to serve when the demands of war forced the government to solicit their inclusion. As soon as hostilities waned, however, they were typically inactivated and processed out of military service. Some progress was made when Congress passed the Army Reorganization Act of 1866, establishing four black infantry units: the Thirty-Eighth, Thirty-Ninth, Fortieth, and Forty-First Infantry Regiments—later organized in 1868 into the Twenty-Fourth and Twenty-Fifth Infantry units, and two cavalry units—the Ninth and Tenth Cavalry.[1] The act, while providing a permanent place in the nation's army for African Americans, was only a modest step toward their larger goals. Those who were able to gain entry soon found themselves deployed to outposts on the edge of the western frontier fighting Native Americans, where the army would not face any issues of cohabitation with the white population. Many African Americans, however, did not gain entry. With only a handful of units organized, the quota for enlistments was quickly met. For the remainder of the century, blacks had little opportunity to gain significant numbers in the military. African American leaders quickly deduced that in order to make greater headway toward equality, racial integration within the armed forces was the major hurdle that they needed to overcome.

Little progress was made in the Spanish-American War at the turn of the century. African Americans clamored to be included in the forces that were organized to fight in Cuba. In the end, official battle reports showed that of the 15,000 troops that fought on July 1, 1898, on the high ground near Santiago, Cuba, as part of Gen. William Shafter's Fifth Army Corps, 2,000 were African American troops. In the two battles that transpired that day—El Caney and San Juan Heights—"blacks and whites, fought side by side, endured the blistering heat and driving rain, and shared food and drink as well as peril and discomfort."[2]

While the Spanish American War lasted only three months, during that time African Americans had fought valiantly and had proven their worth in Cuba and Puerto Rico. The Sixth Massachusetts Regimental National Guard and its Black Company L engaged in a few skirmishes, and when America replaced Spain as the colonial power in the Philippine Islands, two new black regiments—the Forty-Eighth and Forty-Ninth Infantry Regiments—were organized.[3] The government welcomed African American participation in Cuba and Puerto Rico because it believed that black troops could be effectively used to cooperate with Cuban insurgents, who were of a darker complexion as well.[4] A more impressive sign of progress came when, upon being asked if black officers and troops were to be taken, Secretary of War Russell Alger commented that "if a colored company had efficient, soldierly colored officers they were as much entitled to recognition and acceptance in the military service as were the troops themselves."[5] Progress was short-lived, however, as black National Guard units were disbanded after the war.

Although black participation was largely forgotten and the government remained true to its normal practice of pressing them out of military service, the experience in the Spanish-American War had highlighted the importance of the National Guard in securing the right to fight. The National Guard was an important institution for a number of reasons, most important its symbolic connection to nation and citizenship.[6] It was the organized militias, after all, that had defended the colonies before the establishment of a Continental Army and augmented said forces during the War of Independence. The establishment of black National Guard units would also signal a tacit recognition of African American capabilities on a societal level, given that the organization of such units would require the respective state to subsidize the equipping and housing of them.[7] Such acknowledgment would, in turn, signal approval of African American National Guard units being activated, as no state would appropriate funds without the expectation of a return on its investment. The National Guard, then, seemed like a more direct avenue to combat, rather than trying to secure entry into one of the few all-black regular army units.

Choosing to organize National Guard units paid off during World War I. Units were activated to form the Ninety-Third Infantry Division that would participate in the war raging on the European continent. The Ninety-Third Infantry was composed of four segregated units: the 369th, 370th, 371st, and 372nd Infantry Regiments. Initially put to work in labor assignments, the Ninety-Third would soon be transferred and placed under the control of French forces. Gen. Philippe Pétain, commander of the French forces, provided expedited training and sent the African American units to the front to fill gaps caused by the harshness of a trench war that had been raging for three and a half years. The Ninety-Third performed splendidly. More than 170 of its members individually earned the Croix de Guerre or the French Legion of Honour, in addition to the unit receiving this commendation medal.[8] The 369th Regiment—originally the Fifteenth New York National Guard unit—was the only unit never to give up ground to the enemy or lose a soldier by capture.[9]

While the exploits of the Ninety-Third Division demonstrated the fighting ability of African Americans to the world, their own government did not provide similar praise. The unit had been integrated with French troops, but American units remained racially segregated. The Ninety-Second Division, the other all-black outfit sent to France, had been filled with draftees and saw no combat during the war. In post–World War I America, African Americans endured a Jim Crow system that prevented them from enjoying the same benefits as their white counterparts.[10] In the military, any successes of the Ninety-Second and Ninety-Third Infantry Divisions were quickly forgotten, as black separation rates in the army—the rate of those leaving the service—began to outpace recruitment rates. Yet again, racial integration would remain a dream until the next war demanded African American inclusion.

That chance came when the world plunged into war again two decades later. African Americans had little success in their attempts to secure equality in the civilian world during the interwar period and once again looked to the military to provide a route to that goal when America entered World War II. President Franklin D. Roosevelt enacted two key pieces of legislation between 1940 and 1942 that had a profound impact on the future of African Americans in combat and the process of racial integration.[11] The first was the Selective Training and Service Act, signed into law on September 16, 1940. The act was designed to compel all men between the ages of twenty-one and thirty-five to register for the draft and produced the induction of eight hundred thousand draftees.[12] In terms of increasing numbers of places for blacks in the military, the act seemed promising. As for facilitating racial integration, however, it fell short. African Americans clung to a small ray of hope after reading Section 4a of the act, which stated that "there shall be no discrimination against any person on account of race or color."[13] It did not require any of the military commanders to eliminate segregation, however, and a passage in Section 3a stated that "no man shall be inducted for training and service until adequate provision shall have been made for such shelter, sanitary facilities, water supplies, heating and lighting arrangements, medical care, and hospital accommodations, for such men, as may be determined by the Secretary of War."[14]

Angered, African American leaders lambasted the president. They correctly argued that such an arrangement largely excluded African Americans because their participation centered on the ability or willingness of the armed forces to build separate facilities. At a meeting with the president and key defense leaders arranged shortly after the Selective Training and Service Act passed, black leaders' concerns met with apathy from Secretary of War Henry L. Stimson, who recalled that a similar attempt had been made by the Woodrow Wilson administration during World War I. While black leaders and the defense secretaries seemed to be at an impasse, the president needed the support of all parties involved. His solution to the dilemma was to have Steve Early, White House press secretary, announce that the number of blacks inducted into the army would be proportional to their share of the U.S. population, which at that time was approximately 10 percent. All combat and noncombat units, including aviation units, would accept black soldiers. Officer Candidate School (OCS) would begin to admit blacks, but graduates could only serve in black units where white officers held command positions. While the change in policy opening up combat billets certainly was a welcome adjustment, the section of the press release affirming that the policy of "not integrating colored and white enlisted personnel in the same regimental organization" would stand, effectively tabling any further discussion on racial integration.[15]

The second important document during World War II was Executive Order 8802, issued by President Roosevelt on June 25, 1941. The order forbade discrimination in industries holding government contracts for war production and in training for jobs in war industries. It also created the Fair Employment Practices Commission to investigate and take action against discrimination.[16] Executive Order 8802 had a more profound effect on the navy and marine corps, which did not have the history of recruiting African Americans that the army did. In the army, the 10 percent quota that was enacted before the order remained in place, as did racial segregation.

Of the many blacks who were drafted or volunteered for service in the army during the war, only about 15 percent secured combat assignments.[17] In 1942, the army reactivated the Ninety-Second and Ninety-Third Infantry Divisions, the black divisions that had fought in World War I, and organized a new Second Cavalry Division, comprising the Ninth and Tenth Cavalry Regiments.[18] The Ninety-Second Division, which saw combat in Italy toward the end of the war, was the only unit to serve as a full division in combat. The Ninety-Third Division saw little combat during the war. After being deployed from San Francisco in 1944, it was involved in campaigns in New Guinea, the Northern Solomons, and the Bismarck Archipelago, but mainly acted as security forces or laborers, unloading ships and cleaning up battle debris.[19] Several smaller black combat units were also organized. The 969th Field Artillery Battalion supported the defense of Bastogne. The 452nd Antiaircraft Battalion supported the Allied drive across Europe into Germany.[20] The 761st Tank Battalion, which had the first black armored combat commander, reinforced Gen. George S. Patton's Third Army in the Battle of the Bulge and was involved in four major campaigns.[21] Other black combat units, such as the 369th Antiaircraft Artillery Defense Regiment and the 555th Infantry (Airborne) Battalion, had been organized and trained throughout the war but never saw combat. The 369th defended the Hawaiian Islands against the possibility of another attack, and the 555th, nicknamed the "Triple Nickel," deployed to the Pacific Northwest to fight forest fires.

That African Americans proved their merit in their country's time of need was certain, but without fighting in integrated units, securing forward progress on the issue of equality remained elusive. The chance they needed, however, came toward the end of the war, when mounting white casualties as a result of the strong German offensive in the Ardennes forced the War Department to issue a directive to black units calling for volunteers to augment white units.[22] Initially, the need for personnel was so dire that the army planned to integrate black infantry soldiers individually with whites, but due to fears of political reprisals based on the long-standing policy of segregation, it instead formed all-black platoons that were integrated into white infantry companies.[23] These "Fifth Platoons" served as a major step toward integration in the army. They represented the first move to integrate black and white soldiers at the regimental level. In March, April, and May 1945, fifty-two of these platoons went into action along the Rhine to push for the final defeat of Germany.[24]

While the creation of the "Fifth Platoons" had demonstrated that racial integration was feasible, the experiment did not change the army's persistent policy on segregation. At the close of the war, blacks who had fought in these units were returned to their segregated units, and the Ninety-Second Division, the largest all-black unit, was deactivated. To some, however, the success of the integrated companies demonstrated that racial integration provided for a more effective fighting force. In May 1945, the army commissioned a study on the performance of blacks who had volunteered for service in integrated units. The subsequent report, "The Utilization of Black Platoons in White Companies," published one month later by the Research Branch, Information and Education Division, Headquarters, U.S. Army, European Theater of Operations, emphatically recounted that white soldiers had attained a profound respect for the black soldiers who fought alongside them, and many would welcome fighting beside them in the future.[25] Despite the clear evidence that suggested that racial integration was not only effective but accepted, the army delayed publishing the findings of the commission, deferring to its traditional attitudes on this issue. Integration, it seemed, would require a push from a higher authority.

On July 26, 1948, President Harry S. Truman provided that push by exercising his power of executive fiat. Realizing that many inequalities still prevailed in the African American military experience, he signed Executive Order 9981 and made equality of treatment and opportunity for all persons in the armed services official policy without regard to race, color, religion, or national origin.[26] It was the most significant official policy enacted hitherto and was met with jubilant praise from the African American community. Acclaim would be short-lived, however, as the order turned out to be more of a paper exercise with respect to racial integration. Service branch leaders regarded it as more of a guideline than a mandate. Secretary of the Army Kenneth C. Royall only complied with the provisions of the order when forced to by the President's Committee on Equality of Treatment and Opportunity, more commonly referred to as the Fahy Committee after its chair, Charles Fahy, which was organized to enforce the provisions of the order. Arguments over implementation, quotas, and assignments continued for two years, and lasting change toward implementing racial integration in the army would only transpire "when manpower shortages dictated the need to fill understrength units (white or black) with available soldiers."[27] On the eve of the Korean War, 98 percent of African American troops remained in segregated army units.[28] That would not remain the case for long, however, as the demands of war, changing attitudes, and pragmatic leadership facilitated the final move toward racial integration. None of those changes, however, could have transpired without the experience, wisdom, and influence of George C. Marshall.[29]

Marshall served in the army for most of the African American struggle to gain entry into the army in the twentieth century. Commissioned in 1902, he was keenly aware of the historic attitudes within the army toward black troops. Marshall served in a training and organization role for the First Division prior to World War I. While on the staff of the American Expeditionary Forces Headquarters during the war, he was privy to information on the performance of black units in the war. Moreover, he was a key planner of the Meuse-Argonne offensive, a battle in which the African American Ninety-Second and Ninety-Third Infantry Divisions participated.[30] Given his involvement with planning, he was keenly aware of the successes and failures of the all-black divisions, as well as the general attitudes of higher-ranking American officers toward their performance.

Marshall firmly believed in the reciprocal nature of civil-military relations. Leaders had asserted the importance of military service since the founding of the American Republic. George Washington, the leader to whom Marshall is often compared, in his "Sentiments on a Peace Establishment," commented: "It may be laid down as a primary position, and the basis of our system, that every citizen who enjoys the protection of a free Government, owes not only a

proportion of his property but even his personal services to the defense of it."[31]
Marshall believed in this spirit of civic duty as well, as his efforts to promote
universal military training after World War II attested. His experience differed,
however, in that he was frequently confronted with the issue of racial equality
in the armed forces and society as a whole that was gaining momentum during
his time as army chief of staff.[32] Applying his convictions regarding citizenship
to all races, Marshall asserted that "when you are calling on a man to risk his
life in the service of the country, he had every right, it would certainly seem, to
demand the same rights [as] the other fellow who was risking his life."[33]

Such poignant words regarding the treatment of minority personnel were
taken by civil rights leaders at the time, however, as mere lip service. In response
to a memorandum from William H. Hastie, a civilian aide to Secretary of War
Henry L. Stimson, sent in an attempt to pressure the army on racial integration in
September 1941, Marshall claimed that while many of his statements were valid,
"this would be tantamount to solving a racial problem that has perplexed American People throughout the history of this nation. The Army cannot accomplish
such a solution and should not be charged with the undertaking. The settlement
of vexing racial problems cannot be permitted to complicate the tremendous
task of the War Department and thereby jeopardize discipline and morale."[34]
Marshall openly admitted that he was not satisfied with the progress on racial
matters in the army. In stating that it was not up to the War Department to
solve social issues, however, he effectively outlined the position that the army
would take on the issue of racial integration until it was forced to change at
the end of the decade.[35] Maintaining this traditional attitude did nothing to
combat prejudices that civil rights leaders viewed as a systemic problem in the
armed forces. Marshall's actions, however, spoke more of a leader tasked with
organizing the development and mobilization of the nation's largest war effort
hitherto in its history, rather than a man bent on suppressing the advancement
of African Americans.

In his reminiscences to biographer Forrest Pogue in 1957, Marshall openly
admitted his failure to deflect pressures placed on him by his staff and lack of
foresight as to the consequences of his actions regarding policies on training.
Instituting policy based on the normal auspices of sound military planning
regarding weather, terrain, and logistics, Marshall recalled that he "wanted
the camps largely kept in the south, because they didn't have to have such construction as they would in a northern climate, and in addition to that, training
would be much facilitated because they could train outdoors for more days

in the year."[36] What he failed to account for, however, was the treatment that African American soldiers would undoubtedly be subjected to in a Jim Crow South that was largely prejudiced against them and the army's lack of control over busing and transportation in a region that was rigidly prejudiced against supporting African American troops. Characterizing this as one of the "biggest mistakes he made in the mobilization of the Army," Marshall said, "We should have never coagulated the south with these Negro camps . . . my refusal was not based upon that understanding (of the difficulties) . . . there was no hope of settling that at that time . . . anything of that kind would lead to dissension . . . and we had enough on our hands to get a fighting army."[37]

While Marshall made self-professed mistakes regarding African American troops during the war, to claim that he purposely tried to hinder their progress is a stretch. He had authorized Dwight D. Eisenhower to incorporate his "Fifth Platoons" toward the end of World War II. After the war was over, he kept his word to readdress inadequate policies regarding segregated units when he organized the Gillem Board, a committee of three general officers he tasked with preparing "a policy for the use of the authorized Negro manpower potential during the postwar period including the complete development of the means required to derive the maximum efficiency from the full authorized manpower of the nation in the event of a national emergency."[38] Based on the attitudes of senior officers in the army at the time, Marshall was perhaps the greatest ally African Americans had in the army. He not only possessed an equitable outlook on citizenship and service; he was responsible for recognizing the future military leaders who would eventually transform policies on race.

As part of his reorganization of the War Department and army personnel, "he insisted that his subordinates, including combat commanders, be autonomous, self-activating agents."[39] He envisioned a general and civilian aide staff that would rely on their own sound judgment and not bother him with play-by-play details of their decisions. Marshall's conceptions of what made a strong leader formed the basis of how generals would be selected for many years.[40] While this was important in later years in securing victory in World War II and establishing a capable general staff schooled in the art of war, it was also relevant to the process of racial integration as those leaders he selected would be responsible for ultimately steering the army toward that path.

In 1920, when serving as aide-de-camp to Gen. John J. Pershing, Marshall jotted down notes that he thought best exemplified the qualities that successful leaders should possess. Among them were good common sense; someone who had studied his profession; was physically strong, cheerful, and optimistic; displayed marked energy; possessed extreme loyalty; and was determined.[41] Leaders who possessed these qualities were remembered, either stored within the confines of Marshall's exceptional memory or written down in a little black book that he was rumored to have kept.

If these were the qualities that he required in a general, Marshall could have found no more fitting leader than Ridgway, who served in four important assignments under the command of Marshall during the 1920s and 1930s that were instrumental to Ridgway's future success. First, Ridgway served as a company commander under Assistant Regimental Commander Marshall with the Fifteenth Infantry Regiment in Tientsin, China, during the mid-1920s. From 1929 to 1930, Ridgway was a student under Assistant Commandant Marshall at the Advance Course at the Infantry School at Fort Benning, Georgia, which he recalled Marshall had made into one of the "finest and most thorough advanced military courses in the world."[42] Their third meeting came in the mid-1930s, during planning and execution of military maneuvers in the Midwest overseen by Marshall. Serving as the assistant chief of staff, G-3 (operations) of the Second Army and VI Corps Area, Ridgway devised training maneuvers in preparation for the looming world war. Ridgway recalled it as one of the "toughest jobs ever handed to him" and remembered Marshall coming to him at the end of the exercise with kind words of praise that "boosted his spirits."[43] In a letter to Ridgway on August 24, 1936, after the maneuvers, Marshall wrote that "you personally are to be congratulated for the major success of all the tactical phases of the enterprise. . . . I wanted to thank you for the very vital services you rendered to me during the maneuvers in digging me out of a hole two or three times. . . . You did such a perfect job that there should be some way of rewarding you other than saying it was well done."[44] Their fourth assignment together during the period came when Ridgway served as a delegate on a military mission to Brazil in 1939, led by Brigadier General Marshall, to "lay the groundwork for closer collaboration" in the event that the United States became involved in World War II.

As a result of these interactions, Ridgway cemented his reputation with Marshall. His role as assistant chief of staff, G-3 (operations) of the Second Army and VI Corps Area, stood out as a key experience that demonstrated Ridgway's future potential as a capable leader. Nonetheless, these four encounters during Ridgway's development as an officer left a lasting impression on Marshall, whose support proved instrumental in Ridgway's rise to the rank of major general in 1942 when he was given command of the newly activated Eighty-

Second Airborne Division. There and in his subsequent post as commander of the Eighteenth Airborne Corps, he proved to be a capable commander. He battled in Eindhoven, the Netherlands, in the Ardennes, and along the Rhine River against the German "Ruhr Pocket" to link up with Soviet troops in the Baltic region. His performances in those campaigns and others led Marshall to claim later that Ridgway had "firmly established himself in history as a great battle leader."[45]

Continued praise from Marshall was always a blessing as Ridgway considered him both a mentor and a friend. Moreover, such accolades from the man whom multiple world leaders believed to be the organizer of the Allied victory in World War II were of significant importance in catapulting Ridgway into future roles as military adviser to the U.S. delegation to the UN General Assembly, commander of U.S. forces in the Caribbean, army deputy chief of staff in the Pentagon, commander of the Eighth Army in Korea, and commander-in-chief of the Far East Command and UN Forces. It was in this latter role as commander-in-chief of the Far East Command that Matthew Ridgway went down in history as the man who dealt racial segregation in the army its final blow.

The successes and failures of segregated units were not new to Ridgway. He was aware of the accomplishments of the Tuskegee Airmen—originally deemed by the all-white leadership in the army as not possessing of the faculties to operate aircraft—who were proving to be particularly effective escort and attack pilots. Having planned the airborne invasion of Sicily in 1943 and participated with his Eighty-Second Airborne Division, he was invested in the triumph of the Italian campaign. He was transferred to Northern Ireland to help plan the pending invasion of Normandy at the close of 1943. He was kept abreast of how events were unfolding in Italy, however, given that the planning for Operation OVERLORD always depended on how Allied forces were progressing in other theaters. He was keenly aware of the performance of the 370th Regimental Combat Team and the greater Ninety-Second Infantry Division, which got off to a shaky start.

The experiences of the Ninety-Second, commanded by Maj. Gen. Edward M. Almond, provided a glaring example of the wrong way to employ African American troops. Almond, a native Virginian, graduate of the Virginia Military Institute, veteran of World War I, and George C. Marshall's brother-in-law, exhibited the unofficial but enduring belief in the War Department that white southerners provided the best leadership for black units because they supposedly understood the capabilities of African Americans.[46] Almond constantly exhibited his lack of enthusiasm for his assignment, his absence of confidence in the black soldiers under his command, and his reluctance to award commendation medals to blacks.[47] When fighting near the village of Sommocolonia, two platoons of black troops were overrun by German forces. When negative reviews for the Ninety-Second in Italy called the leadership of the division into question, Almond blamed black troops for blemishing his record.[48]

If the Ninety-Second's exploits provided a lesson in poor leadership, the exploits of the fifty-two "Fifth Platoons" in March, April, and May 1945 along the Rhine in the final push against Germany were indicative of the potential success that racial integration could offer.[49] Facing personnel shortages in the later stages of the war, the army issued a directive approved by Eisenhower, the supreme commander of the Allied Expeditionary Force, that went out to all black units asking for volunteers to replace fallen white soldiers as a result of massive losses and a strong German counteroffensive.[50] The army originally planned to integrate black infantrymen individually with whites, but due to fear of political reprisals based on the established policy of segregation, they instead formed all-black platoons that were integrated into white infantry companies.[51] As commander of the XVIII Airborne Corps in the Battle of the Bulge, Ridgway had firsthand knowledge of the performance of these units and of the army-commissioned study, "The Utilization of Black Platoons in White Companies," that followed in 1945. Knowledge of blacks' performance and the positive reviews received from whites who had fought with them were of great importance later, when personnel shortages in Korea forced Ridgway to make more permanent policy changes with regard to racial integration.

When hostilities broke out in Korea in June 1950, Ridgway was serving as the deputy chief of staff for administration under U.S. Army Chief of Staff Gen. J. Lawton Collins. In late December 1950, Walton Walker, commander of the Eighth Army, deployed in Korea, died in a jeep crash. Collins promptly dispatched Ridgway to assume command of the Eighth Army. When he arrived in theater, Ridgway found the Eighth Army devoid of martial spirit. Remembering in his memoirs his first encounters with troops that were holding the line beyond the Han River, he noted, "They were unresponsive, reluctant to talk. I had to drag information out of them. There was a complete absence of alertness, that aggressiveness, that you find in troops whose spirit is high."[52]

In terms of race relations within the army at the time, Ridgway inherited a command of demoralized black units that had been denigrated in the press. Blacks were rebuked by senior officers for "bugging out" in the face of the

North Korean enemy in key battles, such as the fight to break free from the
Pusan Perimeter in July 1950 and at Battle Mountain the following month.
African American soldiers soon came to suspect that they were deliberately "left
undermanned and underequipped so the blame for military failures could be
placed on them."[53] It should be noted that failures by whites were just as common during the first phase of the war. Bradley Biggs recounted: "In July 1950,
ill-equipped, ill-prepared, white U.S. troops reeled from and fled an armor-
heavy North Korean onslaught. Near Hadong, North Korean forces routed the
3d Battalion of the U.S. 19th Infantry Regiment. . . . When the North Korean
4th Infantry Division attacked white 1st Battalion, 34th Infantry, soldiers, the
white unit fled the battlefield, leaving behind heavy weapons, rifles, carbines,
and ammunition on its retreat south to Chonan."[54] Despite obvious examples
of cowardice displayed by white units, none of them received the negative press
that African American units were subjected to or the severity of punishment
for their actions.[55]

Some progress on racial integration had been made prior to Ridgway's arrival.
U.S. forces had gone to Korea severely undermanned and poorly equipped. After
hard fighting in the first months of the war, mounting casualty rates relentlessly
depleted combat units. In response, some battalion commanders began integrating their units to bring them up to strength for the continued fight. Upon
assuming command of the Second Division after its retreat from the Yalu River
in October 1950, Maj. Gen. Clark L. Ruffner found many of his battalions to be
already integrated.[56] Despite this foresight demonstrated by officers in the later
months of 1950, sustained pressure from higher-ranking officials continued to
halt any widespread move toward racial integration. General Almond took the
opportunity to reinforce his position by ordering the resegregation of the Second
Division. Ruffner claimed: "Almond had nearly gotten it back to where all the
battalions were once again segregated. . . . Even after a massive influx of black
replacements arrived, I was under orders from Almond not to place blacks in
white combat units. . . . So I filtered them into white combat-service units. . . .
They did a damn fine job and there was never any trouble from southern whites,
nor any black-white conflict."[57] Such was the situation when Ridgway arrived
at the end of December 1950. Upon assuming command, he was tasked with
breaking the Chinese offensive that had placed U.S. forces on the retreat. His
successes and failures were watched closely by leaders in Washington and by
his immediate commander, Gen. Douglas MacArthur, who remained in Tokyo.
Mounting a successful turnaround depended on fielding an efficient force.

Fundamentally, Ridgway was always a soldier that preferred the field over the desk, which made his assignment as commander of the Eighth Army in Korea all the more fitting.[58] He was a sharp leader that had a talent for inspiring soldiers to work and fight. In *The War for Korea, 1950–1951: They Came from the North,* Alan Millett explains that Ridgway "impressed his fellow officers with his physical courage, force of character, energy, quick intelligence, broad professional knowledge, soldierly skills, self-confidence, ruthlessness, and deft manipulation of others."[59] Ridgway's main concern was with "restoring the Army's fighting spirit, a quality that cannot be imposed from above but that must be cultivated in every heart, from private on up." Martial spirit, Ridgway felt, was "rooted in the individual's sense of security, of belonging to a unit that will stand by him, as units on both sides and in the rear stand by all other units too."[60]

He believed in "the old fashioned idea that it helped the spirits of the men to see the Old Man up there, in the snow and the sleet and the mud, sharing the same cold, miserable existence they had to endure."[61] Such thinking mirrored that of his mentor, George Marshall, who Gen. Alan Brooke, chief of the Imperial General Staff and Marshall's British counterpart during World War II, once claimed had "treated his inferiors almost the same as his peers."[62] For African American troops that had borne the brunt of some of the most harrowing fights in the war thus far and had been the constant scapegoat for commanders of divisions who did not perform well in battle, Ridgway's personal approach went a long way toward curbing further resentment.

Ridgway's character was further confirmed by Harry Summers, squad leader of Company L of the Twenty-First Infantry Regiment, who commented:

> When he got to Korea the first thing Ridgway did was go out and talk to people. He talked to every corps commander and every division commander. He would stop soldiers along the road and talk to them. . . . He had a real empathy for the GI, and also a firm belief in the effectiveness of leadership. . . . I think Ridgway realized that an integrated unit usually performed much better in combat than a segregated one.[63]

Ridgway's journey to the front lines and hands-on approach to leadership facilitated two important changes. First, his surprise at and utter disdain for division commanders who lacked the requisite leadership capabilities led him to purge the Eighth Army of such officers in a fashion reminiscent of Marshall's reorganization of military leadership during World War II. Second, with respect to race, the experience further cemented his belief that racial integration was the "only way to assure the sort of esprit a fighting army needs, where each soldier stands proudly on his own feet, knowing himself to be as good as the next fellow and better than the enemy."[64]

Ridgway had always been more pragmatic when it came to racial integration. He needed men to fight and did not see a point in maintaining segregated units at the expense of progress on the battlefield. As the rotation system sent men home and brought new ones to the front, black troops were integrated into white companies, and vice versa. On February 8, after Ridgway's offensive codenamed THUNDERBOLT had retaken Inchon, the *New York Times* confirmed that "for some weeks now, the Army has been assigning white replacements to black units and black replacements to white units . . . discovering that the removal of the color line among fighting troops is paying dividends both in morale and in battle."[65] Similar reports continued in the following months, highlighting that racial integration was indeed moving forward.

Moreover, Ridgway wrote in his treatise on the Korean War that when he was commander of the Eighth Army he received support from Maj. Gen. William B. Kean, commander of the Twenty-Fifth Division: "An earnest and thoughtful recommendation for the integration of white and Negro troops. . . . Both from human and military point of view, it was wholly inefficient not to say improper, to segregate soldiers this way."[66] Kean had experience observing black troops, including the Twenty-Fourth Infantry Regiment that was then under his command, as well as those that trained at Fort Benning, Georgia, before the war. Ridgway found Kean's assessment to be on par with his own and "planned to seek authorization in mid-March from General MacArthur, who would in-turn sound out Washington, to commence integration at once."[67] While viewing racial integration as a step toward military efficiency and a partial solution to the morale problem affecting black troops, he personally had always felt that maintaining segregation was wrong. He thought it "both un-American and un-Christian for free citizens to be taught to downgrade themselves . . . as if they were unfit to associate with their fellows or to accept leadership themselves."[68]

If it had not been clear before, by the spring of 1951 Ridgway—as well as others—correctly surmised that full racial integration of army units would be the most effective strategy in supplying personnel and boosting the morale of war-weary soldiers. Moreover, as Bernard C. Nalty, prominent historian of race relations in the U.S. military, commented in *Strength for the Fight: A History of*

Black Americans in the Military, "the efficiency of Ridgway's command depended on the prompt arrival of trained replacements, but badly needed black infantrymen idled away their time in Japan because white units could not accept them."[69] That situation simply did not make sense to Ridgway.

With enough evidence of his own to substantiate a more widespread policy of integration, he decided to take his thoughts up the chain of command. He approached the subject with U.S. Army Chief of Staff Maxwell D. Taylor at a meeting in Tokyo. At that meeting, Ridgway implied that if he could get the approval from higher authorities, he planned to "effect full integration beginning with the largest all-black combat units, the 24th IR and the two infantry battalions in the 9th and 15th IRs."[70] Ridgway could have easily instituted integration in the Far East theater given his position as commander-in-chief of the Far East Command. Unlike his predecessor, however, he was savvy enough to recognize that receiving permission from his superiors on major policy issues was sound practice. His decision to do so was based on his command of two National Guard units—the Fortieth Infantry Division from California and the Forty-Fifth Division from Oklahoma—that raised the issue of federal-state relations.[71] His decision soon panned out, as Taylor approved of the move and commissioned a research study for a team of social scientists to travel to Korea to interview black and white soldiers that eventually became known as Project Clear in February 1951.[72] Project Clear would later confirm what Ridgway and other senior military officers had come to realize through their combat experiences in Korea: "that racial integration worked."[73]

In the meantime, the move toward racial integration in Korea was confirmed when Ridgway took over as commander-in-chief of the Far East Command and UN Forces after President Truman relieved Gen. Douglas MacArthur. By April 11, 1951, Ridgway had full control over operations in Korea and continued to push Chinese and North Korean forces until he recaptured Seoul and the Soviet Union called for armistice talks.[74] In June that same year, Ridgway found himself with a unique opportunity to settle the issue of racial integration once and for all, when Secretary of Defense Marshall made a trip to Korea and Tokyo. Marshall agreed with Ridgway's plans on implementing racial integration and took the plans to be approved in Washington, D.C. Support from his mentor was likely the only ammunition Ridgway needed, however. Washington approved his plans as well, and he implemented them throughout his command. His successes soon led the army to facilitate racial integration in all theaters of operations. At the end of February 1954, *Time* magazine reported that "there

U.S. soldiers dropping their trash in containers in Korea. Circa 1951. Courtesy Harry S. Truman Library, Independence, Mo.

were only 10,000 persons still serving in the Army's all-black units, with some 190,000 absorbed in regular outfits."[75]

The process of racial integration was a long struggle that began with African Americans merely seeking the ability to gain entry into the army in significant numbers. Gaining entry soon led to the next logical step: racial integration came to be viewed as the greatest measure of equality. African American leaders assumed that by transcending racial barriers in the armed forces, one of the most conservative institutions in the United States, they could then replicate that experience in broader American society. Numerous studies were conducted by the army on the use of African Americans with positive results. None of those positive reviews, however, could shake the ingrained prejudices held by many white senior officials and military leaders within the army and the War Department. It was only through the foresight and action taken by key individuals that racial segregation in the army was dealt its final blow. That momentous shift began with Marshall and ended with Ridgway. The mutual respect that these men had for one another grew from the first time that Ridgway served under Marshall in China. Ridgway quickly impressed his commanding officer and demonstrated capabilities that Marshall deemed worthy of future commanders. In turn, Marshall exhibited the strength of character he would later become famous for and thereby established the basis for a long-term mentorship of the junior officer. For the next three decades, Ridgway learned from and consulted Marshall not only about the inconsistencies of army policy with respect to race, but on how to lead the army and the government effectively through the transition toward racial integration in the early Cold War.

NOTES

1. The Twenty-Fourth and Twenty-Fifth Infantry Regiments remained segregated until they were disbanded at the close of the Korean War, when the needs of the services dictated that racial segregation would not maintain combat efficiency.

2. Frank N. Shubert, "Buffalo Soldiers at San Juan Hill," paragraph 11, paper presented at the 1998 Conference of Army Historians, Bethesda, Md., http://www.history.army .mil/documents/spanam/bssjh/shbrt-bssjh.htm.

3. "Black Americans in the U.S. Military from the American Revolution to the Korean War: The Spanish American War and the Philippine Insurgency," New York State Military Museum and Veterans Research Center, https://dmna.ny.gov/historic /articles/blacksMilitary/BlacksMilitarySpanAm.htm; Jeremy P. Maxwell, *Brotherhood in Combat: How African Americans Found Equality in Korea and Vietnam* (Norman: University of Oklahoma Press, 2018), 33–34.

4. "Negro Troops Called On," *New York Times*, April 4, 1898.

5. "Second Levy of Troops," *New York Times*, May 28, 1898.

6. Jeffrey T. Sammons and John Howard Morrow, *Harlem's Rattlers and the Great War: The Undaunted 369th Regiment and the African American Quest for Equality* (Lawrence: University Press of Kansas, 2014), 62.

7. Maxwell, *Brotherhood in Combat*, 35.

8. Bill Harris, *The Hellfighters of Harlem: African-American Soldiers Who Fought for the Right to Fight for Their Country* (New York: Carroll & Graf, 2002), 221.

9. Ibid.

10. Michael Lee Lanning, *The African-American Soldier: From Crispus Attucks to Colin Powell* (New York: Citadel, 2004), 161.

11. Maxwell, *Brotherhood in Combat*, 41.

12. Claudette E. Bennett, *We the Americans: Blacks* (Washington, D.C.: U.S. Department of Commerce, Economics and Statistics Administration, U.S. Census Bureau, 1993), 4.

13. President Franklin D. Roosevelt, "Selective Service and Training Act of 1940," *World Affairs* 103, no. 3 (1940): 180.

14. Lanning, *African-American Soldier*, 165.

15. Adjutant General's Office, "War Department Press Release," October 9, 1940, RG 407, National Archives and Records Administration (hereafter cited as NARA).

16. Maxwell, *Brotherhood in Combat*, 47.

17. Lanning, *African-American Soldier*, 173.

18. Ibid., 174.

19. Ninety-Third Infantry Division information found in Department of the Army, *The Army Almanac: A Book of Facts Concerning the Army of the United States* (Washington, D.C.: Government Printing Office, 1950), 510–92. See also Lanning, *African-American Soldier*, 174.

20. Lanning, *African-American Soldier*, 180.

21. Gail Lumet Buckley, *American Patriots: The Story of Blacks in the Military from the Revolution to Desert Storm* (New York: Random House, 2001), 278.

22. Ibid.

23. David Colley, *Blood for Dignity: The Story of the First Integrated Combat Unit in the U.S. Army* (New York: St. Martin's Press, 2003), xiii.

24. Ibid.

25. Maxwell, *Brotherhood in Combat*, 56; Colley, *Blood for Dignity*, 189.

26. "Executive Order 9981," July 26, 1948, RG 11, General Records of the United States Government, NARA.

27. Maxwell, *Brotherhood in Combat*, 75.

28. Arthur H. Mitchell, *Understanding the Korean War: The Participants, the Tactics and the Course of the Conflict* (Jefferson, N.C.: McFarland, 2013), 112.

29. For a comprehensive understanding of the different levels of racism that permeated the military establishment, see James E. Westheider, *Fighting on Two Fronts:*

African Americans and the Vietnam War (New York: New York University Press, 1997), 4–6. As his title suggests, Westheider's analysis centers on racism in the military during the Vietnam War; however, his identification of three forms of racism—institutional, personal, and perceived—is the standard by which historians understand race relations more broadly in the military. Much of this, however, cannot be applied to the Korean War because institutionally the armed services were still segregated, thereby making perceived racism a moot point.

30. Jami L. Bryan, "Fighting for Respect: African-American Soldiers in World War I," *On Point*, January 20, 2015, https://armyhistory.org/fighting-for-respect-african -american-soldiers-in-wwi/.

31. George Washington, "Sentiments on a Peace Establishment," 1783, paragraph 37, https://founders.archives.gov/documents/Washington/99-01-02-11202.

32. Universal military training (UMT) was a method of maintaining a sufficient military posture, one sufficiently strong without the hefty expense of a large standing military establishment, whereby all males, upon turning eighteen, would report for up to one year of basic military instruction. On UMT, see William A. Taylor, *Every Citizen a Soldier: The Campaign for Universal Military Training after World War II* (College Station: Texas A&M University Press, 2014).

33. James H. Willbanks, ed., *Generals of the Army: Marshall, MacArthur, Eisenhower, Arnold, Bradley* (Lexington: University Press of Kentucky, 2013), 46–47; Larry I. Bland, ed., *George C. Marshall: Interviews and Reminiscences for Forrest C. Pogue, Transcripts and Notes, 1956–1957* (Lexington, Va.: George C. Marshall Research Foundation, 1986), 68.

34. Memorandum, CofS for SW, December 1, 1941, sub: Report of Judge William Hastie, Civilian Aide to the Secretary of War, dated September 22, 1941, OCS 20602–219.

35. Maxwell, *Brotherhood in Combat*, 31.

36. Interview with Forrest Pogue, February 14, 1957, in George Catlett Marshall and Forrest C. Pogue, *George C. Marshall Interviews and Reminiscences for Forrest C. Pogue* (Lexington, Va.: George C. Marshall Research Foundation, 1991), 459.

37. Ibid.

38. Quoted in Memorandum, Gen Gillem for CofS, November 17, 1945, sub: Report of Board of General Officers on Utilization of Negro Manpower in the Post-War Army, copy in CSGOT 291.2 (1945) BP, reprinted in Morris J. MacGregor, *Integration of the Armed Forces, 1940–1965*, 153.

39. Debi Unger and Irwin Unger with Stanley Hirshson, *George C. Marshall: A Biography* (New York: HarperCollins, 2014), 161.

40. Thomas E. Ricks, *The Generals: American Military Command from World War II to Today* (New York: Penguin, 2012), 24.

41. George Marshall to Brig. Gen. John S. Mallory, November 5, 1920, in Larry I. Bland and Sharon Ritenour Stevens, eds., *The Papers of George Catlett Marshall*, vol. 1: *"The Soldierly Spirit": December 1880–June 1939* (Baltimore: Johns Hopkins University Press, 1981), 202–3.

42. Matthew B. Ridgway and Harold H. Martin, *Soldier: The Memoirs of Matthew B. Ridgway, as Told to Harold H. Martin* (New York: Harper, 1956), 42.

43. Ibid., 45.

44. George Marshall to Matthew B. Ridgway, August 24, 1936, in Bland and Stevens, *"Soldierly Spirit,"* 504.

45. Foreword to Ridgway and Martin, *Soldier.*

46. Lanning, *African-American Soldier*, 178.

47. A. William Perry Collection (AFC/2001/001/51117), Veterans History Project, American Folklife Center, Library of Congress.

48. Maxwell, *Brotherhood in Combat*, 123.

49. Colley, *Blood for Dignity*, xiii.

50. "Army Eulogizes Negro Soldiers," *New York Times*, January 1, 1945.

51. Colley, *Blood for Dignity*, xiii.

52. Ridgway and Martin, *Soldier*, 205.

53. Christine Knauer, *Let Us Fight as Free Men: Black Soldiers and Civil Rights* (Philadelphia: University of Pennsylvania Press, 2014), 196.

54. Bradley Biggs, "The 24th Infantry Regiment: The 'Deuce-Four' in Korea," *Military Review* 83, no. 5 (September–October 2003): 64.

55. Maxwell, *Brotherhood in Combat*, 111.

56. Lee Nichols, *Breakthrough on the Color Front* (New York: Random House, 1954), 113.

57. Ibid.; Leo Bogart, *Project Clear: Social Research and the Desegregation of the United States Army* (New Brunswick, N.J.: Transaction, 1992), 21.

58. Clay Blair, *The Forgotten War: America in Korea, 1950–1953* (New York: Anchor, Doubleday, 1989), 561.

59. Allan R. Millett, *The War for Korea, 1950–1951: They Came from the North* (Lawrence: University Press of Kansas, 2010), 311.

60. Matthew B. Ridgway, *The Korean War: How We Met the Challenge; How All-out Asian War Was Averted; Why MacArthur Was Dismissed; Why Today's War Objectives Must Be Limited* (New York: Da Capo, 1986), 192.

61. Ridgway and Martin, *Soldier*, 204.

62. Andrew Roberts, *Masters and Commanders: How Four Titans Won the War in the West, 1941–1945* (New York: HarperCollins, 2009), 390–91.

63. Harry Summers interview in Rudy Tomedi, *No Bugles, No Drums: An Oral History of the Korean War* (New York: John Wiley & Sons, 1993), 106–7.

64. Ridgway, *Korean War*, 193.

65. "Mixing of G.I. Units Pays off in Korea," *New York Times*, February 9, 1951.

66. Ridgway, *Korean War*, 97.

67. Ibid., 192.

68. Ibid., 193.

69. Bernard C. Nalty, *Strength for the Fight: A History of Black Americans in the Military* (New York: Free Press, 1986), 259.

70. Ridgway, *Korean War*, 192.

71. Nalty, *Strength for the Fight*, 259.

72. MacGregor, *Integration of the Armed Forces*, 441.

73. Bogart, *Project Clear*, 1.

74. Maxwell, *Brotherhood in Combat*, 103.

75. "Races: The Unbunching," *Time*, February 22, 1954.

CONCLUSION

Good and Faithful Servant

Many observers have commented on George C. Marshall's significant legacy before and during World War II.[1] As both a soldier and a statesman, Marshall's public-service career spanned half a century. Lance Morrow perceived, "The arc of his life was also the nation's trajectory. He molded his life and work to his duty and nation—and those four things became indistinguishable."[2] Indeed. George C. Marshall had already secured an impressive legacy at the conclusion of World War II. Henry L. Stimson, secretary of war during World War II, characterized Marshall as "the finest soldier I have ever known." President Harry S. Truman, the eighth president under whom Marshall served, described him as "at the top of the great commanders in history" and "the greatest living American." Winston Churchill portrayed Marshall as the "true organizer of victory" in World War II.[3] Many others agreed, and most commentators since have hailed him as the architect of Allied success.[4] Marshall's legacy did not end there, however. Just as he had a positive impact on the United States in numerous and significant ways before and during World War II, he also did so in its aftermath. As the preceding chapters of this volume have demonstrated, Marshall's leadership helped steer the United States through a stormy transition from the vast destruction of World War II to the clear emergence of the United States as a global power. Marshall contributed in myriad ways to this formative chapter in U.S. history and helped guide the country during the early Cold War.

The chapters in this volume present many key themes that reveal much about Marshall, the United States, and the early Cold War. In the introduction, "Entering a New Storm," William A. Taylor highlights the manifold ways Marshall influenced the early Cold War. In chapter 1, "The Obligation to Serve," Taylor reminds readers of the difficult yet perennial task of finding the best way for a democracy to mobilize its personnel and the vital relationship between military service and American democracy—militarily, economically, politically, and socially. In chapter 2, "To Mediate Civil War," Katherine K. Reist reveals the obscurities involved in foreign interventions—diplomatically and potentially militarily—as well as the complicated nature of foreign civil wars, even when policy makers tried to fit them within the Cold War's global binary of capitalism versus communism. In chapter 3, "The Advocate of Airpower," John M. Curatola illustrates the challenges of grappling with novel and innovative technology to address the changing nature of warfare. In doing so, Curatola explains the importance of military leaders having the requisite foresight to grasp how new technology might alter warfare while also having an appreciation of history and resulting wisdom to understand that certain aspects of war are timeless and unchanging. Most important, Curatola illuminates that success in innovation depends on identifying and training the next generation of leaders to leverage potential, while equipping and enabling them to maximize their adaptation to the new environment. In chapter 4, "Military Posture for Peace," Sean N. Kalic proves the immense complexity, yet vital necessity, of reforming the U.S. national security apparatus to meet international challenges. Such a noteworthy accomplishment required identifying the elements necessary for national security and having the prescience required to assemble them into an effective whole. In chapter 5, "To Harness Atomic Power," Frank A. Settle Jr. discovers the absolute necessity of understanding the existential nature of weapons of mass destruction and their terrific and awesome power. Settle establishes that seeking controls on proliferation and promoting positive and peaceful uses of atomic energy while refraining from wanton abuse of such absolute weapons were critical components of success during the Cold War and ultimately prevented it from escalating into world destruction. In chapter 6, "The Patient Is Sinking," Michael Holm illustrates the value of prudence to an understanding of the import of postconflict reconstruction and a realization that U.S. power was as much ideological as it was military. Buttressing allies diplomatically, ensuring democracy politically, and reinforcing capitalism economically helped to win the peace in the long term. In chapter 7, "An Alliance by Default," Ingo Trauschweizer elucidates the immense value of alliances in a world where national power was, and is, both precious and finite. The crafting and maintaining of strong alliances helped to bolster national power in an increasingly interconnected world and displayed a recognition of how the U.S. position had shifted dramatically as a result of World War II. In chapter 8, "Return to the Pentagon," Jared Dockery demonstrates the potential, and problems, of coalition warfare. Dockery illuminates the challenges of responding to a surprise attack and the intricacies of conflict in a globalized world, including the application of diplomatic, political, economic, and military power, all while carefully balancing the threat of escalation in a nuclear-armed atmosphere. In chapter 9, "The Freedom to Serve," Jeremy P. Maxwell traces the long struggle of African Americans to achieve equality in military service and to leverage the results to secure similar advances in broader American society. A combination of consistent pressure from civil rights leaders, African American soldiers, civilian policy makers, and such military leaders as Generals Marshall and Ridgway combined with battlefield realities in Korea to bring about racial integration of the U.S. military.

Throughout all these critical episodes, George C. Marshall experienced many successes, including most notably the European Recovery Program that posterity named in his honor. Other endeavors failed, including Marshall's unrelenting advocacy to implement UMT and his unsuccessful and controversial mission to China. In both his successes and failures, however, one thing remained constant: Marshall was always at the center of the storm. This omnipresence attested to his critical and far-reaching influence in the early Cold War. The United States, grateful for his efforts, regaled him for his service. Clifford K. Berryman, the well-known and Pulitzer Prize–winning American political cartoonist, captured the essence of this gratitude in his artistic homage "Well Done, Thou Good and Faithful Servant."

In addition to praise from U.S. sources, Marshall also received international acclaim. On December 10, 1953, George C. Marshall achieved an unprecedented feat: he was the first, and subsequently only, career soldier to win the Nobel Peace Prize.[5] Some observers critiqued Marshall's nomination because of his

"Well Done, Thou Good and Faithful Servant." January 9, 1949. Cartoon by Clifford K. Berryman. Courtesy Center for Legislative Archives, U.S. National Archives and Records Administration.

lifelong connection to the U.S. military. There was even a brief outburst by three communist protesters during the awards ceremony, wherein several agitators shouted, "We protest!" from the gallery and showered the audience below with propaganda leaflets. Countering the interruption, King Haakon VII of Norway immediately stood up and feverishly applauded Marshall, at which point the crowd broke into a raucous cheer, drowning out the protesters.[6] At the awards ceremony in the auditorium at the University of Oslo, Marshall received his award based on his post–World War II economic recovery efforts aimed at Western Europe, most notably the European Recovery Program, or Marshall Plan. In presenting the award, Carl Joachim Hambro, a member of the Nobel Committee, regaled the audience with a detailed summary of Marshall's many accomplishments as a soldier, beginning with his time as cadet first captain at

Virginia Military Institute and covering the voluminous highlights of his most distinguished military career. He emphasized, however, "Nobel's Peace Prize is not given to Marshall for what he accomplished during the war. Nevertheless, what he has done, after the war, for peace is a corollary to this achievement, and it is this great work for the establishment of peace which the Nobel Committee has wanted to honor."[7]

In his acceptance speech, Marshall admitted, "I have been greatly and surprisingly honored in the past twenty-four hours." Having difficulty with a cough due to a severe cold after a lung infection the previous month and somewhat rattled by the unexpected protest, Marshall gathered his thoughts among the uproarious applause led by the king. He continued, relating Pax Romana to World War II and highlighting three areas—improving education, moderating national attitudes, and addressing world poverty—as "great essentials to peace." Marshall concluded, "We must present democracy as a force holding within itself the seeds of unlimited progress by the human race. By our actions we should make it clear that such a democracy is a means to a better way of life, together with a better understanding among nations."[8]

After receiving the Nobel Peace Prize, Marshall and his wife, Katherine Tupper Marshall, retired to a small home in Pinehurst, North Carolina, having decided that the climate there was more favorable than that of their longtime home in Leesburg, Virginia. Throughout retirement, they often alternated between the two homes depending on the weather. With Marshall largely out of the public eye, some observers compared him to Cincinnatus, the famed Roman soldier and statesman who embodied civic virtue, owing to his previous commitment to serve the nation when called out of retirement multiple times—as special presidential envoy to China in 1945, as secretary of state in 1947, and as secretary of defense in 1950—and his willingness to relinquish the reins of power once he had done his duty. Upon his fourth and final retirement in 1951, Marshall quipped, "When I retired, I walked straight out."[9] Afterward, Marshall lived a simple and private life, refusing to write his memoirs despite significant interest from publishers and eschewing the probable financial windfall that would have resulted from their royalties. Instead, he donated the entirety of his private papers to the George C. Marshall Foundation located at VMI in Lexington so that they could be published as detailed and as accurately as possible over time, with all proceeds going not to himself but rather to the foundation.[10]

On June 5, 1957, President Dwight D. Eisenhower honored George C. Marshall at a personal ceremony at Blair-Lee House, the president's guesthouse, in Washington, D.C., to commemorate the tenth anniversary of the European Recovery Program. Foreign ambassadors present at the occasion lavished Marshall with gifts, including a silver medal from Harold Caccia, the British ambassador, and an ornate tapestry from Herve Alphand, France's ambassador, among many others. Envisioning the "economic and political chaos" of Western Europe after World War II, President Eisenhower remarked, "That this tragedy was averted is due in large measure to the bold and imaginative undertaking which you proposed and which rightfully bears your name."[11] Countries around the world also celebrated the momentous occasion, including Denmark and Italy.

While at his home in North Carolina, George Marshall suffered on January 15, 1959, a brain aneurysm and then endured on February 17 a more severe stroke while at Womack Army Hospital at Fort Bragg, North Carolina. After these two major health setbacks, Marshall contracted pneumonia and pituitary gland complications, growing progressively weaker and requiring lengthy hospitalization.[12] On March 11, doctors admitted Marshall to Walter Reed Army Hospital in Bethesda, Maryland, where he would spend the next seven months under constant care. He died there at 6:08 P.M. on October 16, 1959; he was seventy-eight years old.[13] Marshall was survived by his widow, Katherine Tupper Marshall; sister, Mrs. John J. Singer, of Greensburg, Pennsylvania; and stepdaughter, Mrs. James J. Winn, of Leesburg, Virginia.[14]

Upon Marshall's death, President Eisenhower immediately issued a proclamation highlighting Marshall's central role in the early Cold War. Eisenhower remarked, "As soldier and statesman, General Marshall devoted his entire life to selfless service to his Nation. To his resolution and strength of purpose, his steadfast courage and wise decision, this Nation, and indeed the Free World, are deeply indebted for survival at a time of great peril, for the safeguarding of freedom, and for the strengthening of peace."[15] Marshall's passing was the end of an era. From the architect of U.S. victory in World War II to his many positions of responsibility during the early Cold War, Marshall epitomized public service. He encountered a plethora of challenges after World War II, campaigning for universal military training, attempting to mediate the Chinese Civil War, advocating for an independent air force, shaping the National Security Act of 1947, attempting to control atomic weapons, devising the European Recovery Program, helping to formulate the North Atlantic Treaty, leading the war effort in Korea, and integrating the U.S. military. He accomplished all this personally and indirectly through his relationships with other policy makers whom he had cultivated, mentored, and led, including John

M. Palmer, James W. Wadsworth Jr., Dwight D. Eisenhower, Ferdinand A. Eberstadt, Henry H. Arnold, Larry Kuter, Robert A. Lovett, Bernard Baruch, Dean Acheson, Paul Hoffman, George F. Kennan, Charles Bohlen, J. Lawton Collins, and Matthew B. Ridgway. He also shaped the early Cold War through his interactions with other individuals of note whom he debated and countered, including Chiang Kai-shek, Mao Zedong, Douglas MacArthur, and Edward M. Almond. As a result, George C. Marshall influenced the early Cold War in a way unique for any one American.

Eisenhower was not alone in his praise of Marshall's importance to American policy, politics, and society. Former President Truman had referred to Marshall as "the greatest living American," and President Eisenhower previously characterized Marshall as being "in the class I call great."[16] During Marshall's secretary of defense confirmation hearings, Sen. Millard E. Tydings (D-Md.) remarked, "Where is there any man in America who is better qualified? Always the answer comes back to General Marshall."[17] The *Washington Post* reported, "General of the Army George Catlett Marshall ranks among the finest public servants this Nation has ever known."[18] Innumerable condolences and countless praise poured in after his passing.

At the funeral, a couple hundred visitors, including "humble neighbors from his beloved Leesburg as well as many of the best-known Americans of his time," paid their respects to a leader who had been at the center of almost every major crisis during the transition from World War II to the early Cold War. "Many of those persons in the chapel had worked with Gen. Marshall when he was Army Chief of Staff during World War II. Others had assisted him when the Marshall Plan for European recovery was formulated in 1947. In 1953 Gen. Marshall was awarded the Nobel Peace Prize for developing the plan. Some of those in the chapel had been with Gen. Marshall when he was Secretary of State and Secretary of Defense during the Truman Administration," reported the *Washington Post*.[19]

Andrew J. Goodpaster, former supreme allied commander of NATO and chair emeritus of the George C. Marshall Foundation, maintained that Marshall "outlined a vision for the nation, and the world, that remains relevant. It can serve as an instructive and helpful guide."[20] Indeed. As the preceding chapters of this volume have demonstrated, George Catlett Marshall was involved, directly or indirectly, in all the major challenges of his day. His life, leadership, and significance extend much further, however. Several key lessons emerge from Marshall's influence in the early Cold War and resonate still.

Casket bearers consisting of one enlisted service member from the U.S. Army, Air Force, Coast Guard, Marine Corps, and Navy joined by one cadet from the Virginia Military Institute remove General Marshall's casket and prepare to carry it into the Fort Myer Chapel for the private funeral service. October 20, 1959. Courtesy George C. Marshall Library, Lexington, Va.

The impressive career of George C. Marshall as a soldier and statesman illustrates many dictums that apply today. Marshall's relentless, though ultimately unsuccessful, pursuit of UMT shows that service to something larger than oneself—not just military service but service to the nation—is an ideal worthy of emulation. Marshall's failure to mediate the Chinese Civil War presents a cautionary tale of entanglement in foreign conflicts, especially if policy makers do not have a clear grasp of underlying local and cultural dynamics. Marshall's advocacy for an independent air force reinforces the value of basing preparation for war not on the last war but on the next one, however difficult that may be. Marshall's shaping of the National Security Act of 1947 illustrates the necessity to reform periodically the national security apparatus and to align it with international threats—something that contemporary observers have argued is long overdue today. Marshall's attempt to control atomic weapons proves the existential truth that a world with nuclear-armed nations is perpetually dangerous and always capable of global destruction; therefore, harnessing that power and preventing proliferation are vital responsibilities. Marshall's comprehension that the agonizing destruction wrought by total war is not good for anyone, even the victors, reveals that economic stability reinforces political strength and makes winning the peace a necessity. Marshall's exertions to create, strengthen, and maintain alliances highlights the value of international cooperation, even and especially in the furtherance of national interests. Marshall's determination to ensure preparedness—and quickly address its lack when others had allowed peace to generate complacency—evidences that eternal vigilance is necessary in a world replete with military threats. Marshall's determination to guarantee that military service reflected American values confirmed that the U.S. military not only fought for democracy abroad but also encouraged it at home.

Overall, Marshall's influence in the early Cold War reminds us of three key lessons. First, cooperation toward national goals is vital to the future of the United States. This includes not only coordination among the various armed services toward military objectives, but also collaboration among various political affiliations toward national interests and cohesion between the military and civil society writ large. Second, situating national defense within a broader grand strategy is difficult, yet vital, to achieve U.S. national interests. Marshall's advocacy of a small army to minimize expenses backed up by a large pool of trained personnel to signal resolve, provide deterrence, and speed mobilization in case of conflict was but one example. Many Americans have grown comfortable with seeking national security at all costs as an end unto itself, rather than subordinating national defense to such broader societal aspirations as standard of living, individual liberties, and fiscal sustainability. Third, forming, nurturing, and maintaining alliances are vital to secure U.S. national interests and international security. In a globalized and interconnected world, narrow isolation is not only impractical but also runs counter to U.S. national interests. As the sole global superpower, U.S. policy makers must remember, as Marshall did, that power is, and always has been, both precious and finite. They must wisely choose where and how to spend it.

Just as the stormy transition from World War II to the early Cold War posed a challenge to the nation's leadership, epitomized by Marshall, the United States now finds itself at a critical crossroads. Numerous contemporary issues resonate with the themes of this book, including a significant shift in Europe back toward preparedness based on Russia's provocations, including Sweden and Lithuania resuming conscription, Norway opening its draft to women, and France considering mandatory national service.[21] Similar reverberations have echoed even in the United States as evidenced by the formation of the National Commission on Military, National, and Public Service and a federal judge's recent ruling that an all-male draft would be unconstitutional with the implication that women will have to register with the Selective Service System at some point, a case that will likely make its way in due course to the U.S. Supreme Court.[22] In terms of diplomacy, recent administrations have argued forcefully for the United States to take a prominent role in mediating foreign conflicts, illustrated most visibly by U.S. attempts to broker peace in the Middle East.[23] Just as Marshall and other U.S. policy makers grappled with how to integrate the technology of airpower into military strategy during the early Cold War, so too do current leaders have to assimilate remotely piloted vehicles—not only in the air but also on land and sea—into the armed forces, including not only leveraging their technical capabilities but also assessing their legal, ethical, and moral implications.[24] Likewise, the accomplishments of the National Security Act of 1947 were momentous and provided much of the organization and apparatus necessary to wage, endure, and eventually win the Cold War. Its continued presence, however, only reinforces the need to debate and accomplish significant reforms of the current U.S. national security apparatus to ensure its ultimate success.[25] Control of nuclear energy remains highly relevant, if also highly contested, as evidenced by the signing and subsequent withdrawal of the United States from the Iran nuclear deal, formally known as the Joint Comprehensive Plan of Action (JCPOA), North Korea's nuclear development and provocative testing, and nuclear tensions between Pakistan and India over Kashmir.[26] While not the same vast scope as the Marshall Plan, international aid has remained a central aspect of U.S. foreign policy in such places as Iraq and Afghanistan, and the U.S. Agency for International Development continues to perform an important part of overall U.S. grand strategy.[27] The value of alliances likewise has remained most relevant. Questions among European allies regarding the viability—or even desirability—of the European Union have accompanied U.S. domestic debates regarding the cost-sharing arrangements, use, and need for NATO.[28] The issues of preparedness raised during Marshall's tenure as secretary of defense during the Korean War also resonate, highlighting the difficulty, yet absolute necessity, of ensuring national security in a time of international uncertainty and addressing in a firm yet measured manner provocations by North Korea or Russia.[29] Finally, just as Marshall helped to change military service during his day, so too have U.S. leaders made subsequent modifications to ensure that the American military is open to all who are willing and able to serve. Debates about who serves and how, including the opening of combat positions to women and significant questions regarding the fairness, sustainability, efficiency, and effectiveness of the All-Volunteer Force, percolate today.[30]

As new storm clouds gather, a most important question emerges from this plethora of critical disputes for the United States to resolve in the return to great power competition: Which U.S. leaders will rise to the occasion and influence these challenges in a way similar to Marshall? In many ways, the United States today is entering a new storm in international relations. One can only hope that current and future U.S. policy makers will approach this tumultuous time with the vision, foresight, and wisdom that George Catlett Marshall did when he was at the center of the storm.

NOTES

1. On Marshall's legacy, see David L. Roll, *George Marshall: Defender of the Republic* (New York: Dutton Caliber, 2019); Debi Unger and Irwin Unger with Stanley Hirshson, *George Marshall: A Biography* (New York: HarperCollins, 2014); Jack Uldrich, *Soldier, Statesman, Peacemaker: Leadership Lessons from George C. Marshall* (New York: AMACOM, 2005); Ed Cray, *General of the Army: George C. Marshall, Soldier and Statesman* (New York: W. W. Norton, 1990); Mark A. Stoler, *George C. Marshall: Soldier-Statesman of the American Century* (Boston: Twayne, 1989); Leonard Moseley, *Marshall: Hero for Our Times* (New York: Hearst, 1982); Harold Faber, *Soldier and Statesman: General George C. Marshall* (New York: Ariel, 1964); Robert Payne, *The Marshall Story: A Biography* (New York: Prentice-Hall, 1951); and William Frye, *Marshall: Citizen Soldier* (Indianapolis: Bobbs-Merrill, 1947).

2. Lance Morrow, "George C. Marshall: The Last Great American?" *Smithsonian Magazine* 28, no. 5 (August 1997): 107.

3. John G. Norris, "Marshall Was Ranked as a Giant of His Age: Truman Once Called General 'Greatest Living American'; 'True Organizer of Victory' Was Accolade of Churchill," *Washington Post*, October 17, 1959.

4. On Marshall as the organizer of U.S. success, see Jonathan W. Jordan, "Architect of Victory," *World War II* 21, no. 6 (October 2006): 52–58; Stanley Weintraub, *15 Stars: Eisenhower, MacArthur, Marshall—Three Generals Who Saved the American Century* (New York: NAL Caliber, 2007); and Kevin Baker, "America's Finest General: George C. Marshall's Long Slog through the Ranks Took Him to Power, Victory and Greatness—Five Stars, International Acclaim and a Nobel Prize," *Military History* 28, no. 3 (September 2011): 28–35.

5. For a complete list of Nobel Peace Prize winners, see Norwegian Nobel Institute, "All Nobel Peace Prizes," 2018, https://www.nobelprize.org/prizes/lists/all-nobel -peace-prizes/.

6. On protesters see George Axelsson, "Haakon's Tribute to Marshall Drowns Protest of Oslo Reds," *New York Times*, December 11, 1953.

7. Carl Joachim Hambro, "The Nobel Peace Prize 1953: Award Ceremony Speech," December 10, 1953, https://www.nobelprize.org/prizes/peace/1953/ceremony-speech/.

8. George C. Marshall, "Nobel Lecture," December 10, 1953, https://www .marshallfoundation.org/marshall/essays-interviews/george-c-marshall-nobel-lecture/.

9. Jesse M. Donalson, "George C. Marshall: Where Is He Now?" *Washington Post and Times Herald*, March 31, 1955.

10. Chalmers M. Roberts, "'A Great Citizen' Reaches 75," *Washington Post and Times Herald,* December 31, 1955. On the papers of George C. Marshall, see George C. Marshall Foundation, "Papers of George Catlett Marshall," https://www.marshallfoundation .org/library/collection/marshall-papers/#!/collection=7.

11. Jay Walz, "Marshall Is Honored on 10th Anniversary of Aid Plan," *New York Times*, June 6, 1957.

12. "Gen. Marshall Weaker: 'Involvement' of Pituitary Gland Complicates Illness," *New York Times*, February 24, 1959.

13. "Marshall Is Dead in Capital at 78: World War Chief," *New York Times*, October 17, 1959.

14. On Marshall's death, see box 17, folder General Marshall, White House Office, Office of the Staff Secretary Records, Subject Series, Alphabetical Subseries, Dwight D. Eisenhower Library.

15. Dwight D. Eisenhower, "Death of General Marshall: A Proclamation by the President of the United States," October 16, 1959, 1, in ibid.

16. "Nation Mourns Gen. Marshall: Famed War Leader Dies at 78; Funeral Rites Set Tuesday," *Los Angeles Times*, October 17, 1959.

17. "George C. Marshall Devoted Life to Service of Country: Hailed as Soldier and Statesman," *Los Angeles Times*, October 17, 1959.

18. "Gen. George C. Marshall," *Washington Post*, October 18, 1959.

19. Julius Duscha, "President, Truman Bow at Simple Marshall Rites," *Washington Post*, October 21, 1959.

20. Andrew J. Goodpaster, "George Marshall's World, and Ours," *New York Times*, December 11, 2003.

21. Elisabeth Braw, "Europe Takes a Second Look at Conscription," *Wall Street Journal*, August 26, 2018, https://www.wsj.com/articles/europe-takes-a-second-look -at-conscription-1535311309.

22. National Commission on Military, National, and Public Service, "Interim Report: A Report to the American People, the Congress, and the President," January 2019, 1–28, https://www.inspire2serve.gov/NCOS%20Interim%20Report.pdf; Matthew S. Schwartz, "Judge Rules Male-Only Draft Violates Constitution," *NPR*, February 25,

2019, https://www.npr.org/2019/02/25/697622930/judge-rules-male-only-draft-violates
-constitution.

23. Margaret Talev and Jonathan Ferziger, "Pence Says U.S. Must Play 'Preeminent'
Role as Peace Broker," *Bloomberg News*, January 23, 2018, https://www.bloomberg
.com/news/articles/2018-01-23/pence-says-u-s-must-play-preeminent-role-as-peace
-broker-jcrmeyhr.

24. Mark Hamilton, Office of the Secretary of Defense, "The Third Offset, Remotely
Piloted Systems, and Moral Hazards," U.S. Army War College Strategy Research Project, 2017, 1–26, https://publications.armywarcollege.edu/pubs/3427.pdf.

25. On defense reform, see Heidi B. Demarest and Erica D. Borghard, eds., *U.S.
National Security Reform: Reassessing the National Security Act of 1947* (London: Routledge, 2019).

26. Zachary Laub, "The Impact of the Iran Nuclear Agreement," Council on Foreign Relations, May 8, 2018, https://www.cfr.org/backgrounder/impact-iran-nuclear
-agreement.

27. Curt Tarnoff and Marian L. Lawson, "Foreign Aid: An Introduction to U.S.
Programs and Policy," *Congressional Research Service*, April 25, 2018, 1–36, https://fas
.org/sgp/crs/row/R40213.pdf.

28. Carl Bildt, "The Six Issues That Will Shape the EU in 2017," World Economic
Forum, January 18, 2017, https://www.weforum.org/agenda/2017/01/the-six-issues
-that-will-shape-the-eu-in-2017/; Jonathan Eyal, "The Real Problems with NATO:
What Trump Gets Right, and Wrong," *Foreign Affairs*, March 2, 2017, https://www
.foreignaffairs.com/articles/europe/2017-03-02/real-problems-nato.

29. Terrence Mullan, "Global Uncertainty in an Age of 'America First,'" Council
on Foreign Relations, June 28, 2017, https://www.cfr.org/blog/global-uncertainty-age
-america-first; Edward Wong, "Trump's Talks with Kim Jung-un Collapse, and Both
Sides Point Fingers," *New York Times*, February 28, 2019, https://www.nytimes.com
/2019/02/28/world/asia/trump-kim-vietnam-summit.html; Daniel Treisman, "Why
Putin Took Crimea: The Gambler in the Kremlin," *Foreign Affairs*, April 18, 2016,
https://www.foreignaffairs.com/articles/ukraine/2016–04–18/why-putin-took-crimea.

30. Meghann Myers, "Almost 800 Women Are Serving in Previously Closed Army
Combat Jobs. This Is How They're Faring," *Army Times*, October 9, 2018, https://www
.armytimes.com/news/your-army/2018/10/09/almost-800-women-are-serving-in
-previously-closed-army-combat-jobs-this-is-how-theyre-faring/; on historical background, see William A. Taylor, "From WACs to Rangers: Women in the U.S. Military
since World War II," *Marine Corps University Journal*, Special Issue: Gender Integration
(2018): 78–101; and Dianna Cahn, "Pentagon: Military-Civilian Disconnect Could Endan-
ger All-Volunteer Force," *Stars and Stripes*, January 18, 2018, https://www.stripes.com
/pentagon-military-civilian-disconnect-could-endanger-all-volunteer-force-1.507427.

CHRONOLOGY

December 31, 1880	George Catlett Marshall born in Uniontown, Pa.
September 1897	Marshall entered Virginia Military Institute at age sixteen.
February 2, 1902	Marshall commissioned as second lieutenant in the U.S. Army.
February 11, 1902	Marshall married Elizabeth Carter Coles of Lexington, Va.
September 15, 1927	Elizabeth Carter Marshall (née Coles) died from surgery complications.
October 15, 1930	Marshall married Katherine Boyce Tupper Brown of Baltimore, Md.
September 1, 1939	Marshall sworn in as chief of staff of the army.

December 16, 1944	Marshall promoted to general of the army (five-star rank).
April 12, 1945	President Franklin D. Roosevelt died, and President Harry S. Truman assumed office.
July 17, 1945	Potsdam Conference began.
August 2, 1945	Potsdam Conference ended.
August 15, 1945	Japan surrendered in World War II.
November 18, 1945	Marshall retired as chief of staff of the army.
November 1945	President Harry S. Truman appointed Marshall as special presidential envoy to China with the rank of ambassador.
December 15, 1945	Marshall mission to China authorized.
December 20, 1945	Marshall arrived in Shanghai to begin his China mission.
March 5, 1946	Winston Churchill delivered "Iron Curtain" speech.
January 7, 1947	Marshall departed China.
January 21, 1947	Marshall sworn in as secretary of state.
January 29, 1947	Marshall mission to China officially ended.
March 12, 1947	Truman announced Truman Doctrine before joint session of Congress.
June 5, 1947	Marshall delivered European Recovery Program speech at Harvard University.
July 26, 1947	President Truman signed the National Security Act of 1947.
April 3, 1948	President Truman signed the Economic Cooperation Act.
June 24, 1948	Berlin Blockade began.
July 26, 1948	President Truman signed Executive Order 9981.
January 20, 1949	Marshall resigned as secretary of state.
January 1949	Marshall appointed chair of the American Battle Monuments Commission.
April 4, 1949	North Atlantic Treaty Organization formed.

May 12, 1949	Berlin Blockade ended.
August 29, 1949	Soviet Union detonated first atomic bomb, "Joe-1."
October 1, 1949	Marshall appointed president of the American Red Cross.
April 7, 1950	NSC-68 presented to President Truman.
June 25, 1950	Korean War began.
September 15, 1950	X Corps landed at Inchon, South Korea.
September 21, 1950	Marshall sworn in as secretary of defense.
December 1, 1950	Marshall resigned as president of the American Red Cross.
December 23, 1950	Gen. Walton H. Walker died in a jeep accident in Korea.
April 11, 1951	Truman relieved MacArthur with Marshall's support.
June 7, 1951	Congress passed the Universal Military Training and Service Act.
June 19, 1951	President Truman signed the Universal Military Training and Service Act.
September 12, 1951	Marshall resigned as secretary of defense.
December 31, 1951	European Recovery Program ended.
July 27, 1953	Delegates signed the Korean Armistice Agreement.
December 10, 1953	Marshall awarded the Nobel Peace Prize in Oslo, Norway.
October 16, 1959	Marshall passed away at Walter Reed Army Hospital in Washington, D.C.

CONTRIBUTORS

JOHN M. CURATOLA is a professor of history at the U.S. Army School of Advanced Military Studies (SAMS) at Fort Leavenworth, Kansas. A retired U.S. Marine Corps officer, Curatola served in uniform for twenty-two years and participated in Operation Provide Hope in Somalia in 1992, Operation Iraqi Freedom in 2003, and was the J-4 logistics lead during the Indian Ocean Tsunami Relief efforts in 2005. Upon retiring from the U.S. Marine Corps, he finished his doctorate at the University of Kansas. His published works focus on World War II, airpower, and the Cold War. He has given numerous presentations at such venues as the National Archives and various public libraries, as well as a number of nationally televised lectures on C-SPAN. His recent book *Bigger Bombs for a Brighter Tomorrow: The Strategic Air Command and American War Plans at the Dawn of the Atomic Age, 1945–1950* (2016) examines the state of the American nuclear monopoly during the early Cold War.

JARED DOCKERY is an associate professor of history at Harding University in Searcy, Arkansas. He teaches American Military History, among other classes, and received the Teacher Achievement Award from Harding in 2016. He is a graduate of Harding, having received a bachelor's degree in history in 1994. He earned both a master's degree and a doctoral degree in history from the University of Arkansas, in 1997 and 2008, respectively. His dissertation explores the World War II career of J. "Lightning Joe" Lawton Collins, and he has presented papers on Collins at numerous history conferences. He has written book reviews for the *Arkansas Historical Quarterly, Michigan War Studies Review,* and *H-War.* Prior to his appointment at Harding, he worked as a sportswriter for the *Northwest Arkansas Times,* and also as the youth minister for the Bella Vista, Arkansas, Church of Christ. He and his wife, Natalie, have two daughters, Elizabeth and Emma Grace.

MICHAEL HOLM is a historian and a senior lecturer at Boston University. He received his master's degree in history in 2007 from McGill University and his doctoral degree in U.S. history in 2013 from Boston University. A specialist in the Truman presidential era, Holm is the author of *The Marshall Plan: A New Deal for Europe* (2017). He has furthermore published "Also Present at the Creation: Henry Cabot Lodge, Jr., and the Coming of the Cold War," *Journal of the Historical Society* (June 2010); coauthored with Andrew David, "The Kennedy Administration and the Battle over Foreign Aid: The Untold Story of the Clay Committee," *Diplomacy and Statecraft* (2016); and is the author of the chapter "All Paine: The American Mind and the Creation of the League of Nations and the U.N.," in *The Legacy of Thomas Paine in the Transatlantic World,* edited by Sam Edwards and Marcus Morris (2018). Holm's current work explores the impact of the atomic bomb on American political culture between 1945 and 1955.

SEAN N. KALIC is a professor in the Department of Military History at the U.S. Army Command and General Staff College at Fort Leavenworth, Kansas, where he has taught since 2004. He holds a bachelor's degree in political science from the University of Denver, a master's degree in defense and strategic studies from Missouri State University, a master's degree in history from Youngstown State University, and a doctoral degree in history from Kansas State University. Kalic is the author of several works, including *Spies: The U.S. and Russian Espionage Game from the Cold War to the 21st Century* (2019); *The Russian*

Revolution of 1917: An Essential Reference Guide (2017); *U.S. Presidents and the Militarization of Space, 1946–1967* (2012); *Thinking about War: Past, Present and Future* (2011); and *Combating a Modern Hydra: Al Qaeda and the Global War on Terrorism* (2005). He has also written several chapters for a variety of anthologies, including "Framing the Discourse: The Rhetoric of the Global War on Terrorism," in *Erbe des Katlen Kriegs* (2013); "Terrorism in the Twenty-First Century: A New Era of Warfare," in *An International History of Terrorism: Western and Non-Western Experiences* (2013); "Post–Cold War Conflicts," in *The Routledge Handbook of American Military and Diplomatic History, 1865 to the Present* (2013); "Dwight D. Eisenhower," in *Generals of the Army: Marshall, MacArthur, Eisenhower, Arnold, Bradley* (2013); and "Reagan's SDI Announcement and the European Reaction: Diplomacy in the Last Decade of the Cold War," in *The Crisis of Détente in Europe: From Helsinki to Gorbachev, 1975–1985* (2009). Kalic has presented lectures for the U.S. Naval War College, Slovenian General Staff, Slovenian Command and General Staff College, and the U.S. Army's Future Study Group.

JEREMY P. MAXWELL is an assistant professor in the Department of Military History at the U.S. Army Command and General Staff College at Fort Leavenworth, Kansas, where he recently moved from his prior post as the Defense POW/MIA Accounting Agency (DPAA) Postdoctoral Fellow of the Dale Center for the Study of War and Society at the University of Southern Mississippi. He holds a bachelor's degree in history from Loyola Marymount University, a master's degree in history from Ball State University, and he received his doctoral degree in history from Queen's University Belfast. His research interests include the study of military, social, diplomatic, racial, and ethnic history. He is the author of *Brotherhood in Combat: How African Americans Found Equality in Korea and Vietnam* (2018), which was a finalist for the U.S. Army Historical Foundation Distinguished Writing Award, and is currently working on his second book about the legacy of the Montford Point Marines. He attends and presents his work at regional and national conferences and is involved in a number of collaborative projects.

KATHERINE K. REIST is an associate professor of history at the University of Pittsburgh at Johnstown, where she has been the History Department chair for twenty-five years. Her recent publications include "Training a Reluctant Ally: The U.S. Naval Advisory Mission to China, 1945–1949," in *Naval Advising and Assistance: History, Challenges, and Analysis,* edited by Donald Stoker and Michael T. McMaster (2017); "The American Military Advisory Missions to China, 1945–1949," *Journal of Military History* (October 2013); articles in the *Wiley-Blackwell Encyclopedia of War* (5 vols.); and a forthcoming chapter, "Training a National Army in Time of Civil War: The American Military Advising Mission to China, 1945–1949," in *War and the American Pacific: New Dimensions of the American Military in the 1940s Pacific and East Asia.* She has served as a member of the Society for Military History Board of Trustees.

FRANK A. SETTLE JR. is the author of *General George C. Marshall and the Atomic Bomb* (2016). A professor emeritus of chemistry at Washington and Lee University and director of the Alsos Digital Library for Nuclear Issues, Settle was professor of chemistry at the Virginia Military Institute from 1964 to 1992. Before coming to Washington and Lee in 1998, he was a visiting professor at the U.S. Air Force Academy, a consultant at Los Alamos National Laboratory, and a program officer at the National Science Foundation. He is also a coauthor of *Instrumental Methods of Analysis,* 7th ed. (2018) and the editor of *The Handbook of Instrumental Techniques* (1997). He has published extensively in scientific, educational, and trade journals. At Washington and Lee University, he developed and taught courses on nuclear history, nuclear power, and weapons of mass destruction for liberal arts majors. Settle received a bachelor's degree in chemistry from Emory and Henry College and a doctoral degree in chemistry from the University of Tennessee, Knoxville.

MARK A. STOLER is professor emeritus of history at the University of Vermont, where he taught from 1970 to 2007, and editor of *The Papers of George Catlett Marshall,* volume 6 of which received the Link-Kuehl Award for Documentary Editing from the Society for Historians of American Foreign Relations (SHAFR). He has also written or edited numerous other volumes on U.S. and Allied strategy and diplomacy during World War II and the Cold War, including *George C. Marshall: Soldier-Statesman of the American Century; Allies at War: Britain and America Against the Axis Powers; Major Problems in the History of World War II; Debating Franklin D. Roosevelt's Foreign Policies;* and *Allies and Adversaries: The Joint Chiefs of Staff, the Grand Alliance and U.S. Strategy in World War II,* which won the Distinguished Book Award from the Society for Military History. He is also a past council member of that society and a past president of SHAFR.

WILLIAM A. TAYLOR is an award-winning associate professor of global security studies, previous department chair, and holder of the Lee Drain Endowed University Professorship in the Kay Bailey Hutchison Center for Security Studies at Angelo State University in San Angelo, Texas. Taylor is the editor for the new book series Studies in Civil-Military Relations with University Press of Kansas and the author of three books, including *Contemporary Security Issues in Africa* (2019); *Military Service and American Democracy: From World War II to the Iraq and Afghanistan Wars* (2016); and *Every Citizen a Soldier: The Campaign for Universal Military Training after World War II* (2014), which won the Crader Family Book Prize Honorable Mention in 2015. Taylor has won fourteen national fellowships and research grants and won the 2019 Angelo State University President's Award for Faculty Excellence in Leadership/Service, 2016 Angelo State University President's Award for Faculty Excellence in Research/Creative Endeavor, and the 2016 Texas Tech University System Chancellor's Council Distinguished Research Award. His books are housed in more than 1,000 libraries throughout the United States and in more than forty countries around the world. He has contributed to nineteen other books and has published more than eighty reference articles and book reviews.

INGO TRAUSCHWEIZER is the director of the Contemporary History Institute and professor of history at Ohio University. He has published widely on the Cold War and contemporary strategy and policy, including his award-winning book *The Cold War U.S. Army* (2008); an edited collection with Steven M. Miner, *Failed States and Fragile Societies: A New World Disorder?* (2011); and *Maxwell Taylor's Cold War: From Berlin to Vietnam* (2019). In his teaching and ongoing scholarship, Trauschweizer is broadly interested in the changing nature of war and warfare throughout early modern and modern history, the role of alliances in maintaining peace and waging war since the end of World War II, and the effects of wars on American society and political culture.

INDEX

Page numbers in *italics* indicate illustrations.

Marshall mission to China: assessments of, 55–56; cease-fire agreements, 47–48, 53; Committee of Three, 47, 49, 52–53; criticism of, 52; Executive Headquarters, 48; Manchuria and, 50–51; Marshall and Chiang, 44, 48–49; Marshall recalled for, 41; Marshall's concept of government and military, 47; Political Consultative Conference, 48–49, 51, 53–54; Third Party Group as focus in, 53–54; three stages of, 46; truce teams, 48, 50
Marshall Plan. *See* European Recovery Program
Marshall Plan Anniversary Dinner, 170, 245–46
Martin, Glenn, 69
Martin, Joseph, 206
Martin Aircraft Company, 69, 79n30
Masaryk, Jan, 147, 149, 166
Maxwell, Jeremy P., 6–7, 243
May, Ernest R., 55–56
McAllister, James, 162
McCain, John, 74
McCloy, John J., 12, 138, 173
McLain, Raymond S., 28
McMahon, Brien, 129–30
Meuse-Argonne offensive, 193, 225
military assistance for Europe, 167; cost of, 175; Marshall support for, 169, 171, 180
military draft, 250
Millett, Allan, 190, 203, 208, 232
Mitchell, Billy, 62
mobilization, 26; NSRB role in, 95–96; perpetual, in postwar security planning, 84
Moch, Jules, 161, 173, 175
modernization theories, 155
Molotov, Vyacheslav, 147
Monnet, Jean, 153
Montgomery, Bernard Law, 169

Morgenthau, Henry, 163
Morrow, Lance, 241
Moscow Conference, 41–42, 163–64
Mott, Quentin R., 29
Moulton, Harold, 137
Murphy, Robert, 122
Mutual Defense Assistance Act, 171
Mutual Defense Assistance Program, 170, 180
Mutual Security Act, 181

Nagasaki bombing, 21, 76–77, 106
Nalty, Bernard C., 233–34
National Assembly (China), 51–52
National Commission on Military, National, and Public Service, 250
National Defense Act (1920), 13, 14–15
National Guard, 25, 234; African American units, 220–21
National Military Establishment, 77
National Security Act (1947), 83, 248–49; agencies created by, 91; amendments to, 99, 101, 103n43; background to, 88–89; CIA's duties delineated in, 94; Marshall's confirmation as exception to, 191; Marshall's influence on, 84–85, 96–97, 100–101; purpose of, 89–90
National Security Council, 91; in developing CIA functions, 94; membership on, 93; purpose of, 92–93
National Security Council Report 68. *See* NSC-68
national security planning, 7
National Security Resources Board, 87, 91; mission of, 95–96
National Security Training Commission, 28, 29–30
National Security Training Corps, 28
NATO 1948 (Kaplan), 170
Netherlands, the, 167
New York Herald Tribune, 30, 108

CPSIA information can be obtained
at www.ICGtesting.com
Printed in the USA
LVHW111152010820
662145LV00004B/1135